Integration Otherwise

Inspiration Kit

INTEGRATION OTHERWISE
INSPIRATION KIT

A Guide for Practitioners, Policymakers, and Community Builders

Authored by

Luce Beeckmans, Dounia Salamé, Martina Bovo, Mary Hogan,
Shila Hadji Heydari Anaraki, Karel Arnaut, Paschalis Arvanitidis,
Kristen Biehl, Márton Bisztrai, Gideon Bolt, György Csepeli,
Athina Zoe Desli, Laura Guérin, Heike Hanhörster,
Tina Gudrun Jensen, András Kováts, Emma Krasznahorkai,
Zsuzsa László, Carolien Lubberhuizen, Sarah Makar, Bruno Meeus,
Tamlyn Monson, Antal Örkeny, George Papagiannitsis, Lucie Revilla,
Alexandra Sandor, Marhabo Saparova, Reiner Staubach,
Cornelia Tippel, Charalampos Tsavdaroglou, Zacharias Valiantzas,
Ilse van Liempt, Penelope Vergou, Aimilia Voulvouli,
Susanne Wessendorf, and Dennis Zilske

LEUVEN UNIVERSITY PRESS

ReROOT has received funding from the European Union's Horizon 2020 research and innovation programme under grant agreement number 101004704.

The content reflects only the authors' views, and the European Commission is not responsible for any use that may be made of the information it contains.

ReROOT

Author Contribution Statement

- This Kit has four main authors placed in order of their contribution (not alphabetically): Luce Beeckmans, Dounia Salamé, Martina Bovo, and Mary Hogan;
- The other authors have co-authored as the fifth author and are placed in alphabetical order;
- Martina Bovo has copyright over all drawings (which are based on field researchers' notes and photos); Aamina Shadid and Aliki Tzouvara have copyright over the maps that introduce the fieldwork sites; the diagrams are co-authored by the four first authors and the copyright for the photos is mentioned separately in the Illustration credits.

Published in 2025 by Leuven University Press / Presses Universitaires de Louvain / Universitaire Pers Leuven. Minderbroedersstraat 4, B-3000 Leuven (Belgium).

ISBN 978 94 6270 473 2 (Paperback)
ISBN 978 94 6166 675 8 (ePDF)
ISBN 978 94 6166 676 5 (ePUB)
DOI: https://doi.org/10.11116/9789461666758
D/2025/1869/22
NUR: 759
Design: Crius Group
Cover: Daniel Benneworth-Gray

TABLE OF CONTENTS

EXTENDED TABLE OF CONTENTS

INTRODUCTION

"[A]ctual, existing circumstances are always imbued
with the possibility of being otherwise."

—PANDIAN, ANAND, AND STUART MCLEAN. 2017. *CRUMPLED PAPER BOAT:
EXPERIMENTS IN ETHNOGRAPHIC WRITING.* SCHOOL OF AMERICAN RESEARCH
ADVANCED SEMINAR SERIES. DURHAM: DUKE UNIVERSITY PRESS, 19.

A. INTEGRATION OTHERWISE

Looking at integration in another way

'Integration' is a much-debated term in policy, academia, and elsewhere. While expectations, ideas, policies, and practices regarding the integration of newcomers into a host society can differ substantially from place to place, two dominant views can be distinguished. Either newcomers are not doing enough to integrate, or society is not welcoming enough. With this *Integration Otherwise Inspiration Kit* we do not want to further polarise the debate — quite the contrary. By shedding light on how integration is already happening on the ground, we instead aim to encourage you to look at integration otherwise.

This *Integration Otherwise Inspiration Kit* intends to offer another perspective on integration — one that seeks to break open the polarised debate and move beyond the prevailing narrative that integration is a failure, with either newcomers or society falling short. Yet, while we confront dominant and dominating ways of seeing and doing integration and make visible other ways, weighing their limits and possibilities, the set of people, places, governments and organisations involved in the integration process we discuss is not radically different. Rather, we provide another, grounded, bottom-up perspective, drawing from our four-year study across nine European sites (see below), on how newcomers, in interaction with others, in very banal and everyday ways, 'do integration'.

Indeed, despite the many debates in newspapers and academic journals about what integration is or should be, newcomers are always integrating, in some way or another, into the social and spatial environments in which they live. This process is not fundamentally different from that of less recent newcomers — those who have lived in a place for a longer time — and other residents who also integrate and socialise to varying degrees in different life domains, such as work, family, education, or leisure, and constantly adapt to changing life environments. Hence, we did not venture into an abstract study of what integration in a host society is; rather, we explored the many 'minor integrations' newcomers make do in specific localities and depending on their different relationships and capacities — as a mother or colleague, as a churchgoer or employee, as a pupil or client, etc.

Shifting our perspective from a polarised discussion on how to define integration – a term which will remain nevertheless undefined and contested (and therefore unattainable and often replaced by 'inclusion' or 'incorporation') – to the many minor integrations that are happening anyway, and that we urgently need to start to render visible, understand, recognise, and reflect upon allows us to better weigh the relative successes and failures of everyday integration processes. Through stories from the ground with concise takeaways, as well as via reflection and action tools, this Kit seeks to inspire you to also see (Part I) and do (Part II) integration otherwise – inspiration you can carry forward into the future.

'Minor integrations'

With the concept 'minor integrations' the editors of the book *Infrastructuring Arrival* (the academic complement of this **Integration Otherwise Inspiration Kit**), aim to expose the often vague and sometimes damaging mainstream ideas about integration, which have at least two causes. First, they are often unidirectional and top-down, projecting expectations on migrants. Second, integration is very often 'totalising' in the sense that migrants are expected to integrate into bounded and homogeneous 'wholes' such as 'communities', 'countries', or 'neighbourhoods' to which they are considered not to belong previously.

The 'minor' in 'minor integrations' goes against and beyond these unattainable objectives (Arnaut and Meeus in Chapter 11 of *Infrastructuring Arrival*, 2026). As such, it is an invitation to stimulate alternative imaginings based on how integration happens in everyday practice, recognising that practices and aspirations of integration are multidirectional, inevitably fragmentary, changing over time and in fact do not differ fundamentally from that of longer-established residents. Monson and Jensen in Chapter 10 of *Infrastructuring Arrival* (2026) for instance highlight how newcomers establish a range of "attachments in different places, via different relationships, and across different life domains". The concept of 'minor integrations' shows affinities with the insights from other researchers who recognise integration as a fluid, fragmented, and multidirectional process (Mavrommatis 2018, Grzymala-Kazlowska and Phillimore 2018).

A very important dimension of the concept of 'minor integrations' is the exploration of grassroots agency in migration situations, while keeping an eye on the structural forces which limit and channel this agency, ranging from geo-economical forces and national regimes of exclusion to more local social, ethnic, or racial forms of structural exclusion. This is for instance articulated in the way migrants' labour and lives are eagerly captured by host economies because of their low wages. To counter this, 'minor integrations' seeks to open up avenues by further developing the idea of 'migratory careers' (Martiniello and Rea 2014). 'Minor integrations' furthermore 'de-migranticise' these careers or physical and social mobility paths by situating them in arrival contexts in which old and new residents relate and interact. These arrival contexts, as Glick Schiller and Çağlar (2009) rightly pointed out, are always locally embedded as well as extending nationally and transnationally, resulting in a polycentric network which Lionnet and Shih (2005) aptly called 'minor transnationalism' (see concept box 5 on 'transnationalism').

References:

Glick Schiller, Nina, and Ayse Çağlar. 2009. 'Towards a comparative theory of locality in migration studies: Migrant incorporation and city scale', *Journal of Ethnic and Migration Studies*, 35: 177–202.

Grzymala-Kazlowska, Aleksandra, and Jenny Phillimore. 2018. 'Introduction: rethinking integration. New perspectives on adaptation and settlement in the era of super-diversity', *Journal of Ethnic and Migration Studies*, 44: 179–96.

Lionnet, Françoise, and Shu-mei Shih. 2005. 'Thinking through the minor, transnationally' in Françoise Lionnet and Shu-mei Shih (eds.), *Minor transnationalism* (Durham & London: Duke University Press).

Martiniello, Marco, and Andrea Rea. 2014. 'The concept of migratory careers: Elements for a new theoretical perspective of contemporary human mobility', *Current Sociology*, 62: 1079–96.

Mavrommatis, George. 2018. 'Grasping the meaning of integration in an era of (forced) mobility: ethnographic insights from an informal refugee camp', *Mobilities*, 13: 861–75.

See the academic complement of this *Integration Otherwise Inspiration Kit*, the edited volume *Infrastructuring Arrival* (Arnaut, Beeckmans, and Meeus, 2026), in particular:
– Chapter 1 (Arnaut, Beeckmans, and Meeus, 2026)
– Chapter 10 (Monson and Jensen, 2026)
– Chapter 11 (Arnaut and Meeus, 2026)

From 'arrival infrastructure' to 'arrival infrastructuring'

Our entry point into integration is 'arrival'. The arrival of newcomers in a new locality marks both a moment and a place in their migration trajectory. Often this journey begins somewhere long before their arrival and may continue elsewhere afterwards. In some cases, arrival in a specific place is carefully planned. In others, newcomers find themselves there quite unintentionally after a long journey through many other locations. Moreover, once they have 'landed' in a place, this is often only the first step in the process of settling into a new society. In fact, we could even say it is often not always clear when arrival ends and newcomers stop being 'newcomers'.

Not surprisingly then, we see arrival less as an endpoint and more as a point of departure. In our understanding, arrival is a situation – always temporary, but possibly quite long-term – from where newcomers prepare for their future lives while remaining connected to their past and places elsewhere. It is, therefore, a situation of getting one's bearings, making a new home, inhabiting and connecting to a new environment, and re-rooting. We refer to the social and spatial environment where arrival occurs as an 'arrival infrastructure'.

Often spaces of arrival are situated in what some have termed 'arrival cities' or 'arrival neighbourhoods': cities or neighbourhoods where there is a long history of newcomers settling down. However, processes such as gentrification and, more recently, the suburbanisation of migration have significantly diversified the spaces of arrival, increasingly including other locations in the broader urban region and even in rural areas.

'Arrival infrastructure'

The concept of 'arrival infrastructure' invites us to look with an open mind at how – in the process of arrival – newcomers transform themselves and their environment as much as the environment transforms newcomers and itself. This complex, lively process was already envisaged when the term was initially coined by Meeus, van Heur and Arnaut (2019:1): "We broadly define arrival infrastructures as those parts of the urban fabric within which newcomers become entangled on arrival, and where their future local or translocal social mobilities are produced as much as negotiated". The most important reason for choosing the 'infrastructure' terminology is that, in essence, infrastructure is about mobility and connections: it brings together the 'things' that make social life possible as people move on in life.

'Arrival infrastructure' builds further on concepts such as the 'transition zone' (Burgess 1925/1967) and 'arrival city' (Saunders 2011). These forerunners equally highlight the transformative force of migration for newcomers and more established residents and situate these interactions in concrete urban environments that are themselves in transition. The term 'urban fabric' in the above definition widens the perspective on these environments. It derives from French urban sociologist Henri Lefebvre (1967), who tried to grasp the urban as a tissue that extends across the boundaries of the city, a fabric that is constantly remade and renewed, repurposed, or abandoned. Arrival infrastructure highlights or connects the particular patches or parts of that tissue where transformative interactions between newcomers and their environment take place.

In line with the booming literature on infrastructure, the editors of the book *Infrastructuring Arrival* (the academic complement of this *Integration Oth-*

erwise Inspiration Kit) stress three further aspects in their infrastructural understanding of newcomers' arrival situations: (a) the unequal material conditions in which minor integrations into a new setting take place, for example finding a home, a school, or a place to start looking for work (Amin 2014); (b) the channelling of newcomers' physical and social mobility, of moving on in life and negotiating one's immediate and longer-term aspirations (Kleinman 2014); and (c), emphasising the continuous work of maintaining and renewing the urban fabric, the liveliness, the sheer diversity of everyday socialising, labour, and leisure, cultural, and religious activities (Larkin 2013), not least those related to upbringing and care and often referred to as aspects of 'social reproduction' (Hall 2020).

Arrival infrastructure has generally been studied within local and translocal fields of interaction, variably called arrival neighbourhoods, areas, zones, regions, etc. Several authors, including some of those who contributed to the edited volume *Infrastructuring Arrival* and this Kit, have looked into areas with, for example, industrial agriculture (Chapter 9) or spatially isolated asylum centres and (informal) refugee camps (Chapter 5), while others have focused on social or commercial infrastructures (Wessendorf and Gembus 2024) within 'urban arrival areas' (Hans and Hanhörster 2020) or 'urban emplacement' in migrant hostels (Mbodj-Pouye 2023).

As a noun, 'arrival infrastructure' can be used in both singular and plural. Some authors use the countable form: the library as an arrival infrastructure, two ethnic shops as arrival infrastructures. Other use the non-countable form to describe the arrival infrastructure that is relevant for particular groups. This is very similar to how recent scholars in the United Kingdom combine the use of the term 'social infrastructure' in a countable and a non-countable form: the community centre and the playground are countable social infrastructures; together they are 'the social infrastructure' (Latham and Layton 2022; Horton and Penny 2023). Hence, think of how we use the term 'public transport', which cannot be reduced to a bus, a bus stop, a bus driver, or the timetable. Together, 'in concert', they form a public transport system that gets you to some places and not to others. The library, the community worker, the Pentecostal church: together they are an arrival infrastructure that provides conditions for newcomers to shape their arrival and future.

References:
Amin, Ash. 2014. 'Lively Infrastructure', *Theory, Culture & Society*, 31: 137–61.
Burgess, Ernest W. 1925/1967. 'The growth of the city: An introduction to a research project' in Robert E. Park and Ernest W. Burgess (eds.), *The city: Suggestions for investigations of human behavior in the urban environment* (Chicago: The University of Chicago Press).
Hall, Sarah Marie. 2020. 'Social reproduction as social infrastructure', *Soundings*, 76: 82–94.

Hans, Nils, and Heike Hanhörster. 2020. 'Accessing resources in arrival neighbourhoods: How foci-aided encounters offer resources to new-comers', *Urban Planning*, 5: 78–88.

Horton, Amy, and Joe Penny. 2023. 'Towards a Political Economy of Social Infrastructure: Contesting "Anti-Social Infrastructures"', *Antipode*, 55: 1711–34.

Kleinman, Julie. 2014. 'Adventures in infrastructure: making an African hub in Paris', *City & Society*, 26: 286–307.

Larkin, Brian. 2013. 'The politics and poetics of infrastructure', *Annual Review of Anthropology*, 42: 327–43.

Latham, Alan, and Jack Layton. 2022. 'Social infrastructure: why it matters and how urban geographers might study it', *Urban Geography*, 43(5): 659–68.

Lefebvre, Henri. 1967. 'Quartier et vie de quartier', *Cahiers de l'Institut d'aménagement et d'urbanisme de la région parisienne*: 9–32.

Mbodj-Pouye, Aïssatou. 2023. *An address in Paris. Emplacement, bureaucracy, and belonging in hostels for West African migrants* (New York: Columbia University Press).

Meeus, Bruno, Bas van Heur, and Karel Arnaut. 2019. 'Migration and the infrastructural politics of urban arrival' in Bruno Meeus, Karel Arnaut, and Bas Van Heur (eds.), *Arrival infrastructures: Migration and urban social mobilities* (London: Palgrave Macmillan).

Saunders, Doug. 2011. *Arrival city: how the largest migration in history is reshaping our world* (London: Windmill Books).

Wessendorf, Susanne, and Malte Gembus. 2024. 'The social front door: the role of social infrastructures for migrant arrival', *Journal of Ethnic and Migration Studies*, 50: 2822–38.

See the academic complement of this *Integration Otherwise Inspiration Kit*, the edited volume *Infrastructuring Arrival* (Arnaut, Beeckmans, and Meeus, 2026), in particular:
– Chapter 1 (Arnaut, Beeckmans, and Meeus, 2026)
– Chapter 5 (Arvanitidis, Papagiannitsis, and Voulvouli, 2026)
– Chapter 9 (Lubberhuizen, 2026)

The interactive process through which newcomers, together with others, build and transform their arrival situation and carve out their future social and spatial mobility is what we call 'arrival infrastructuring'. In a twofold adaptation, we have redefined the term 'infrastructure' beyond its conventional usage. Firstly, we extend the concept beyond what is traditionally classified as 'hard infrastructure' – such as roads, electricity networks, and other provisioning systems. This is the 'structure' that supports or underpins ('infra') daily life in often invisible ways, only becoming noticeable when it breaks down. Secondly, while we include what are increasingly termed 'social infrastructures' – such as libraries, schools, health centres, and various social services, often provided by the government – we further expand the concept. These social infrastructures, to which newcomers have varying degrees of access depending on their legal status, represent only part of the broader notion of 'arrival infrastructure' we aim to highlight.

We use 'arrival infrastructuring' as a verb then to refer to the many ways in which people – newcomers in particular – infrastructure the arrival situation of new-comers in social and spatial ways. For instance, newcomers' arrival is often infra-structured through practices like sharing homes with co-nationals or providing food, information, and support via church services. Through these 'infrastructuring practices', which often make use of both hard and social infrastructures, the arrival situation, and the process of integration, is socially and spatially supported or 'infra-structured'.

We sometimes use the term 'infrastructuring work' instead of 'infrastructuring practices' to emphasise the substantial and often invisible – or invisibilised (intentionally made invisible) – care work and reproductive labour that characterises arrival infrastructuring. Frequently, arrival infrastructuring takes place within existing, historical places of arrival, where it plays a significant role in shaping, altering, and transforming their socio-spatial characteristics. Yet, in other cases, arrival infrastructuring results in the creation of entirely new parts of the arrival infrastructure. Arrival infrastructuring often encompasses both formal and informal dimensions. Compared to what is typically understood as social infrastructures, such as libraries or schools, arrival infrastructuring is less fixed in place, less standardised or institutionalised in nature, and less visible, as it often addresses gaps in formal systems of care and support to which newcomers have no access.

Sometimes governments – through their services, representatives, and policies – play a pivotal role in supporting the 'infrastructuring practices' of newcomers and others. However, this is not always the case. Governments often channel certain groups into 'permanent arrival' – such as people who spend years waiting in asylum centres – or into 'permanent temporariness' – as seen with those whose asylum applications are rejected, rendering them illegalised and even criminalised, in this way often countering the minor integrations or arrival infrastructuring work that has already happened.

At the same time, newcomers, often in collaboration with others, infrastructure arrival using whatever is at hand, including parts of government infrastructures. The notion of 'arrival infrastructuring' thus allows for a critical, bottom-up perspective as it highlights how infrastructuring practices can support arrival ('infra-structure' arrival) within, against, and beyond government infrastructures.

Our goals

Our goal with this *Integration Otherwise Inspiration Kit* is to make visible diverse forms of arrival infrastructuring and the wide range of people, organisations, and institutions involved. We aim to highlight instances where we find they contribute to valuable 'minor integrations', so that others can be inspired by them or make space for them in their policy or practice. At the same time, we strive to acknowledge the limitations and challenges inherent in processes of arrival infrastructuring, as we are cautious not to romanticise the often difficult realities newcomers face, since arrival infrastructuring is not immune to exploitation and abuse. By bringing to the fore a variety of arrival infrastructuring practices, we also do not intend to say that they should serve as an excuse for governments to retreat from investing in integration – quite the contrary.

Our overall objective is to work towards a different narrative on integration – one that goes beyond the current state of polarisation about integration. We simply find that a lot of knowledge about other ways of doing integration already exists and is embedded in the work of people on the ground. This *Integration Otherwise Inspiration Kit* aims to make it visible and encourage you to activate this knowledge in your own context.

About us

We are a group of 38 researchers. Most of us are academics, but some are social and spatial practitioners. We are based at six universities, two research institutes, and two NGOs in eight countries in Europe, including Turkey and the UK. We were brought together by a Horizon 2020 research project called 'ReROOT: Arrival Infrastructures as Site of Integration for Recent Newcomers' that has been running since Spring 2021.

When we applied for funding, we never imagined that the European Research Council would give us the opportunity to both revolutionise and depolarise how we approach integration in Europe. Grateful for this chance, we collaborated intensively from 2021 to 2025. Some of us worked as fieldwork researchers, others as trainers or tutors. We met regularly, both online and in person, in small groups and larger gatherings, and in the meantime have developed a strong network.

One of the more action-oriented outcomes of this intense journey is this *Integration Otherwise Inspiration Kit*. This publication is complemented by an academic book, *Infrastructuring Arrival: Envisioning the Migration-Integration Nexus Beyond Crisis* (edited by Karel Arnaut, Luce Beeckmans, and Bruno Meeus, Leuven University Press, 2026). Where relevant, we have included cross-references between the two, as you may have already noticed above.

Our imagined audience

When we created the *Integration Otherwise Inspiration Kit*, our imagined audience was everyone involved in or interested in local integration processes and arrival, and even more generally everyone who engages with newcomers on a regular basis. The specific audience we had in mind are social and spatial practitioners, local public administrations and policymakers, community builders, civil society organisations, NGOs and activists, and of course newcomers old and new.

B.   INSPIRATION KIT

How to use the Kit?

The *Integration Otherwise Inspiration Kit* consists of two parts: Part I 'Seeing Integration Otherwise' and Part II 'Doing Integration Otherwise'. Part I 'Seeing Integration Otherwise' sheds light on the diverse forms of arrival infrastructuring we have encountered during our research and aims to inspire you with another perspective on integration by highlighting the many minor integrations we witnessed on the ground. Part II 'Doing Integration Otherwise' reflects on our own collaborative actions of engaging in 'integration otherwise' and aims to inspire you to take action yourself. Both parts are subdivided into chapters. For Part I 'Seeing Integration Otherwise', we grouped similar forms of arrival infrastructuring by chapter, namely: resourcing, bridging, coming together, and claiming. For Part II 'Doing Integration Otherwise', we clustered actions with similar objectives into each chapter, namely: raising awareness, coalition-building, and empowering.

The inspiration in this Kit is provided in two main ways. Firstly, through stories that give insight into a variety of infrastructural practices and will enable you to 'see integration otherwise' (Part I) and in a variety of ways to take action and 'do integration otherwise' (Part II). Insights into what we find valuable or what we think might be problematic are summarised after each story as 'takeaways'. Secondly, we provide you with a set of tools, with reflection tools in Part I that encourage you to 'see otherwise', and action tools in Part II that support you in 'doing otherwise'. It is possible to use the tools separately from the stories, but we often use a story to demonstrate the context in which a tool works well. Lastly, we have the 'Reflection and Advice' section that concludes each part. Here we provide some advice from the field researchers themselves for you to reflect upon regarding issues of ethics and positionality – the awareness of how one's own social, cultural, and political context influences one's research.

The various components of the *Integration Otherwise Inspiration Kit*

- *Stories*: The stories from the field aim to illustrate arrival infrastructuring work in depth. They always start with a problem statement and then tell the full story.

- *Titles of stories*: All titles have a descriptive first part, and a more analytical second part that concisely explains the 'integration otherwise' in the particular site. The life domain of the 'minor integration' is mentioned first in case you want to immediately go to the domains that are most relevant to you.

- *Takeaways*: The takeaways are lessons learned from the research with regard to the 'integration otherwise' and are situated at the end of the stories.

- *Tools*: Reflection and action tools can be found throughout the Kit and are linked to one story (or more). They have a different layout from the stories so that they stand out.

- *Reflection and advice*: Both Parts I and II end with 'Reflection and Advice' sections that provide 'umbrella' reflections on the two parts.

- *Concept boxes*: This is where we expand on concepts that we use often but that might sound very academic.

- *Visual material*: Our Kit is not just text-based. We have four types of visual material in this Kit:

    1. 'Drawings' that add some additional, non-textual argumentation to the stories.

    2. 'Diagrams' that provide templates for engaging with the tools.

    3. Maps that introduce the fieldwork sites so you have an idea of their geographical location.

    4. Photos taken by our researchers.

The words we use matter

Here, we share some reflections on language and terminology. As you may have noticed, in this introduction, we have used the term 'newcomers' rather than, for example, 'migrants' or 'refugees'. This choice reflects our conviction that the term 'newcomers' to some extent transcends the rigid categories imposed by governments on people, although we do acknowledge that it remains a label that reduces people's identities to their migratory status (while the people who can move freely in this world are not categorised in similar ways).

Throughout the Kit, you will see that we also sometimes use other terms instead of 'newcomers'. This is because we thought that it was relevant to do so there, or because our participants identified themselves in those terms. We also do not want to pretend that these categories do not exist or that they do not significantly influence people's lives. Therefore, choosing the right terminology was sometimes a difficult call for us to make, and we hope that people feel represented in the most accurate and respectful way possible.

How was the Kit made?

This Kit is the result of a rigorous co-production process and is therefore co-authored. The 'author contribution statement' explains the co-authorship (see p. 4). The co-production of the Kit had many stages, starting with the ethnographic fieldwork and action research, continuing on to the second stage of translating site-specific insights into more general findings and reformulating them in a language that is accessible. The last stage consisted of testing the Kit internally and within the original fieldwork sites.

Here, we briefly reflect on research ethics and data management. It is important for you to note that all content in this Kit is pseudonymised. This means that we do not use the real names of people in order to protect their privacy. The same is true for place names when revealing them could cause our participants harm. Of course, we always made sure to obtain informed consent, either written or orally.

Our main principle of fieldwork was 'do no harm'. Additionally, we tried to work to a non-extractive and transformative form of research, one that in fact results in a mutual benefit for both the 'researcher' and the 'researched' and breaks the hierarchy between them. Part II testifies to this transformative ambition, although we acknowledge our own shortcomings and limitations and reflect upon them in the Reflection and Advice sections. We recognise that our knowledge is partial and that our research participants are the experts in their own experience.

> Further reading: You might be interested in consulting the Ethics Charter of the Atlas research project for further advice on ethics and positionality when working in arrival contexts: https://atlas-bxl.eu/.

The Kit Team

The team that developed this *Integration Otherwise Inspiration Kit* based on their involvement in the ReROOT project from day one and on an intensive co-production trajectory with the field researchers consists of Luce Beeckmans, Dounia Salamé, Martina Bovo, and Mary Hogan.

C. NINE EUROPEAN SITES

The *Integration Otherwise Inspiration Kit* is based on ethnographic (action) research conducted across nine European sites as part of the ReROOT project. In this section, we briefly introduce you to the nine fieldwork sites, providing geographical and contextual background information to help orient you. Some of the sites consist of more than one location, even in more than one country. We have taken them together because they are connected by migratory dynamics or provide an interesting basis for comparison.

Additionally, we present the research team for each site, along with the team responsible for developing this Kit. This section also credits individuals from outside the ReROOT project where required. The sites are ordered alphabetically.

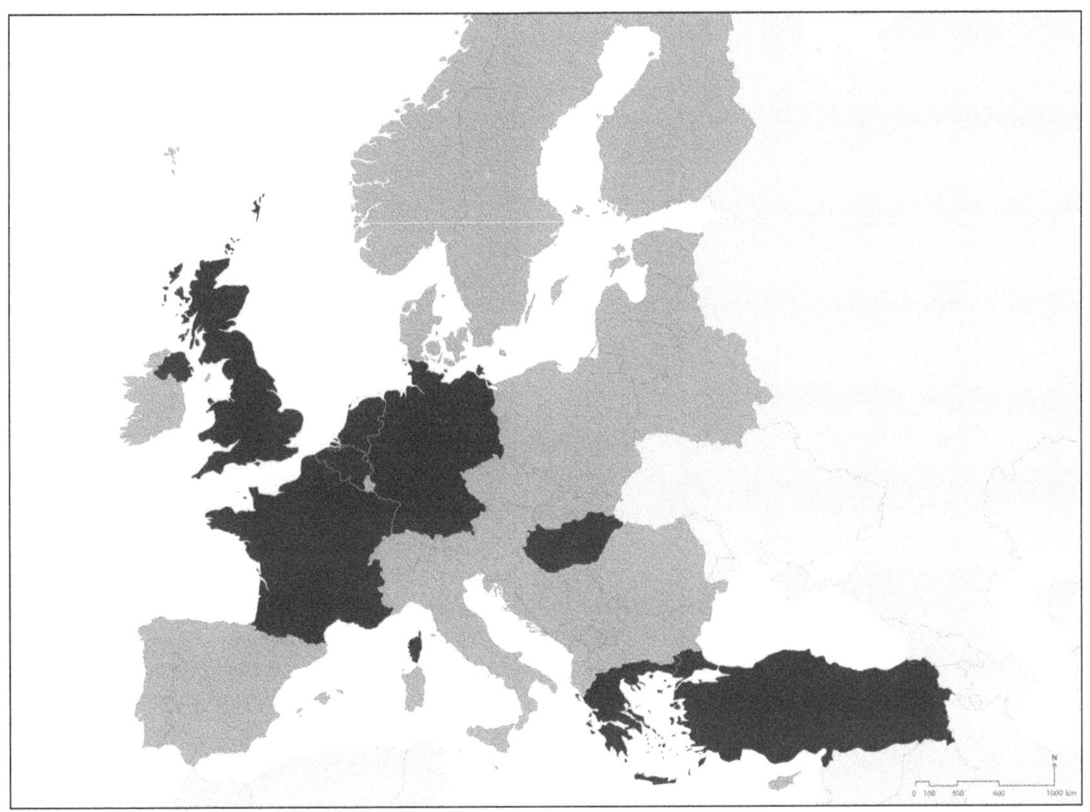

Figure 1. Map of all nine research sites

1. Brussels

Figure 2. Map of Brussels site

About the site

The field research in Brussels (Belgium) focuses on people on the move who are commonly (but not unproblematically) referred to as 'transit migrants' or 'transmigrants' – newcomers moving and dwelling outside the state-run reception and asylum centres. The Brussels field of inquiry consists of multiple co-constructed and interrelated environments, ranging from online networks and platforms to private homes, occupations and squats, camps, churches, organised shelters, parks, and streets. Within this site, the topic of care – care of the self and of others, protection and empowerment, voicing and advocacy – in difficult conditions, in different settings, and in different forms has emerged as the most prevalent research focus.

Broader context

The broader context for this research is a 'hostile environment': the post-2015 landscape of a lingering so-called 'refugee crisis' in a political climate in which subsequent Belgian Secretaries of State for Asylum and Migration stressed the unmanageable numbers of refugees and characterised their policy as that of reclaiming control over migration by limiting the 'influx' and speeding up the 'outflow'.

More specifically, the site research focuses on squats and private hosting. The continued and politically created shortage of accommodation for asylum-seekers supplemented by a lack of housing for undocumented and documented people alike is addressed in Brussels by activism of different sorts directed at bringing (violations of) housing and asylum rights to the attention of the general public. This activism consists of (a) occupations of empty buildings, leading to the mobilisation of support and the opening of temporary shelters in the city, and (b) legal procedures, leading to multiple convictions of the state for the non-provision of reception. This offers a legal base legitimising the occupations and other protest actions. Furthermore, the 2015 reception crisis led to the creation of the Citizen Platform (now BelRefugees) that, among other things, organised private hosting. This was an immediate success and families started hosting people on the move, even unmediated by the Citizen Platform.

Ethnographic research

The ethnographic research consisted of participating in and initiating provision of service and leisure activities, dwelling in parks and the city alongside newcomers, following individual trajectories, voluntary work, etc. The ethnographic work carried out was comprised of interviews with hosts and guests, and collaborative and at times activist interactions with interlocutors. After an initial two years, the research method was expanded to include action research with the purpose of co-politicising, co-activating and co-living. Concretely, this action research involves participating in and sometimes co-organising events to bring attention to the issues facing unhoused people on the move in Brussels.

Research team

Shila Anaraki (field researcher, KU Leuven), Karel Arnaut (KU Leuven), Ilse van Liempt (Utrecht University), and Bruno Meeus (Hogeschool Utrecht).

2. Budapest

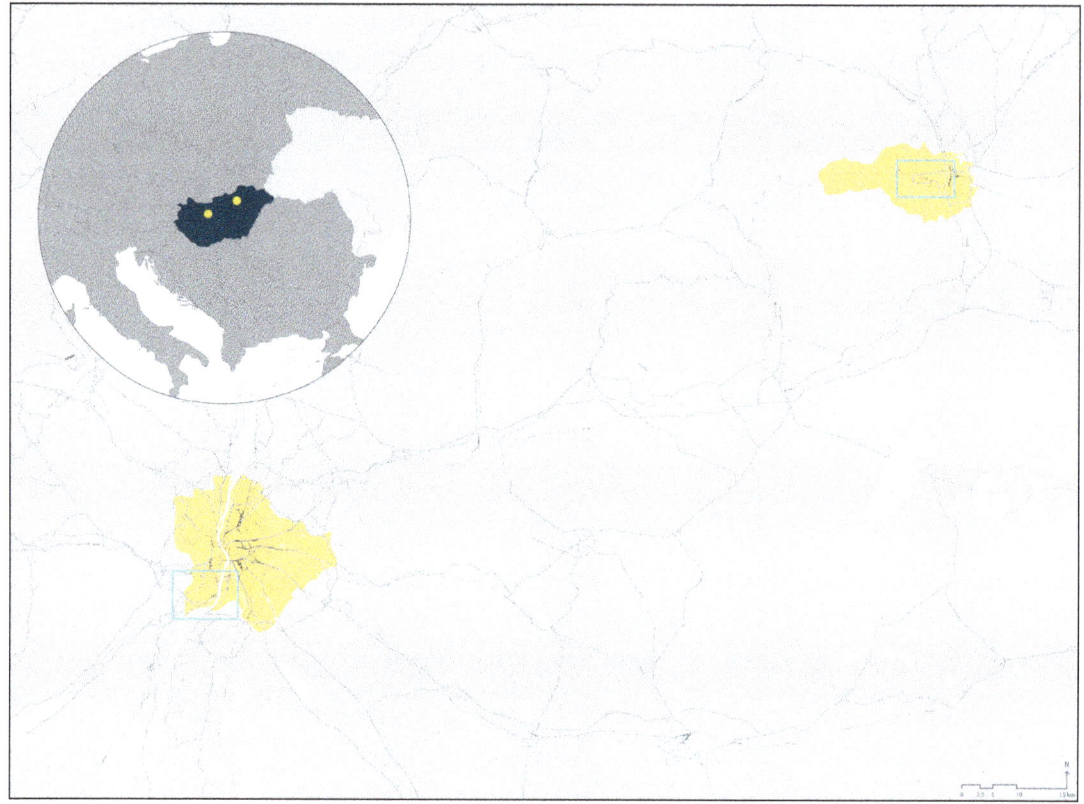

Figure 3. Map of Budapest site

About the site

The research site explores the life worlds of international students present in Budapest and its hinterland (Hungary) within the framework of the Stipendium Hungaricum international scholarship programme. This programme allows people from the Middle East, Central Asia, Eastern Europe, broader Africa and South/Southeast Asia to study at Hungarian universities. The research focuses on various aspects of life of newcomer-students at Semmelweis University, Eötvös Loránd University ELTE in Budapest, and the University of Miskolc in eastern Hungary. This includes social networks, housing, parochial spaces, online platforms, events, cultural practices, and NGOs that students make use of, invest in, occupy, and transform during their time as students in Hungary.

Broader context

Newcomers arrive in Budapest for many reasons. Often these reasons include education, business ventures, and improved opportunities for the future. Because migration is strictly regulated in Hungary, newcomers face limited support from the state. However, other stakeholders, such as universities and civil society organisations, provide necessary services and support to make up for the gaps left by the state. This research focuses on international students, because taking up an international scholarship at a Hungarian university is common channel for moving to and living in Hungary, and more broadly the EU. Even though the scholarship programmes are not created specifically for settling in Hungary, many students do not return to their home countries and aspire to settle elsewhere in the EU.

Ethnographic research

During the research period, the research team engaged with universities in the country where students from the Stipendium Hungaricum international scholarship programme were studying. Additionally, research was carried out in Budapest with grassroots groups, informal providers and official NGOs providing frontline services to newcomers.

Research team

Márton Bisztrai (field researcher, Menedék Hungarian Association for Migrants), Sarah Makar (field researcher, Menedék Hungarian Association for Migrants), Alexandra Sandor (field researcher, Menedék Hungarian Association for Migrants), Emma Krasznahorkai (field researcher, Menedék Hungarian Association for Migrants), András Kováts (Menedék Hungarian Association for Migrants), György Csepeli (Menedék Hungarian Association for Migrants), Antal Örkeny (Menedék Hungarian Association for Migrants), and Zsuzsa László (Menedék Hungarian Association for Migrants).

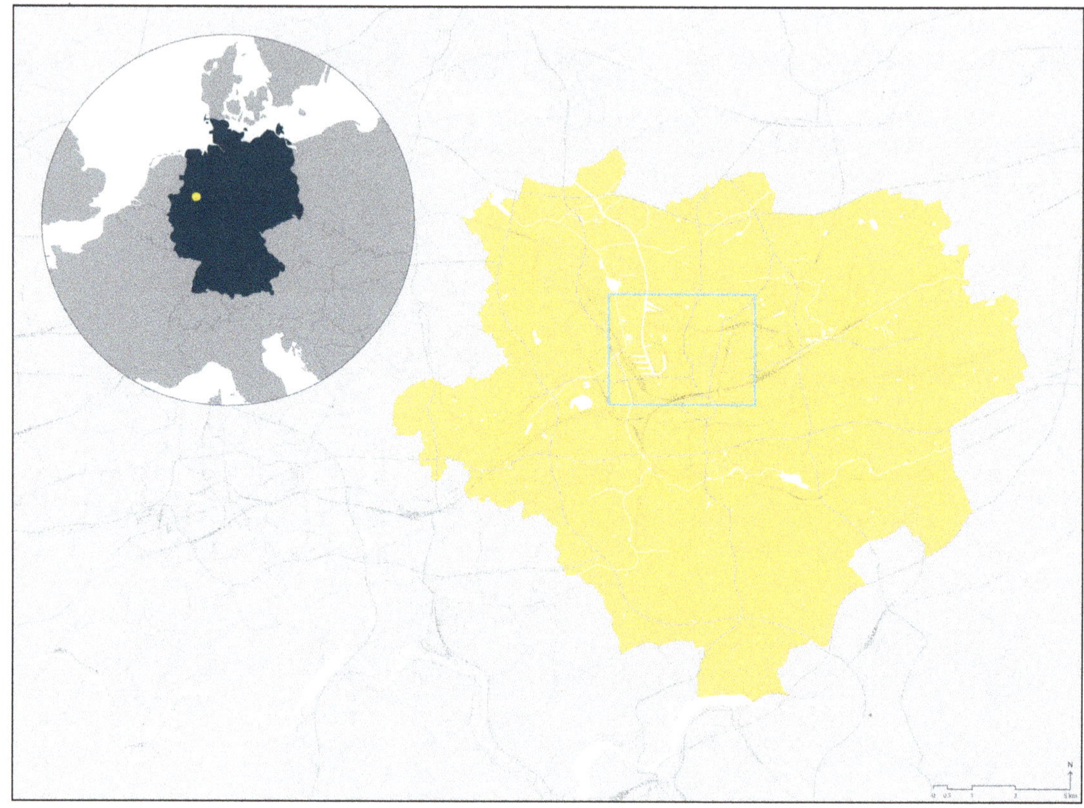

Figure 4. Map of Dortmund-Nordstadt site

About the site

The district of Nordstadt in Dortmund (Germany) has a historical path as a traditional arrival neighbourhood and is shaped by multiple layers of migration processes. Nowadays, Nordstadt is characterised by a high population turnover that has become even more marked in recent decades. It is, at the same time, the poorest and youngest district in Dortmund. Against this backdrop, the district has been subject to various political and urban interventions and offers a dense landscape of formal and informal support structures addressing migrants from various backgrounds. However, newcomers are confronted with structural gaps when it comes to the provision of child- and youth-related infrastructure and housing, gaps which affect migrants' life situations significantly.

Broader context

Although Germany has been shaped by various migration processes since the Second World War, its political acknowledgement as a country of immigration followed slowly in the late 1990s to early 2000s. In the light of projected demographic change and related skills shortages, a shift in German migration policies then took place that is reflected in the legal differentiation between labour and humanitarian migration, which affects migrants' access to rights and resources. As integration is seen as taking place at the local level, the importance of arrival neighbourhoods has been increasingly politically acknowledged. There is consensus among local stakeholders that arrival processes need to be governed as early as possible after arrival.

Ethnographic research

The field research comprised interviews, observation and informal conversations, and the analysis of migration-related policy documents. First, the research engaged with many stakeholders at the expert level and, in the next step, with selected stakeholders on the ground. A wide range of stakeholders were interviewed, from ministry officials to informal brokers offering support of various kinds. Two primary schools and two public migration advice services were selected to delve deeper into organisations that are relevant to migrants' life situations. These organisations were an important entry point for further observations and conversations with staff and newcomers, for example at the school gate.

Research team

Cornelia Tippel (field researcher, ILS Research), Dennis Zilske (PlanerLaden), Heike Hanhörster (TU Berlin), and Reiner Staubach (PlanerLaden).

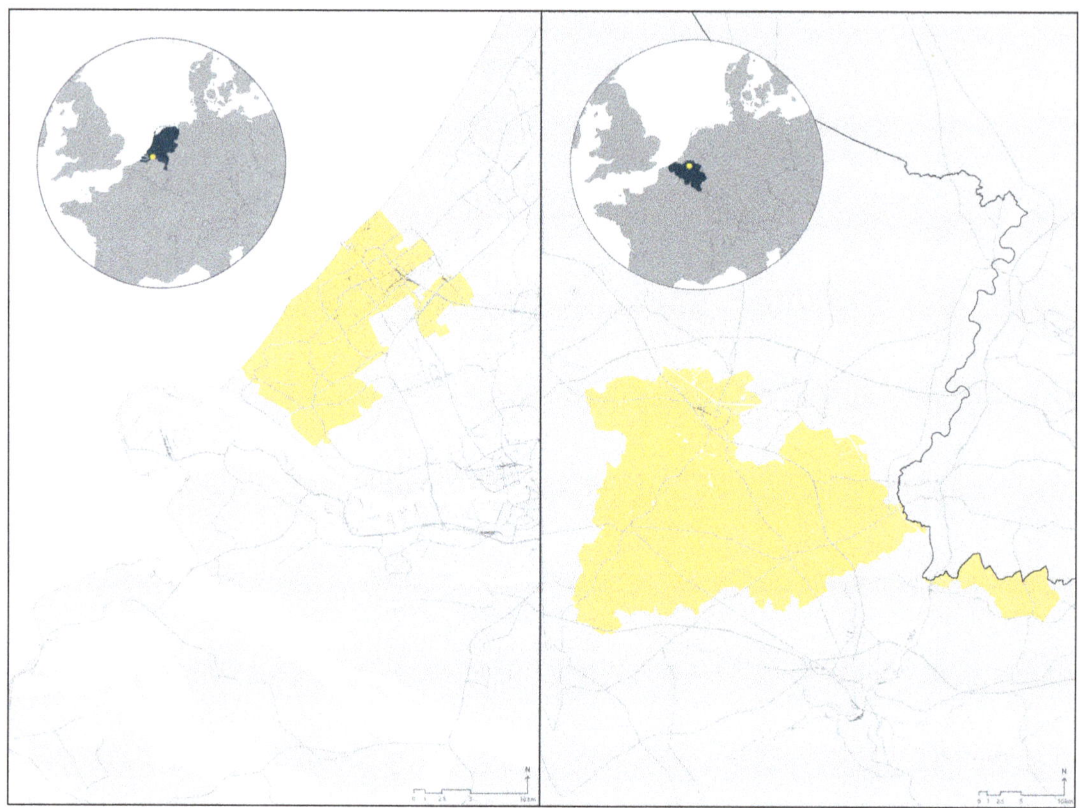

Figure 5. Map of Haspengouw/Westland site

About the site

This site revolves around the mobile lifeworlds of agricultural migrant workers in the municipality of Westland (the Netherlands) and the region of Haspengouw (Belgium). In Haspengouw, known for its fruit cultivation, and Westland, known for its greenhouse agriculture, many Central and Eastern European (CEE) migrant workers are employed in the orchards and greenhouses on temporary contracts. Research at this site focuses on the ways migrant workers get their bearings upon arrival in these agricultural areas through work, housing, shops, services, digital spaces, and informal networks, all within a context where there is a constant need for flexible, dismissible labour. In this context, migrant workers are often seen and treated as either temporary or seasonal newcomers, or as (potential) victims of exploitation.

Broader context

The relationship between agriculture and migration in Westland and Haspengouw precedes the expansion of the European Union in 2004 and 2007. Turkish and Moroccan guest workers already present in the Netherlands and Belgium and Sikh refugees coming to Belgium often found informal employment, which alleviated a demand for cheap and flexible labour. Together with national legislation allowing more flexible and temporary labour, the expansion of the EU made it possible for growers to employ citizens from mainly CEE countries. From these emerging mobilities, (in)formal transnational migration industries have developed in which employment agencies, farmers, and brokers became important stakeholders and profit participants channelling agricultural migrant workers into temporary work and housing.

Ethnographic research

The ethnographic entry points were various orchards, greenhouses, and factories in Westland and Haspengouw. There, research was conducted in order to better understand the ways in which agricultural labour and migration policies and practices work out in the repetitive physical labour in the fields and in social interactions between migrant workers and employers. From these entry points, the research followed different people, trajectories, communities, and infrastructures involved in the arrival situation and (temporary) settlement of migrant workers. Spatially, this also meant following people from agricultural workplaces to urban areas like The Hague and Brussels, where many migrant workers live and organise themselves.

Research team

Carolien Lubberhuizen (field researcher, Utrecht University), Ilse van Liempt (Utrecht University), Karel Arnaut (KU Leuven), and Gideon Bolt (Utrecht University). The field researcher was supported by a project assistant, Winona Boomkens. In addition to the 12 visual contributors to the photovoice project, she collaborated with the geographer Noor van der Vorst to make an audioscape.

5. Istanbul-Fatih

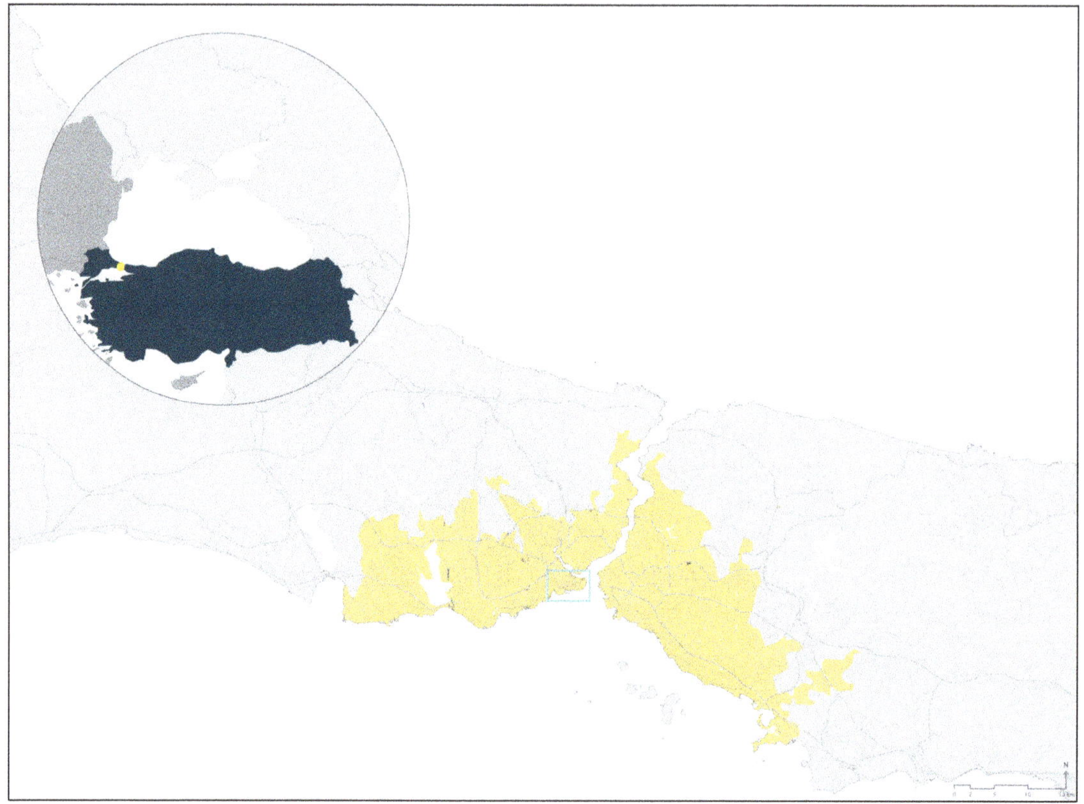

Figure 6. Map of Istanbul-Fatih site

About the site

The localities of Aksaray, Laleli, and Kumkapı, part of the historical district of Fatih in Istanbul (Turkey), form a transnational migration hub that connects the Middle East, Central Asia, Eastern Europe, North Africa, and South/Southeast Asia. Since the 1990s in particular, migrants with various legal statuses, migration motives and opportunities have been arriving into this already existing local context of diversity. The localities comprise a wide range of business both small and large, formal and informal, such as shops, call centres, cargo agencies, hotels, barbers, real estate agencies, and ethnic restaurants, which serve as an arrival infrastructure for newcomers. While Aksaray and Laleli are known for their vibrant commercial wholesale trade landscape, Kumkapı has remained a residential area, providing housing infrastructure for long-term inhabitants, passers-by, and newcomers.

Broader context

An important broader context is the gendered nature of arrival infrastructures. Women suitcase traders arriving in the area in the 1990s continue to play a significant role in organising work relations and social life along lines of gender and intimacy. The loosely regulated mobility of suitcase traders facilitated the mass arrival and further (labour) migration from former Soviet Union countries. In other words, women suitcase traders have been the primary mediators of post-1990s arrivals in these localities. While the arrival of women suitcase traders is supported by the presence of different infrastructures in the area, it is also discouraged by the simultaneous development of migrant sex work in these localities that have reinforced the area's public reputation as a place of prostitution. This reputation makes movement through public space and finding employment and housing particularly difficult and sensitive, in particular for (young) women newcomers. Women who are particularly marked as 'foreign' in this space, including the many domestic workers we interviewed, shared experiences of verbal and/or physical sexual harassment and violence. This all happens against the backdrop of increased regulation and restrictions of migration by the Turkish state in recent years.

Ethnographic research

Ethnographic research was conducted in Aksaray, Laleli, and Kumkapı in commercial spaces like shops, real estate agencies, cargo transport infrastructure, and in a private clinic that is one of the very few institutionalised spaces providing services to migrants. Participant observation included spending many hours on different days and times of the week in the previously mentioned spaces and chatting and hanging out with shopkeepers, waiters, carriers of goods to be shipped by the cargo agencies, real estate agents, café managers, and patients and medical staff of the clinic, all of whom provided insights into the multi-layered arrival situation in the area where the boundaries of formality and informality are blurred.

Research team

Marhabo Saparova (field researcher, Sabancı University) and Kristen Biehl (Sabancı University).

6. Karditsa/Katerini

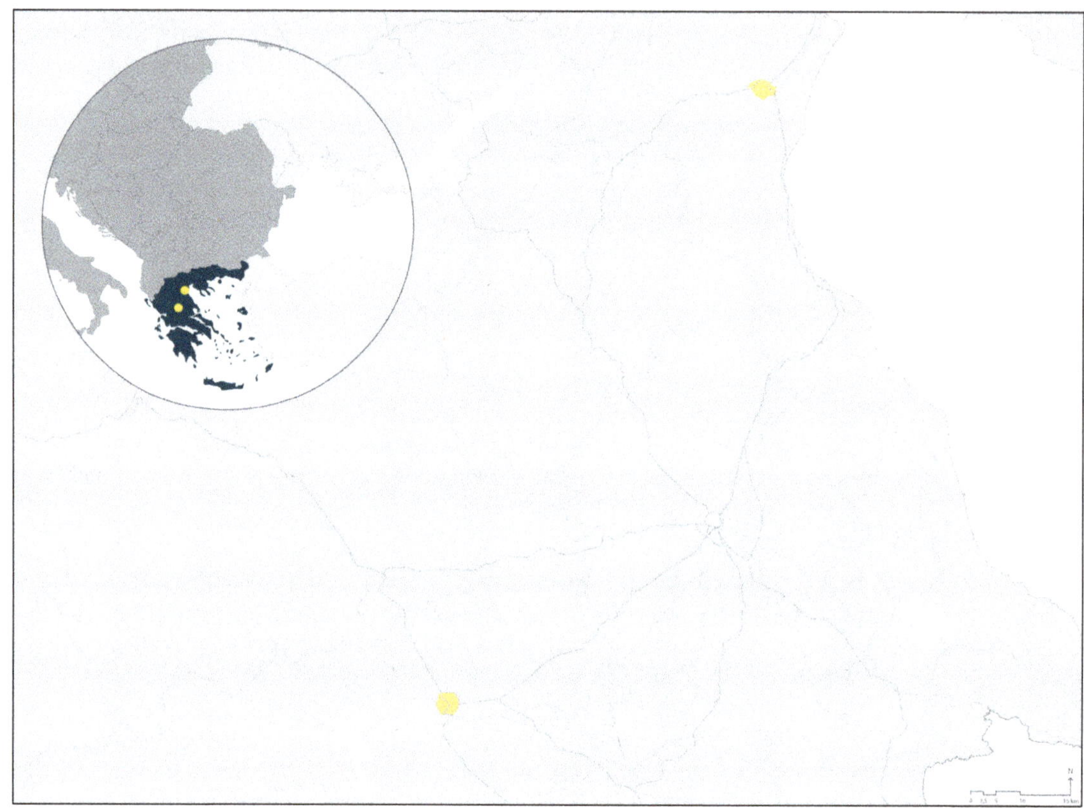

About the site

The research site is comprised of two typical small, disempowered cities, Karditsa and Katerini, located in central Greece, that exhibit similar characteristics in terms of demographics, economy, and migrant arrivals. The arrival situation is shaped by the implementation of the ESTIA programme (Emergency Support to Integration and Accommodation) funded by the EU in the two cities, which provided accommodation to a substantial number of newcomers (asylum-seekers) who entered the country during the so-called 'refugee crisis' in 2015–2016. Newcomers, local municipalities, implementing stakeholders, grassroots organisations, NGOs, and established immigrants constitute the arrival situation under study. Yet, despite the similarities between the two cities, local responses to immigration and to formation of arrival infrastructures have been quite different, as will be outlined in the stories.

Broader context

In an attempt to deal with the pressing issue of accommodating the newcomers, the EU, in collaboration with the Greek government, UNHCR, and many other implementing partners and NGOs, introduced the ESTIA programme, which was applied in a series of selected cities. To fulfil its objectives of addressing the needs of recently arrived asylum-seekers in Greece, the programme drew on local stakeholders to set up local structures of implementation. These structures were neither fixed nor identical in each city and reflected the local conditions, capacities, politics, and dynamics, as well as the existing formal and informal arrival infrastructuring practices.

Ethnographic research

In order to deal with the complexity and multidimensionality of the subject matter, the research employed a range of methods. Institutional mapping during the first steps helped to delineate the relevant stakeholders and the basic structure of the site. We used a variety of ethnographic methods such as participant observation, diaries, and fieldnote-taking, as well as conducting semi-structured interviews. In order to gain the trust of newcomers, the researchers also got involved in volunteering work, participated in social events, and actively assisted with job searching.

Research team

George Papagiannitsis (field researcher, University of Thessaly), Penelope Vergou (field researcher, University of Thessaly), Aimilia Voulvouli (field researcher, University of Thessaly), Athina Zoe Desli (field researcher, University of Thessaly), and Paschalis Arvanitidis (University of Thessaly).

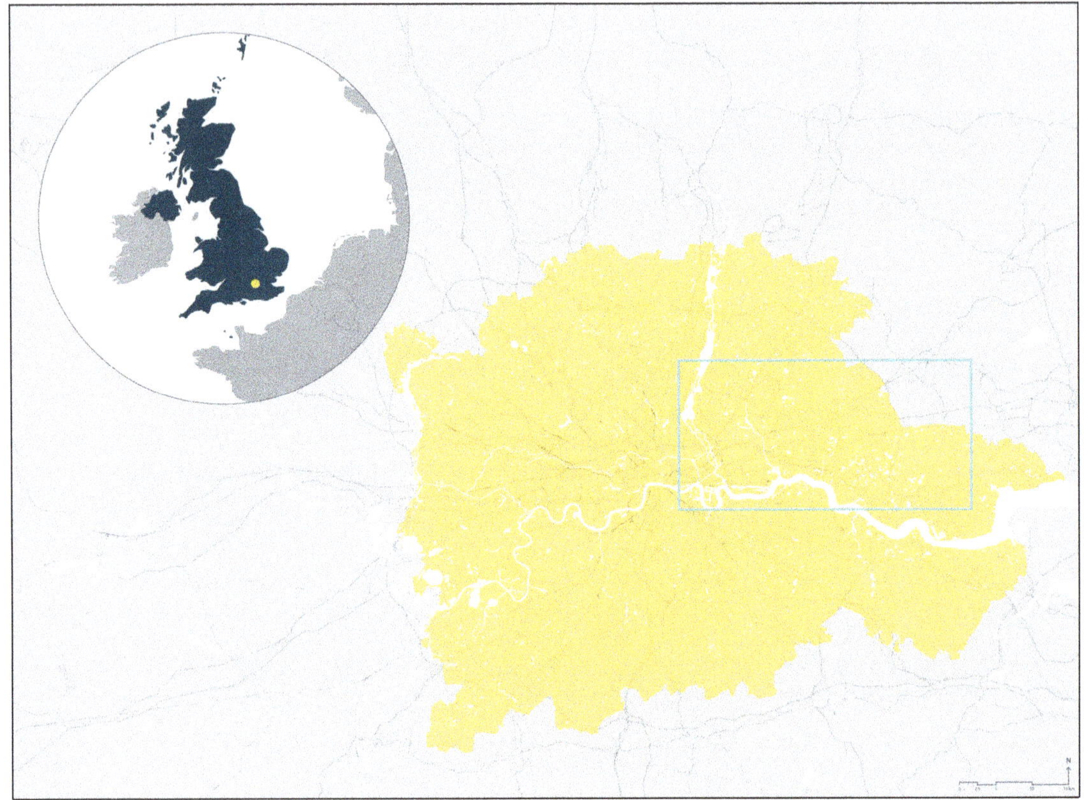

Figure 8. Map of London site

About the site

The London borough under scrutiny, anonymised to protect the privacy of the research participants, is a deprived neighbourhood in East London that has experienced swift demographic change in recent years. The municipality seeks to ensure socio-economic inclusion for longer-established residents, while also meeting the needs of a changing population. It is a task complicated by the political history of the area, funding restrictions, the UK's dysfunctional housing market, and the effects of the national government's hostile policies on migrant residents.

Broader context

The London borough has a strong social integration policy that recognises that both international migrants and established residents may suffer exclusion in a context of deprivation. Central government cuts to municipal budgets have narrowed the space for municipalities to provide support beyond the minimum that they are legally obliged to offer. Wider dynamics of social exclusion, social housing supply, and housing affordability in the city lead vulnerable arrivals, both British and foreign-born, to reside and seek support in the borough. Finally, many residents have experienced severe poverty or prolonged social exclusion due to national-level policies and practices directed at migrants, as will be explained at length in the stories.

Ethnographic research

The ethnographic research took place in everyday spaces such as libraries, markets, cafés, shops, and homes, as well as in services targeting specific needs or publics. These included free food provision services, English teaching services, and services for particular cultural, linguistic, or faith groups. Initial fieldwork did not reveal any visible, targeted services for international migrants or other newly arrived residents. However, the municipality, charities, and community groups deliver a range of different and often changing services to residents, frequently including different types of newcomers in the local area, whether British or foreign-born.

Research team

Tamlyn Monson (field researcher, Coventry University) and Susanne Wessendorf (Coventry University).

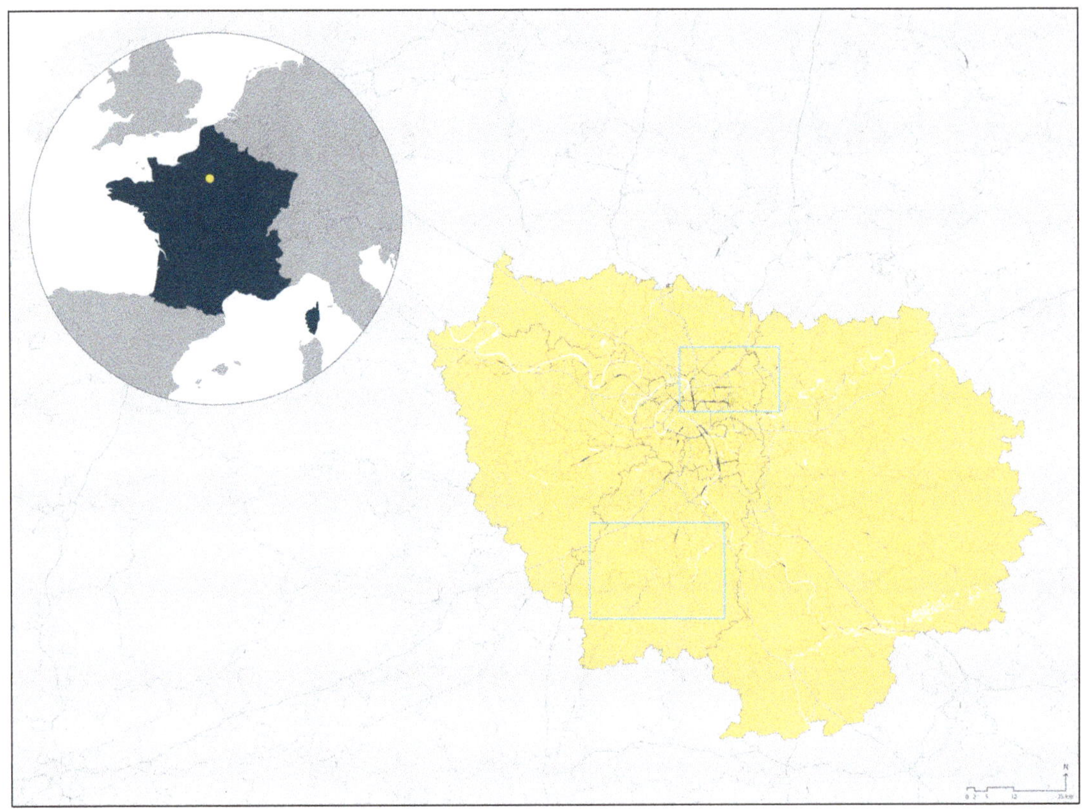

Figure 9. Map of Paris site

About the site

In 2015, informal camps in the northern part of Paris made the issue of migrant arrivals suddenly highly visible. This situation revealed the scarcity of accommodation for migrants and became problematised by the French government as a political crisis. The Paris research focuses on the many ways the state responded to the so-called 'migration crisis' – from relying on historical accommodation infrastructures to creating a large range of new housing structures for asylum-seekers. It also explores how migrants themselves have reacted to these interventions, taking advantage of them or circumventing them. A specific focus on housing for migrants in the so-called *'foyers'* – a form of social housing for migrant guest workers from West Africa designed in the 1950s – has allowed for a fine-grained exploration of the interplay between distinct stakeholders – state and non-state, migrant and non-migrant – in their joint infrastructuring of new-comers' arrivals.

Broader context

The year 2015 accelerated a trend of creating new types of 'mixed' accommodation dedicated to migrants, compared to older types of segregated accommodation like the *foyers* originally planned for West Africans. Meanwhile, since 1997 the *foyers* too have been subjected to a national transformation plan to turn them into more standardised social housing. This transformation has happened alongside a major reduction of collective spaces, limiting the daily appropriations of the buildings as much as collective mobilisation processes. Despite two decades of calls to close the Parisian *foyers*, the 2015 reception crisis saw their reactivation by the state to accommodate newcomers. The research sheds light on the strong postcolonial continuity between old modes of accommodation for migrants and so-called new types of accommodation for newcomers.

Ethnographic research

The ethnographic inquiry unfolded across these different types of accommodation. It involved qualitative research with the managers of the *foyers*, who are at the forefront of the dynamics regarding migrants' accommodation. Furthermore, it consisted of ethnographic research with Sudanese newcomers who arrived in (or after) 2015 at reception structures and *foyers*. The networks deployed by different generations of arrival are compared through their varying embeddedness in the *foyers*.

Research team

Laura Guérin (field researcher, Ecole d'Architecture de Paris-Val-de-Seine), Lucie Revilla (field researcher, CNRS), Stefan Le Courant (field researcher, CNRS), and Aïssatou Mbodj (CNRS).

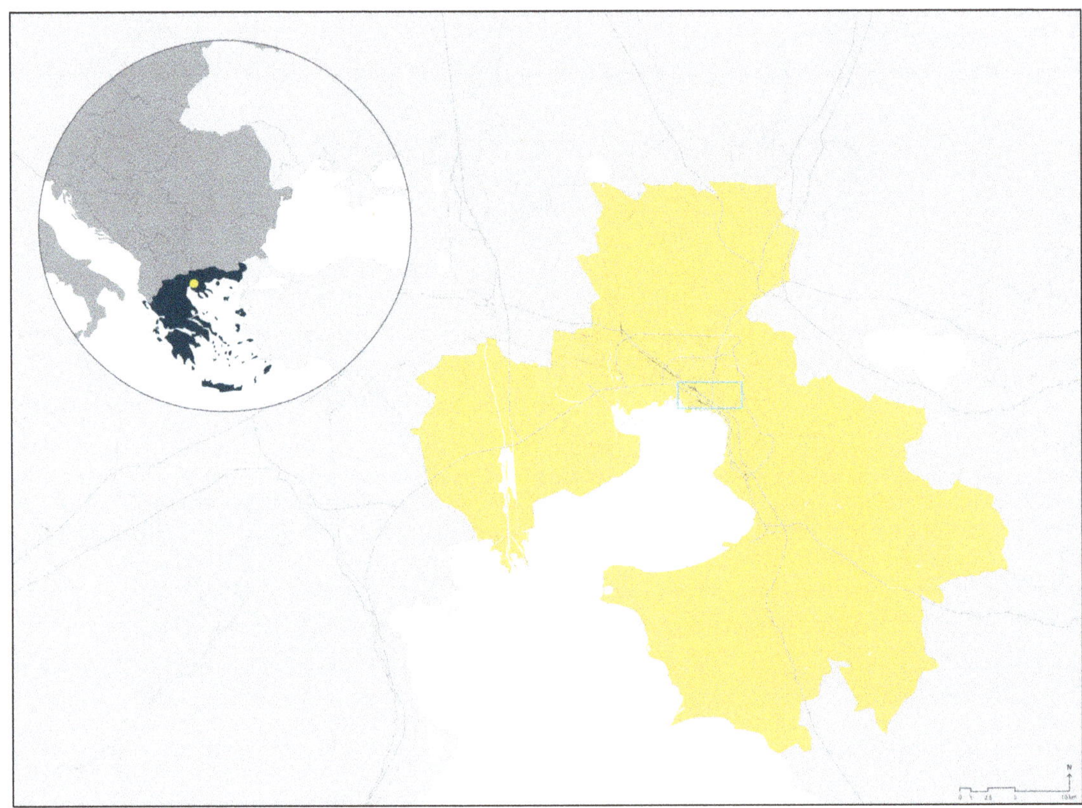

Figure 10. of Thessaloniki

About the site

Thessaloniki (Greece) is an important city that functions as a hub in the movement of migrants from Turkey to the Balkans and further on to northern Europe. The research focuses on two specific areas that concern homeless people on the move. The first is located on the western side of the city, in an area of abandoned train wagons, which are occasionally used by undocumented people on the move to recover from their difficult journeys. The second is located in the upper town, where abandoned wall houses next to the medieval city walls have been occupied by newly arrived migrants.

Broader context

Apart from registered refugees and asylum-seekers, an increasing number of newcomers merely pass through Thessaloniki or stay for short periods of time. The people on the move there are mainly undocumented newcomers, who are aiming to cross Greece and the rest of the Balkan countries on their way to Europe, being careful not to be detected by the authorities, so that they can then apply for asylum directly in a central or northern European country of their choice. In the struggle of people on the move to remain invisible and not be recorded by the authorities, alternative infrastructures such as the abandoned train wagons area and the wall houses play a decisive role.

Ethnographic research

The research consisted of participant observations in the abandoned train wagons and the wall houses because they constitute unique cases where newcomers find shelter and which substantially inform their mobility paths. Semi-structured interviews were also conducted with newcomers and grassroots organisations. Additionally, a participatory mapping project was organised involving several newcomers.

Research team

Charalampos Tsavdaroglou (field researcher, University of Amsterdam), Zacharias Valiantzas (field researcher, Aristotle University of Thessaloniki), and Paschalis Arvanitidis (University of Thessaly).

TOOL 1
ARE YOU IN AN ARRIVAL INFRASTRUCTURE?

MATERIALS: Bingo card [see below].

TOOL SUMMARY: This tool invites you to study your surroundings and look for clues that indicate whether you are in an arrival infrastructure. By using our arrival infrastructure bingo, you can assess what indicators are present in your area, and perhaps even add indicators from your own experience. This tool is a first step for thinking about and 'seeing' the arrival infrastructuring taking place around you.

START THE BINGO!

STEP 1: Study the bingo card below. Do you recall similar images in your area?

STEP 2: Take the bingo card out with you into the world! Take a walk around your neighbourhood. Do you spot similar instances in your area? What might you add to your own arrival infrastructure bingo card?

REFLECTION

Using the arrival infrastructure bingo card is an engaging way to become more aware of the arrival infrastructuring practices happening around you. By actively looking for indicators in your surroundings, you can gain a deeper understanding of your neighbourhood as an arrival infrastructure and the several forms of arrival infrastructuring in it. This exercise not only helps in recognising existing arrival infrastructuring practices but also encourages you to think critically about what might be missing or could be improved. Reflecting on your findings can lead to meaningful discussions with others about arrival processes and how they can be enhanced to better support newcomers.

> **FURTHER READINGS:** This tool is inspired by the bingo method developed by Tina De Gendt for the exhibition 'The Gates – On the edge of the city' in the City Museum of Ghent (Belgium, 2025). She also wrote a book (in Dutch): De Gendt, Tina. 2024. *De Poorten Een Verborgen Geschiedenis van de Wijken Die de Stad Veranderden*. Tielt: Lannoo.

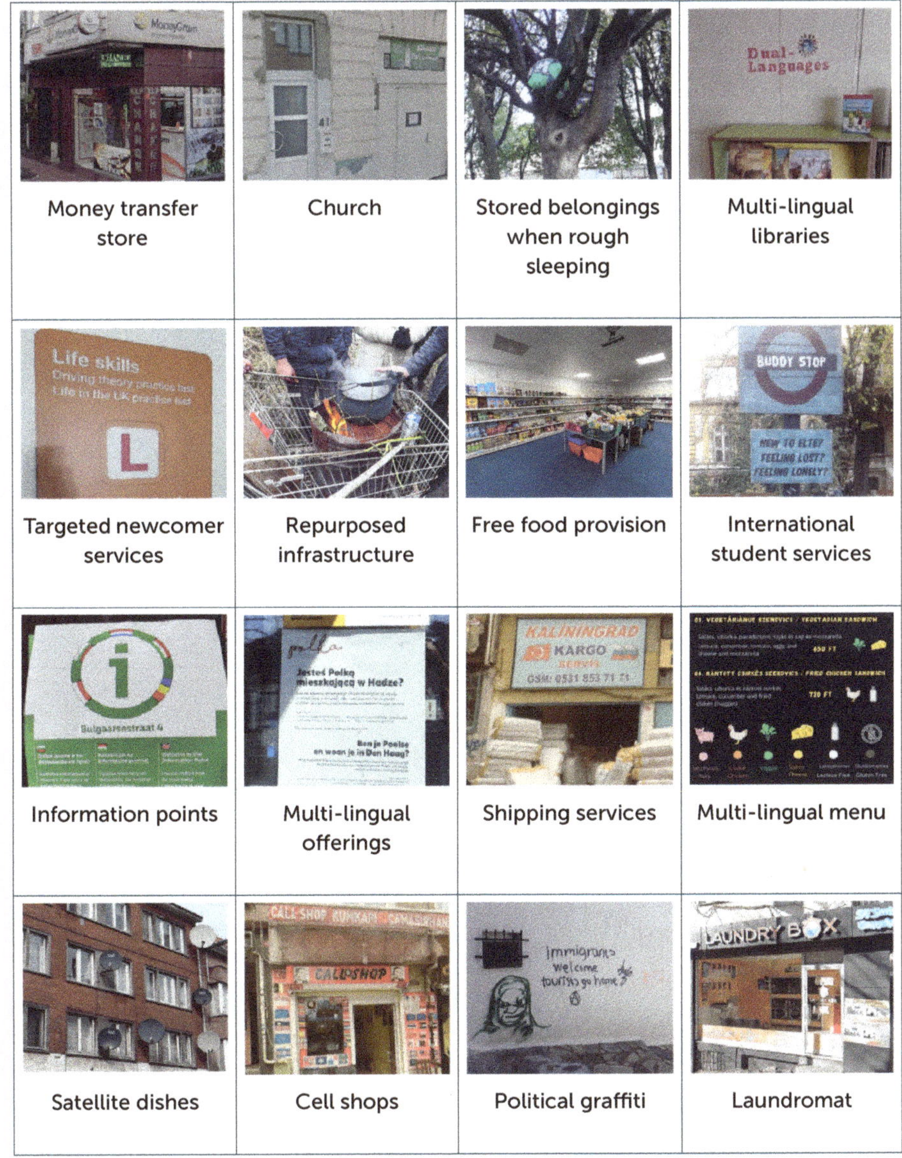

Figure 11. Arrival infrastructure bingo

SEEING INTEGRATION OTHERWISE

INTRODUCTION: ARRIVAL INFRASTRUCTURING

Part I 'Seeing Integration Otherwise' explores the diverse forms of arrival infrastructuring identified during our research. We have grouped these into four chapters: resourcing, bridging, coming together, and claiming. As outlined in greater detail in the introduction to the Kit, we define 'arrival infrastructuring' as the process by which newcomers, in interaction with others, build and transform their arrival situations.

Through stories from the field, we introduce a variety of infrastructuring practices (or what we sometimes refer to as infrastructuring work, as it often involves significant caring and sharing efforts). These narratives, like our research, focus on integration and arrival at the hyper-local level, offering a perspective distinct from that of state-driven, formal reception and integration programmes.

The four forms of infrastructuring work we present were observed across diverse contexts in Europe and manifest differently depending on the specific setting. The stories illustrate how these practices, carried out both by individuals and in coalitions, actively shape the ways in which people arrive and settle in Europe.

As you progress through the chapters, you will encounter other narratives around migration and integration, which challenge prevailing polarised discourses by introducing nuance and complexity. In particular, the 'takeaways' sections highlight what we find valuable about specific forms of arrival infrastructuring, while also addressing their potential limitations.

1. RESOURCING

This chapter highlights infrastructuring practices that sustain the lives of newcomers by providing essential resources that would otherwise be unavailable to them. These resources include (a) material support such as food and clothing, (b) services like childcare, and (c) shelter.

Providing such resources raises critical questions: Who qualifies as a newcomer? Which newcomers are (officially) entitled to receive support? These questions point to the often reductive and problematic categorisation of people by the state, while also revealing how organisations strive to circumvent such categorisations by developing innovative solutions that prioritise human dignity.

In the London site, support is for example organised primarily around needs rather than rigid categorisations. Similarly, place-based distribution of material resources avoids the stigma often associated with categorisation-based provision, offering a more inclusive approach to addressing needs.

At times, providing resources serves objectives that extend beyond sustaining lives. For example, in Dortmund, organisations distribute food, clothing, alarm clocks, and vaccines to enable children to attend school and access their right to education. In Istanbul, childcare initiatives not only allow mothers to work but also create spaces for social interaction, helping to combat isolation.

1.1 MATERIAL SUPPORT

Arrival often brings with it urgent material needs. To address these, the provision of food, clothing, and other essentials is organised locally, with approaches varying across contexts. In our stories, these resources are distributed by local organisations – both institutional and non-institutional (Katerini) – and by self-organised activists (in Thessaloniki).

While sustaining everyday survival, these organisations also introduce new forms and models of solidarity. In Thessaloniki, activists support the movement of people whose mobility is stigmatised as illegal or criminal, enabling them to pursue their personal aspirations.

In Katerini, a local organisation has adopted a 'social supermarket' model, where beneficiaries volunteer in exchange for goods. Unlike traditional aid programmes that distribute goods as charity, this approach dissolves the rigid distinction between 'helper' and 'helped', fostering a unified community of mutual support.

ESSENTIAL MATERIAL SUPPORT
Self-organised community centre next to the abandoned train wagons in Thessaloniki: solidarity beyond borders

A rhetoric of solidarity is employed at various levels: at the supranational level by the European Union, by nation-states, by networks of municipalities like the European Municipal Network of Refugee Solidarity Cities, and by international humanitarian organisations. Often, however, institutional solidarity with migrants is confined to humanitarian aid, restricted by numerous access criteria and limitations. To circumvent these rigid criteria, alternative structures of solidarity have emerged. This story features one such example in Thessaloniki, where the provision of material support aims to surpass the restrictive criteria applied elsewhere.

Abandoned train wagons as arrival infrastructure

In the western part of Thessaloniki, for many years there have been areas with abandoned train wagons. These train wagons have been deserted for several years, mainly since 2010 when, due to the economic crisis, the state railway company was privatised and a large part of the rolling stock was abandoned. Many people on the move from countries in West Asia and Africa find refuge in these forgotten railway infrastructures. People on the move seek to cross Greece and the rest of the Balkan countries without being detected by the authorities so that they can apply for asylum and be recognised as refugees in a more central or northern European country. To achieve this goal, the abandoned wagons in Thessaloniki are crucial as they provide a roof during the long and tough journey across the Balkans. Because of their remote location and people's self-chosen invisibility, food, medical care, warmth, and information are however largely lacking. In response to this precarious situation, a solidarity structure in the form of a community centre was created near the abandoned train wagons by self-organised humanitarian organisations such as Wave, Medical Volunteers International, Mobile Info Team, and the Border Violence Monitoring Network. There, food, clothing, hygiene items, shoes, medicines, first aid, and legal support are provided to people on the move.

"These people saved my life"

Said is from Morocco; he arrived in Turkey by plane, then jumped over the fence in the river Evros and in this way entered Greece. After walking for about 30 days through forests and mountains, he arrived in Thessaloniki. Here he found shelter in the abandoned train wagons and received first aid from the self-organised community centre. In his words: "I would say that these people have saved my life. Their help is excellent, they do not discriminate, and they do not ask where you are from, if you have papers, etc. They offer food, clothes, sleeping bags, medicine, all the basics. For me that's enough. They helped me a lot with my leg. I had broken it when I

Figure 12. Abandoned train wagons in Thessaloniki frequented by people on the move.

jumped the fence between Turkey and Greece. Even though I was very dirty, it didn't make any impression on them, they helped me a lot. A few months [after my arrival at the wagons], a friend from Morocco arrived through Turkey here in Thessaloniki. He was with a group of five, six other people, but unfortunately, the others were arrested by the police and sent back to Turkey, only he managed to be saved, even though the policemen beat him very badly. He came to the wagon where I live, I hid him for 15 days, the doctors from Medical Volunteers International took care of him, gave him medicines, he had wounds on his legs and they healed him, and now he has arrived in France" (Interview with Said, Thessaloniki, March 2022).

Solidarity beyond borders

For people on the move in Europe, candidacy for residence permits is increasingly determined on how people are categorised. If you come from a war zone or if you are from European territory, such as those recently displaced from Ukraine, then you can apply for asylum; if you are from a rich family, then you can apply for a 'golden visa'; if you have a higher-education diploma, then you can claim a 'talent visa'. The community centre in the area of the abandoned wagons goes beyond the above distinctions and categorisations. According to the words of a volunteer in the community centre: "for us, solidarity is non-negotiable, it knows no borders of colour, religion, language and nationality" (Peter, volunteer, Thessaloniki, May 2022).

Activist organisations play an important role in providing essential material support to people who are otherwise bypassed by the restrictive criteria applied within frameworks of solidarity provided by states and humanitarian aid.

Activist organisations often provide essential material support and regularly also implicitly challenge state narratives about migration and solidarity.

Non-discriminatory practices have a profound impact in creating a safe and trustworthy environment for people on the move, fostering human dignity in precarious situations.

The abandoned train wagons represent an intersection of global issues: migration, the aftermath of austerity measures, and the inadequacies of state-led support systems. These interconnections reveal broader systemic vulnerabilities.

ESSENTIAL MATERIAL SUPPORT
Volunteering in exchange for material support in Katerini: from charity to dignity and autonomy

In many arrival contexts, recipients of aid often find themselves in passive roles. However, in this story, a refreshing approach is being embraced. An organisation in Katerini has reimagined material support through a 'social supermarket', where beneficiaries volunteer in exchange for goods. This innovative model blurs the rigid lines between 'giver' and 'receiver', fostering a united community where everyone contributes and benefits.

The 'old tobacco' community centre

In Katerini, O topos mou (My place), a grassroots initiative with no political affiliation founded in September 2007, constitutes a movement of volunteers aiming to raise awareness, mobilise society, and engage in civic action related to ecological, economic, political, and social matters. The group runs a community centre located in the historical Tobacco Station building, which is the inspiration behind the centre's name: Kapnikos Stathmos, or 'tobacco station'. To fund its actions, the group organises various events through the year, such as a Christmas market, flower exhibitions, and summer cinema festivals. Kapnikos Stathmos is not just another charitable organisation, but a place where newcomers and those in need, whether locals or not, find space and time to help and be helped without feeling stigmatised for receiving charity.

Volunteering in exchange for the local currency

At Kapnikos Stathmos, food, clothing, and other essential items are gathered, either from citizens or through donations from organisations — both local and from other Greek cities. There is a wide variety of food and essential items, sufficient to meet all the basic needs of a family, as well as toys and clothing for all ages. In order to distribute these goods to those in need and to find a way for the organisation to become functional and sustainable, a new method of work compensation was devised. Those in need of food and clothing offer a certain number of hours of work at Kapnikos Stathmos, performing tasks related to cleaning, organisation, and sorting of collected goods, in exchange for 'Casta'. 'Casta' is a currency invented by the organisation to compensate those who perform this type of work. They can then exchange the 'Casta' they have earned to 'purchase' essential goods. As one of the administrators points out: "We are an organisation that does something unique in the city, maybe there is nothing similar in the entire country. We help anyone in need, but we are not charity. Refugees come and work here, get paid in Casta, a currency we created, and get food and basic grocery stuff. [...] We maintain warehouses which can provide food for over 200 people for a few days in case of need. We have guestrooms and we can provide shelter to those need it. We also collect clothes, medicines, etc. to support those in need" (Interview with Kostas, Katerini, December 2021).

Fostering autonomy and dignity

An important point to note is that by enacting this compensation model, those in need are not only assisted in satisfying their basic needs, they are also provided with a sense of dignity and autonomy. Instead of passively receiving aid, they actively participate in the maintenance and functioning of the community centre. By working in the centre, the perspective of newcomers is valued and incorporated to improve the centre's offering. They are even asked to weigh in on which goods to stock at the community store. One volunteer at the community centre said: "I recently started working here and I like it. I work occasionally at the tomato factory, but I also come here so I can get food and milk for my child. In this way, I can help my family more" (Interview with Sani, Katerini, May 2021).

TAKEAWAYS

\# Some organisations actively redefine aid and challenge models of charity by promoting mutual benefit, challenging the traditional one-way dynamic of giver and receiver, and encouraging shared responsibility, ownership, and collaboration.

\# The use of an alternative local currency can ensure the sustainability of an initiative by reducing dependence on external funding and strengthening community-based resource management.

\# The adaptive reuse of historical buildings for communal purposes highlights the importance of preserving and repurposing heritage sites as hubs for community engagement and innovation.

TOOL 2
REFLECTING ON AGENCY IN AID PROVISION

MATERIALS: Paper, writing utensils, computer for more in-depth engagement (optional).

TOOL SUMMARY: This tool aims to explore various methods of providing assistance and their impacts on recipients. It encourages understanding the conditions, nature, and philosophy behind aid initiatives, and examines the dynamics between helpers and those receiving aid. This tool can help you to evaluate policies and aid provision channels with the aim of enhancing the agency and empowerment people in need of aid. There are many ways to offer assistance to those in need, often linked to the aim of aid provision, which can range from relieving an urgent material need, to empowering the receiver, to changing relationships of solidarity, or a combination of the above. This tool aims to offer an understanding of the different ways aid can be provided, and the impact it has on the receiver of that aid.

STEP 1: Think of an aid initiative you work with or know about.

STEP 2: To better understand the impact this aid has on the recipient, answer the following questions.

- What are the conditions to receive the aid? Are those conditions decided jointly with the receiver? Are there conditions of deservingness, such as good behaviour, sobriety, proof of inability to work, proof of need, or proof of citizenship?
- What is the nature of the aid? Does the receiver have a choice about what they are receiving? Do they decide the frequency or nature of the aid? Are they active or passive receivers of aid?
- Are there hierarchies in the relationship between the 'helper' and the 'helped'? Does the receiver of aid get a chance to give something in exchange?
- What is the philosophy behind the initiative? Does it have any explicit (political) principles?
- Who is behind the initiative? Who founded it, and how is it funded?

You can of course add your own questions to the list!

REFLECTION
This tool is a helpful first step to examine or evaluate the degree of agency bestowed upon aid recipients via an aid programme. By answering the questions, you are prompted to consider avenues for the development and incorporation of certain policies that might give more agency to people in need of aid.

1.2 SERVICES

Beyond material support, the arrival infrastructure is teeming with initiatives that provide missing or additional services for newcomers. Sometimes local government institutions adapt their services to the needs of people they aim to serve. For instance, in Dortmund, additional vaccination hours have been scheduled for people without health insurance to provide them with the necessary certificates they need to be allowed to attend school. In the London borough, services challenge categorisation-based provision. In Istanbul, in turn, commercial entities, such as insurance companies or brokers, step in to navigate complex bureaucratic regulations, assisting newcomers in securing residence permits.

Within government institutions, committed individuals often create specialised services to foster trust and support among their target communities. In Karditsa, for instance, French and Arabic language classes have been introduced to facilitate integration. At the same time, self-organised initiatives play a vital role in addressing gaps within the existing arrival infrastructure. Examples include migrant-focused childcare, which enable mothers to participate in the workforce.

All these infrastructuring practices exemplify the concept of 'welfare bricolage', where diverse stakeholders combine and adapt resources to meet the needs of underserved communities. For further insights into this concept, refer to the concept box below or explore the illustrative stories that follow.

'Welfare bricolage'

Welfare bricolage, as conceptualised by Phillimore (2018), refers to the process through which individuals and groups combine and adapt resources from diverse formal and informal sources to meet their welfare needs in contexts where state or institutional provision is limited, inadequate, or inaccessible. This concept highlights the agency of individuals and communities in navigating complex welfare landscapes by creatively assembling support from a variety of providers.

Welfare bricolage illustrates both resilience and systemic shortcomings. While it showcases how people create solutions amidst structural inadequacies, it also underscores the need for more equitable and inclusive welfare systems to reduce dependence on fragmented, ad hoc arrangements.

Welfare bricolage relates to 'tinkering' as it involves individuals and communities creatively assembling welfare resources through trial-and-error approaches, adapting what is available to their specific needs in the absence of systemic solutions. It intersects with 'street-level bureaucracy' by highlighting how frontline workers and local stakeholders shape access to welfare,

ESSENTIAL SERVICES
Universal services in a London borough: challenging categorisation-based provision of support

While integration is often depicted as a process managed by nation-states in a top-down manner, this story illustrates the complexity of 'the state' when it comes to how integration evolves on the ground. It not only demonstrates how national government policies can sometimes create challenges for local integration and social inclusion efforts, it also shows how concerted efforts emerge in response, in order to address the inequalities produced in localities by national migration and integration policies. The cooperative efforts of the municipality in our London site to support and collaborate with charity, faith-based, and voluntary organisations is a case in point.

Integration for everyone?

The borough has an integration policy that sees all residents, including the locally 'born and bred', as needing integration support. 'Integration' is understood in both the economic and social sense, since neighbourhood deprivation and housing challenges exist alongside population growth, fluctuation, and diversity. Yet, while the borough's strategy seeks to 'leave nobody behind', national immigration policies prevent the council from providing equal support to all residents. For instance, a staff member of the municipality estimated that the borough receives around 10 times more funding to support arriving Ukrainian nationals than it does per arriving asylum-seeker. In addition, the rules that govern access to funded courses at the local adult education college clearly discriminate in favour of residents with refugee status over those with asylum-seeker status.

Universal provisioning as a tool of integration

An important barrier to obtaining support is having 'no recourse to public funds' (NRPF), which refers to holding a migration status that does not entitle the bearer to benefit from mainstream public welfare support such as Universal Credit (income support) or social housing. 'NRPF residents' include residents with a clear, legal migration status, such as people with a work or study permit, as well as those whose visa has expired or who never held a formal status. Some NRPF residents also have restrictions on their ability to work, which makes them even more vulnerable. In addition to these restrictions, NRPF residents often face obstacles to service access given the fact that eligibility for many services requires access to public funds.

The power of a local municipality

Against this backdrop, the local municipality developed 'universal services'. These services have no barriers to entry, enabling NRPF residents to access them. The 'universal services' provided by the municipality include information, advice, and guidance services, access to libraries and children's centres, and signposting to free activities or support that enhances well-being. When residents approach universal services, they may be signposted on to services that are subject to exclusion criteria, such as those applicable to the adult education college, and when a resident is blocked by such policies, frontline staff try to make a plan to resolve the disadvantage they are facing. As a council staff member described it, in this way the council provides forms of support to relieve the pressure on destitute residents with NRPF, such as access to food banks, charity services, or nursery places. Partnerships with or signposting to charities, such as to the free weekday lunch service run by a Christian charity in the borough, or to the free data provision offered in partnership with a national charity and mobile phone company, is an essential part of this work.

A question remains as to how far these efforts can really go to counteract the suffering and disadvantage imposed by discrimination that is built in by national government policies. For some, the universally available resources support day-to-day survival, but the prospect of a better future or of social mobility remain out of reach. Nevertheless, it illustrates how a municipality can, through service design and partnership working, treat all residents as deserving of support.

TAKEAWAYS

\# Local institutions are crucial in the everyday infrastructuring of arrival.

\# Local government and civil society stakeholders are often constrained by the terms and conditionalities of national immigration policies.

\# Local stakeholders may be actively working to counteract or minimise the worst effects of discrimination and inequality implicit in exclusionary national policies.

\# The role of the government in shaping arrival situations is complex and should be approached in a nuanced way, not least because local and national government may work towards different purposes.

TOOL 3
INTERVIEW GUIDE TO ASSESS THE LOCAL IMPACT OF NATIONAL POLICIES

MATERIALS: Paper, writing utensils.

TOOL SUMMARY: This tool aims to support researchers and practitioners to explore the local impact of national immigration policies. It includes prompts to discuss how higher-level policies impact on local social inclusion efforts and how local practices either reinforce or mitigate inequalities created by national immigration policies.

In the London borough, the local council, while respecting the rules set by state policy, found a way to serve all of its residents by creating accessible frontline information services for anyone who asks. If someone then cannot access a service because of their migration status, that frontline service tries to support them in finding a solution.

To explore how national policy and practice impact the support provided to migrants in a specific local context, integrate related questions into your interview guide (if you are an external researcher) or team discussion (if you are exploring within your own organisational context).

Your questions or prompts could include questions like:

- In what ways is y/our work to support migrant residents constrained by policies and practices imposed by higher authorities?
- How do you/we work to promote social inclusion in the context of external policies and practices that produce inequality for migrant residents?
- In what respects do [our] local practices reinforce inequalities created by immigration policy?
- In what respect do [our] local practices mitigate inequalities created by immigration policy?

REFLECTION

This tool enables researchers and practitioners to explicitly explore the impacts of national immigration policies at the local level, and the extent to which local responses purposefully or unknowingly support or counteract the social inequalities and exclusion that national immigration policy can produce.

Easing access to school in Nordstadt (Dortmund): identifying barriers and overcoming assumptions

> Often barriers to accessing services like education are numerous and not immediately apparent. In Dortmund, frontline caregivers – social workers and teachers – have made significant efforts to understand what truly prevents newcomer children from attending school. By going beyond their traditional responsibilities and adopting an integrated approach to support newcomer families, they have managed to make a meaningful difference in their lives.

Nordstadt: the youngest district in Dortmund

Nordstadt serves as an arrival neighbourhood for Dortmund and the entire region. At the same time, it is the youngest district in Dortmund, as a high share of the population is between 6 and 18 years old. As government-run infrastructures are not adequately equipped to address this demographic, many child-related social infrastructures are overwhelmed.

One of these overwhelmed infrastructures is child healthcare. The pressure is two-pronged: on the one hand, there is a shortage of paediatricians, and on the other hand, many newcomer children do not have health insurance. These two issues prevent newcomer children from accessing childcare facilities, as vaccinations are required for entry. When children, especially newcomers, cannot attend childcare, they miss out on the opportunity of language acquisition and important preparation for the transition to primary school. Their parents, moreover, are unable to work or do other activities.

To address this, the public health authority has been offering a vaccination hour for children without health insurance. Although this vaccination hour targets children without health insurance, it also welcomes children impacted by the shortage of paediatricians.

Understanding barriers to attending school

In our research, we found that schools and individuals working in schools are increasingly focusing on the basic needs of the whole family in order to reduce barriers to school attendance. This includes providing food, clothes, school materials, and access to health services, as well as a range of other items such as alarm clocks.

Caro is a teacher in a primary school in the district who noticed that one of her pupils was frequently tardy. Rather than searching to find a structural solution, which is often beyond the resource capacity of schoolteachers, Caro bought an alarm clock and gave it to him as a gift and a manageable solution to tardiness.

Lea is a social worker in the local family services office of Dortmund's Youth Authority. She noticed that the tardiness of schoolchildren was sometimes related to the family not having a clock or the parents' inability to read one. To cope with this, parents waited by their windows, watching out for when other children were heading to school, and then sent their own children at the same time. As a result, their children were often slightly late. Thus, the office organised a workshop where people were given an alarm clock and taught how to read it.

Welfare bricolage in the field of education

This story shows how local organisations in an arrival neighbourhood go beyond unquestioned assumptions, such as "everyone knows how to read a clock". By doing so, they acknowledge the role of parental practices in sending children to school and the difficulties parents face doing so. In reaction to this, schools and childcare facilities are becoming increasingly informed about and involved in the basic care of families, beyond their educational mission. The informal collaboration described above shows how they resort to 'welfare bricolage' to overcome regulations and routines that prevent newcomer children from attending childcare facilities and pre-schools, especially in arrival neighbourhoods.

TAKEAWAYS

By identifying the underlying issue (no electricity to charge a phone and thus inability to use the phone's alarm clock) behind the apparent issue (children arriving too late at school), frontline caregivers provide essential arrival infrastructuring work and foster inclusion.

By recognising that barriers like tardiness may stem from structural issues rather than neglect, caregivers challenge entrenched assumptions about newcomers and work to foster understanding and inclusion.

Addressing barriers to accessing services is a fundamental aspect of the arrival infrastructuring work carried out by frontline caregivers, such as teachers and social workers. To overcome these obstacles, they often go beyond their primary duties, transcend their main working domains and extend their official responsibilities.

A holistic approach to the struggles of newcomer families allows caregivers to address not just the child's needs but the family's circumstances as a whole, fostering a more inclusive and effective support system for newcomers.

Enhancing social infrastructures and support systems in arrival neighbourhoods like Nordstadt not only benefits newcomers, it also strengthens the entire community by addressing systemic weaknesses and fostering integration.

TOOL 4
IDENTIFYING UNEXPECTED BARRIERS TO EVERYDAY LIFE TASKS

MATERIALS: Paper, writing utensils.

TOOL SUMMARY: This tool helps you identify hidden obstacles that may prevent individuals from carrying out everyday tasks. It is particularly valuable for understanding why people might struggle to engage with services or behave in unexpected ways. By listing the necessary preconditions for achieving specific goals, the tool highlights the particular barriers individuals face. It encourages a closer examination of everyday material challenges to help ensure smoother and more inclusive day-to-day lives for everyone.

People often make assumptions when they see others not respecting what they consider to be basic rules. When trying to understand the reasons behind such behaviour, they frequently use their own experiences as a reference point or rely on certain biases towards others.

To overcome assumptions and biases, we think it is useful simply to list what the necessary preconditions are to comply with certain regulations or advice, instead of listing why they are not followed. This method will allow you to identify the barriers that some people face to comply with regulations.

“In Dortmund, a social worker at a school realised that parents of children who were arriving late to school did not know to read a clock or did not possess one. The school assumed that everyone would have one, and did not identify this as a need.”

STEPS:
Make a list of things one needs to achieve in order to …….
[a goal you are not seeing achieved in others]

Inspired by the social worker in the story above, identify what might be missing for certain people to achieve this goal and think about how you could alleviate this barrier.

For instance:

A list of things one needs to get to school or work on time:

- GO TO BED EARLY: FINISH WORK EARLY, HAVE DINNER READY, BE RELAXED ENOUGH TO FALL ASLEEP

- SLEEP WELL: HAVE A COMFORTABLE BED, NOT HAVE NIGHTMARES, HAVE QUIET NEIGHBOURS

- WAKE UP ON TIME: HAVE A WORKING ALARM CLOCK, ENOUGH BATTERY

- HAVE CLEAN CLOTHES: HAVE TIME THE DAY BEFORE TO WASH CLOTHES, HAVE A WASHING MACHINE

- HAVE BREAKFAST AND COFFEE: HAVE FOOD IN THE FRIDGE, MEANS TO HEAT IT, HAVE WATER AND ELECTRICITY TO MAKE COFFEE

- 3 FLOORS DOWNSTAIRS: BE IN SHAPE, HAVE NO INJURIES, NO REMAINING DOMESTIC WORK

- WALK TO SCHOOL: HAVE SOMEONE STAY AT HOME WITH BABY, BE REGISTERED IN A SCHOOL WITHIN WALKING DISTANCE

Figure 13. Diagram for making a list of things one needs to get to school or work on time.

REFLECTION

This tool highlights the fact that some resources that we take for granted are sometimes not available to everyone. To identify them, we should closely examine the material elements of everyday life. This is the first step towards filling that gap and supporting people in having an easier day-to-day life.

> IF YOU FOUND THIS TOOL USEFUL, HAVE A LOOK AT **TOOL 8**: 'Visualising obstacles to service access' (p. 112-113).

Paperwork facilitation for residence permits in Istanbul: profiting from people's needs or enabling access to rights?

Restrictive migration policies, particularly the increasing complexity of residence permit requirements, often give rise to intermediary figures who facilitate the paperwork process for obtaining such permits. These intermediaries often operate outside of formalised frameworks, giving rise to a range of practices, spaces, and in some cases opportunities to exploit people's need for assistance. While the formal and informal practices of intermediaries can be a cause for concern, they are also crucial for newcomers navigating bureaucratic complexities upon arrival, as illustrated by this story from Istanbul.

Increasingly complex requirements: a maze for newcomers

Obtaining the necessary documents, especially residence permits, has become one of the central concerns in migrants' everyday life in Turkey over the last decade. In 2013, Turkey passed its first comprehensive immigration law categorising foreigners into different statuses and outlining residency requirements. This law has led to an increase in bureaucratic processes surrounding migration regulations, such as residence permits. In 2020, in response to the growing arrival of diverse migrant groups, the Turkish government began imposing limitations on the issuance of residence permits. In addition, Turkish migration bureaucracy is increasingly characterised by extreme ambiguity, frequently changing regulations, and opaque decision-making. As a result, many migrants remain undocumented or become undocumented due to the changing regulations and the inability to meet bureaucratic requirements for applications. Because the Turkish government has made residence permits or at least a foreigner ID number essential for accessing numerous essential services, many migrants lack access. Moreover, residence permits are now required for many types of procedures, including signing work contracts or tenancy agreements, acquiring bank accounts, registering with a school, getting Covid-19 and other vaccinations, going into hospital, and accessing certain social services.

This is for instance the experience of two Ugandan newcomers, Havva and Maryam, who arrived in Istanbul in December 2020. They explained that their lack of proper documentation has affected their prospects of opening a business or finding a better, long-term job: "We are working on a daily basis in the factory now because we do not have a residence permit. We want to open a cargo business and need to open a bank account and also get a document confirming our fixed address but for all these processes we need the residence permit first." (Havva and Maryam, Istanbul, December 2020).

Formal and informal gap-filling in bureaucratic cavities

The long and frequently changing list of documents required for a residence permit application has given rise to business opportunities in this area. For newcomers, the density of unfamiliar procedures can be overwhelming and require not only language proficiency but also appropriate bureaucratic literacy, cultural fluency, and continuing determination. As a result, many venues and services offering to assist in securing migrant documentation have emerged since 2015 in the localities of Aksaray, Laleli, and Kumkapı, which are located in the historical arrival neighbourhood of Fatih in Istanbul.

The service providers and spaces of provision range from formal businesses to informal multi-purpose initiatives, for example shops, hotels, internet cafés, launderettes, and estate agencies. The walls and windows of these various commercial non-state establishments are often lined with paper advertisements and posters where service providers publicise their offerings. These services vary but generally relate to various kinds of documentation, such as translation, health insurance for foreigners, residence permits, work permits, and others.

Figure 14. A storefront in the Fatih area of Istanbul used by arrival brokers to advertise services.

Newcomers in the arrival context encounter or are signposted by more established newcomers or friends to these non-state offerings. For instance, one of the residence permit requirements is proof of health insurance coverage for one year. Migrants who cannot afford to pay for comprehensive health insurance go to the Fatih area to acquire a specific health insurance document that is accepted for the residence application but is not technically valid for medical services beyond emergency situations. Similarly, the estate agencies in the area provide tenancy agreements for a fee that can be used for the application. However, in most cases, the addresses in the agreements do not reflect the actual home address of the applicant.

In Fatih, the arrival infrastructure involves both formal and informal stakeholders and processes. In addition to registered intermediary businesses that specialise in applying for and obtaining residence permits, work permits, and other legal documents for migrant populations, many self-organised and informal brokers provide these services. With such a range of stakeholders (both formal and informal) offering arrival-related services, we found that the infrastructuring practices, in this case residency documentation, also vary in formality. In other words, in the arrival neighbourhood of Fatih multiple businesses infrastructure the arrival of newcomers by 'fixing' their statuses.

TAKEAWAYS

Essential infrastructuring work, such as facilitating the acquisition of official papers, often occurs in the grey area between formality and informality.

Commercial individuals and organisations, whether formal or informal, acting as intermediaries or 'brokers' between newcomers and the state often both profit from newcomers and provide them with essential services that broaden their access to resources and rights. Hence, they often act as enablers and gatekeepers at the same time.

The frequent changes, lack of transparency, and ambiguity in migration regulations result in precarious situations where migrants are at constant risk of becoming undocumented, underscoring the need for more stable and accessible policy frameworks.

Success in navigating complex migration systems depends on more than just financial resources; it requires cultural and bureaucratic literacy that many newcomers lack, further complicating their arrival experience.

TOOL 5
UNDERSTANDING THE ARRIVAL INFRASTRUCTURING WORK OF OTHERS

MATERIALS: Paper, writing utensils.

TOOL SUMMARY: This tool can help you understand and even appreciate the arrival infrastructuring work of others, especially those whose work might be viewed critically. By reflecting on the value, risk, and stakes for newcomers and those who support their arrival, the tool allows you to explore the conditions that make these roles necessary. It ultimately helps with recognising that certain infrastructuring practices arise in response to specific policies and structural conditions.

Sometimes you might have mixed feelings about the infrastructuring work of certain people, organisations, or institutions in the arrival infrastructure in which you are active. Perhaps their methods and missions are not aligned with yours. In these cases, it can be useful to learn more about what these people or organisations offer to newcomers and what their role is in infrastructuring arrival.

STEP 1: Identify at least one person or organisation that you are critical of.

STEP 2: Identify what is at stake for that person or organisation in the arrival infrastructure.

STEP 3: Consider what power they have within the arrival infrastructure.

STEP 4: What kind of strategies do they use to reach, serve, and direct newcomers?

STEP 5: What is the value of this person or organisation for newcomers?

STEP 6: What potential risks does this person or organisation pose for newcomers?

STEP 7: Consider whether the presence and/or practices of the person or organisation in question emerge in response to or in the absence of certain policies or conditions.

We completed this exercise for the story above. You can add your own responses to the diagram for a specific person or organisation whose arrival infrastructuring work you would like to better understand.

Steps	Arrival brokers	Person or organisation
What was your first impression of this person/ organisation?	Arrival brokers offer services to newcomers to assist with securing residence permits at high costs, without transparent processes, and which can lead to exploitative work/living situations.	
What is at stake for them?	Arrival brokers make a living, develop useful working relationships with civil society and state institutions, and improve their upward mobility.	
What power do they have in relation to newcomers?	Because of their knowledge of the detailed bureaucratic processes related to securing resident permits and relative security, arrival brokers are in a position of power in relation to newcomers employing their services.	
What strategies do they employ?	Arrival brokers make their services strategically available to newcomers by using methods such as targeted communication campaigns in languages used by newcomers and positioning these campaigns (flyers, posters, etc.) in places frequented by newcomers (launderettes, money transfer shops, print shops, and shipping offices). They also offer expedited processes.	
What value do they hold for newcomers?	The tailored and geographically situated specificity of arrival brokers holds value for newcomers who often face unclear, exclusionary state residence permit trajectories.	
What risks do newcomers face when engaging with this person/ organisation?	When employing the services of arrival brokers, newcomers can face unregulated fees and/or exploitation, and this can result in situations of ongoing precarity.	
What are the policy implications related to their practices?	In the context of this story, arrival brokers pose the following policy implications: Tailored arrival processes adaptable to the specific needs of newcomers improve residence permit acquisition for newcomers. Make residence permit processes linguistically and geographically accessible for newcomers.	
After compiling the information in this table, what is your second impression of this person/ organisation?	Arrival brokers, while posing some risks to newcomers, offer services to newcomers that are otherwise unavailable. The practice of tailoring and targeting offerings based on the languages newcomers speak and the areas they frequent significantly increase the chances of them securing residence permits.	

Figure 15. Diagram for learning about the infrastructuring work of others.

This tool aims to bring nuance to our understanding of the infrastructuring work of certain people and organisations in the field for newcomers. Even though their work might sometimes be questionable, it might at the same time be important for newcomers. It also helps with understanding that these 'questionable' infrastructuring practices around migration and integration come into being in response to exclusionary policies and other structural exclusionary conditions. Additionally, understanding the outreach and facilitation capacity of other stakeholders in the arrival infrastructure can further inform your own role.

LANGUAGE
Mother-tongue language courses by asylum-seekers in Karditsa: nurturing transnational communities and cultivating trust in institutions

Integration policies often assume that individuals will gradually assimilate into the host society and relinquish their original cultures and identities. However, this expectation is often unrealistic, as many migrants relocate specifically to support their families back home and thus maintain strong transnational connections. These national policies can also hinder integration by isolating individuals and limiting their access to local institutions. The story of language classes in Karditsa illustrates how institutions, when they tune into the specific needs of newcomers, can enhance access, promote transnational communities, and foster socialisation.

Support and integration beyond basic needs

In 2017, the municipality of Karditsa approved the implementation of the ESTIA programme (Emergency Support to Integration and Accommodation) run by UNHCR. The scope of the ESTIA project was the temporary accommodation of newcomers and the facilitation of their access to basic infrastructures or services due to need or obligation, i.e. healthcare or compulsory attendance of formal education for children. However, in addition to meeting the requirements of the funding project, the ESTIA funding beneficiary organisation ANKA (a development agency partnering with the municipality) undertook initiatives that went far beyond its initial mission.

One such initiative concerns the coordination of mother-tongue language courses. The need for such courses was initially expressed by newcomer groups with French and Arabic as their mother tongues. In both cases, adults with teaching degrees volunteered to help the children of the communities learn their mother tongue (Arabic or French), the languages that the children would be taught if they had the opportunity to attend school in their own country.

In between two countries

The underlying idea was initially expressed during a discussion held between core members of the organisation's team and members of the Arabic-speaking community in Karditsa. One of them commented: "Having our children participate in formal education here is great… But what if one day my children are deported or decide of their own will to visit our country? … They won't be able to read a newspaper or shop signs on the streets, or submit an application to a public service… Their communication there would have to be only verbally based on what they hear and learn at home" (Interview with Agnes, Karditsa, June 2022).

This comment activated the ANKA team members, who sought to find ways to satisfy this request. The first step was to identify adult members of the relevant communities with teaching degrees who could volunteer as tutors. The second was to communicate and collaborate with UNICEF, mainly to acquire access to relevant educational material. The course teachers were eventually supplied with primary education books from the schools of the countries of origin. Thirdly, upon receiving the course material, afternoon classes began to operate in the wider context of Greek language courses at the Stavrodromi Intercultural Centre, with the help of volunteers from the respective communities.

—INTERVIEW WITH AGNES, KARDITSA, JUNE 2022.

Expanding existing offerings, gaining trust, and promoting local integration

Although ANKA already organised afternoon Greek language courses for new-comer adults as well as for minors, the addition of mother-tongue language courses had multiple side effects. First, the additional courses contributed greatly to connecting newcomers and especially newcomer children. Given that the children were enrolled in different schools during the day (as part of their compulsory attendance of formal education), ANKA organisers discovered that many students did not know each other. Thus, the language courses began to function simultaneously as an opportunity for socialisation and as a meeting place, which in turn resulted in new friendships blossoming.

Second, the teachers were provided with an opportunity to practise (even informally) their profession, which given their prolonged state of uncertainty (regarding their legal status), was a kind of psychological boost. Third, the participation rates in language courses increased, and the newcomers became more actively involved. Finally, this informal initiative and the underlying respect the organisers demonstrated for the needs of the different communities resulted in a significant increase in the level of trust between the organising team at ANKA and newcomers benefiting from the ESTIA programme in the Karditsa area.

Arrival infrastructuring involves equipping newcomers with tools to navigate their new environment, such as learning the local language, while also providing the space to keep their old and new identities together as this can significantly enhance their integration process.

Addressing the specific needs of newcomers within your arrival infrastructure helps tailor integration and build trust in the service provider and/or institution.

The provision of specific services to newcomers often intertwines various types of infrastructuring work. For instance, a language course can also serve as a platform for building trust, socialising, and connecting with others.

CONCEPT BOX 5

'Transnationalism'

'Transnationalism' refers to the processes by which migrants maintain, create, and navigate connections across national borders, often blending social, cultural, economic, and political practices in ways that transcend traditional notions of state boundaries.

In the work of Smith and Eade (2008), transnationalism is framed as the result of globalisation and migration, highlighting how migrants' lives are not bound to a single national context. Instead, they actively engage with multiple locales, creating hybrid identities and transnational spaces that influence both their host societies and countries of origin.

Nina Glick Schiller et al. (1992) introduced the concept of 'transnational social fields', which describe the network of connections and interactions that migrants maintain across borders. For Glick Schiller and Wimmer (2002), transnationalism challenges the idea that society is naturally contained within the borders of nation-states by highlighting how migrants engage in social, cultural, and economic activities that connect them to multiple states and communities. This framework focuses on understanding the agency of migrants and how their practices reshape nation-states' influence and identities.

'Transnational connections' or 'transnational ties' refer to the ongoing relationships and networks that migrants sustain across national boundaries. These ties encompass familial, economic, social, cultural, and political linkages.

Smith and Eade (2008) view transnational connections as multidimensional, involving flows of people, goods, money, and ideas between the sending and receiving countries. They highlight how these ties influence migrants' identities, economic behaviour (many migrants send money to their home countries, so-called 'remittances'), and sociopolitical engagements, such as advocacy or voting in home-country elections.

For Glick Schiller et al. (1992), transnational ties are integral to the concept of transnational social fields. These connections are not merely symbolic but are embedded in daily practices and institutions, influencing both the micro (personal) and macro (institutional or societal) scales. Migrants' engagement in these ties may challenge nation-state-centric perspectives on citizenship, belonging, and participation, as migrants navigate dual or multiple loyalties and affiliations.

'Transnational communities' are then the networks of individuals and groups who maintain strong social, cultural, economic, and political ties across national borders, creating shared spaces of identity and interaction that transcend the limitations of a single geographic or political context.

In summary, transnational perspectives underscore that migration is not a unidirectional or one-time process. Instead, transnationalism and transnational ties reflect ongoing, dynamic interactions that reshape individual identities and broader societal structures across nation-state boundaries. These frameworks have become central to understanding migration in a globalised world.

References:

Glick Schiller, Nina, Linda Basch, and Cristina Szanton Blanc. 1992. *Towards a Transnational Perspective on Migration: Race, Class, Ethnicity, and Nationalism Reconsidered* (New York: New York Academy of Sciences).
Smith, Michael Peter, and John Eade, eds. 2008. *Transnational Ties: Cities, Migrations, and Identities* (New Brunswick, NJ: Transaction Publishers).
Wimmer, Andreas, and Nina Glick Schiller. 2002. 'Methodological nationalism and beyond: nation–state building, migration and the social sciences,' *Global Networks*, 2: 301–334.

See the academic complement of this *Integration Otherwise Inspiration Kit*, the edited volume *Infrastructuring Arrival* (Arnaut, Beeckmans, and Meeus, 2026), in particular:
– Chapter 1 (Arnaut, Beeckmans, and Meeus, 2026)

TOOL 6
VISUALISING MULTIPLE IDENTITIES

MATERIALS: Paper, writing utensils.

TOOL SUMMARY: This tool aims to help you understand how migration adds new identities to the existing ones, emphasising that both migrants and non-migrants live in multiple and sometimes transnational communities. It encourages you to visualise and reflect on the different roles and identities you hold, and how these evolve over time, especially after significant life changes like migration. The tool highlights the complexity of integration, showing that it involves blending and negotiating multiple identities rather than replacing old ones.

We often think of migration as an exceptional moment where a new potential aspect of our identity is added to the multiple labels that we already bear. It can be helpful to think of all of us, migrants and non-migrants, as living and growing in multiple communities in which we socialise or integrate. Instead of replacing each other, these identities multiply when we integrate into new communities, whether after a migration or not.

STEP 1: Think of a moment when you acquired a new layer to your identity: you became a parent, or you moved from one neighbourhood to another, or from one country to another, or you changed job or career. Make a list of roles you had before this change and after it.

In the case of the member of the Arabic-speaking community in the above story:

Before moving to Karditsa:

- Volunteer
- Mother
- Resident of Damascus, Syria
- IT technician

After moving to Karditsa:

- Mother
- Migrant
- IT technician
- Temporary resident in Karditsa
- Caretaker of family in home country

STEP 2: Illustrate each list by drawing circles for each aspect of your identity. Size your circles according to how much time you spend on each role. You should have one set of circles for each list.

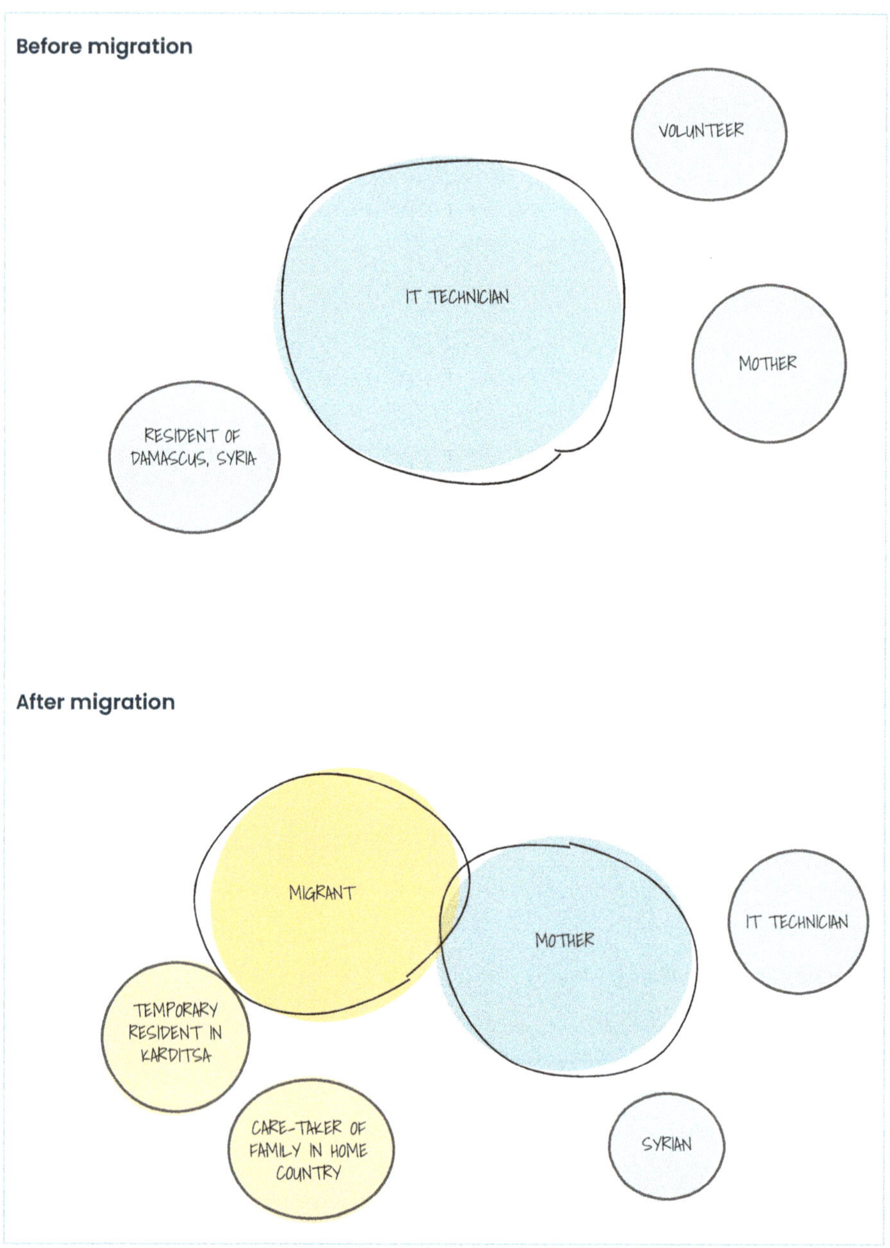

Figure 16 Diagram for visualising multiple identities.

In Karditsa, newcomers were allowed to blend their new and old identities through the combination of Greek language courses and mother-tongue language courses for their children. Greek courses allowed them to integrate better into their arrival context. Arabic and French courses also did the same by allowing them to feel accepted and to meet other newcomers from the same origin as them, thus activating new solidarity networks.

REFLECTION

This tool illustrates how individuals, both migrants and non-migrants, consistently socialise and integrate into multiple communities linked to their diverse identities. Yet migration often leads to the multiplication of identities and related roles. Not only does the migration process lead to new identities, but migrants' identities are also frequently tied to both local and transnational contexts. Therefore, integration into the host society is much more complex than simply relinquishing a pre-migration identity and embracing a new one. It involves the incorporation, blending, and negotiation of multiple identities, resulting in integration across various communities simultaneously (so-called 'minor integrations', see concept box 1). Often these multiple identities are at odds with expectations of integration policies.

Affordable childcare in Istanbul: mutual support facilitating access to work for migrant women

> Newcomers often face a multitude of barriers to accessing certain services, such as daycare for children. Economic challenges, racial discrimination, and lack of documentation are just a few of the obstacles that migrants encounter upon arrival. This story from Istanbul highlights how the inaccessibility of daycare prevents migrant mothers from finding work, which is crucial for supporting themselves and their families. Yet it also showcases the infrastructuring work of migrant mothers, who have established home-based nurseries to care for each other's children in the absence of access to public or private daycare facilities.

A feminised arrival infrastructure

The high visibility of migrant women in the localities of Aksaray, Laleli, and Kumkapı in the arrival neighbourhood of Fatih dates back to the 1990s, when many young and middle-aged women from former Soviet Union countries started to cross borders to purchase merchandise in small quantities (so that it could fit in their suitcases), and sell it back home in local, mostly open-air markets and bazaars. This socio-economic phenomenon gave these localities their peculiar characteristic as places where young and middle-aged women from post-Soviet Eastern European countries, Central Asia, and Sub-Saharan Africa do business. This work often takes the form of so-called 'suitcase trading' or other transnational trading and is likely to be supplemented with low-paid jobs in the service and textile sectors and in the entertainment/sex work industry. Among many other services, migrant women are not able to access state-provided or private childcare services and rely on their networks and economic capital to make different arrangements. One such arrangement, and an important component of the arrival infrastructure, is home-based childcare services.

Mothers face discrimination and financial barriers to childcare

Many working migrant women with children face difficulties in enrolling their children in public nurseries. This is often because they lack the necessary documents or due to the unclear decision-making processes of the nursery's administration, which tend not to provide valid explanations for rejections. Aisha (an African woman in her late twenties) applied to several public nurseries close to her residence. Yet she was rejected by administrators, who stated that "they do not mix races and nationalities". She found an international private nursery that accepted migrant children and enrolled her son there. However, private nurseries are very expensive and many migrant families or a migrant single parent on a low income cannot afford them. This barrier forces women with children either to stop working in order to take care of their children or to take hourly, temporary, often unsustainable jobs that pay very little.

Home-based nurseries: a win-win solution

Those who cannot afford to pay for a private nursery take their children to a self-arranged home-based nursery. Several women from the migrant community use their flats as a nursery space and offer childcare services in Kumkapı.

Most migrant families send their children to these home-based nurseries since they work daily. For them, this service is affordable and there is no need to provide documents or worry about the racial harassment of their children and themselves. It is also a service with flexible payment and scheduling arrangements.

An Uzbek woman who works in a beauty salon in Laleli takes her three-year-old daughter to a home-based nursery and emphasises that she encouraged her neighbour, another elderly Uzbek woman, to open such a space: "Now I can work without worrying about my daughter, you see. And it is a double benefit – my neighbour Shaira was very tired of her employers but could not quit because she needed money. Now she earns money and takes care of the kids as if they were her own grandkids" (Interview with Ela, Istanbul, February 2022).

Adverts offering childcare services can be found on walls in Aksaray, Laleli, and Kumkapı more frequently now. These home-based nurseries are examples of the infrastructuring work that migrant women do to support each other's access to the labour market and other opportunities.

TAKEAWAYS

When access to state or private childcare services is denied, migrant networks often step in to fill the gap, demonstrating the importance of informal support systems in overcoming structural exclusions.

Migrants often perform key infrastructuring work by self-organising micro-services, such as home-based nurseries. In doing so, they navigate the barriers that prevent fellow migrants from accessing essential services while enabling them to fulfil other needs, such as earning money.

A crucial aspect of infrastructuring work is the care provided to (fellow) newcomers, alongside the reproductive labour performed by migrants.

> For a related case, have a look at another story in this volume: Easing access to school in Nordstadt (Dortmund): identifying barriers and overcoming assumptions (p. 61).

1.3 SHELTER

Finding shelter is an essential part of newcomers' arrival. Housing, as a particular type of arrival infrastructure, serves, moreover, as a vital entry point for accessing other essential services and information. The stories in this chapter showcase various ways in which newcomers find shelter when they cannot access state-funded housing or the private housing market because they lack documentation or resources.

The examples below include state-funded housing, such as student dormitories in Hungary or migrant workers' housing in Paris. Additionally, civil society organisations often step in to develop solutions where states falls short in providing accommodation, like the initiative of hosting newcomers in citizens' homes in Brussels. Migrants themselves also exhibit remarkable resourcefulness, as seen in Thessaloniki, where they self-organise to occupy empty urban spaces and create decent shelters for people on the move.

HOUSING

Occupying abandoned buildings as temporary shelter in Thessaloniki: vacancy as resourcefulness in the city

For various reasons, many people find themselves (or choose to be) excluded from formal accommodation systems like camps or asylum centres. For these people, squatting abandoned buildings often becomes the only option for securing shelter. This is exemplified in Thessaloniki, where people on the move began occupying the abandoned houses in Ano Poli as a response to state neglect and policies of abandonment.

Squatting as method

Usually, those who cross the land or sea borders from Turkey to Greece and get arrested by the authorities are transferred to state-run camps. However, camp life is subject to several restrictions and in most cases the camps are located outside the cities in remote and isolated places. In the wider area of the city of Thessaloniki, 13 camps were created in 2016, of which six are still in operation today (2024). In the camps, newcomers live isolated and cut off from the social life of the city. For this reason, many newcomers try to look for alternative housing solutions within the city, usually by occupying abandoned buildings within the urban fabric such as the historic wall houses in Ano Poli. Additionally, those who manage to enter Greek territory and wish to continue their journey without being detected by the authorities find shelter for a few days in abandoned train wagons at the western entrance of the city. Occupying abandoned infrastructures or 'squatting' is therefore a crucial method by which newcomers infrastructure their arrival and transit.

From abandoned train wagons to abandoned wall houses

Abdu arrived in Thessaloniki from Syria in 2017 and stayed in the state-run camp of Diavata, which is located outside the city. But his asylum application was rejected and he thus no longer had the right to stay in the camp. Like many other homeless people in Thessaloniki, he first found refuge in the area with the abandoned train wagons on the west side of the city. In the abandoned train wagons, he met several more homeless newcomers, most of whom had arrived a few days earlier and intended to continue their journey on to the next Balkan countries. Abdu wanted to leave too, but because he did not have enough money, he ended up staying in the train wagons for over a month. In one of the train wagons, he made a place to sleep, with a mattress as well as a small storeroom for his personal belongings. Life in the wagon was difficult especially in winter, and eventually he heard about the abandoned wall houses in Ano Poli, close to the city centre. These houses have a rich and long history of offering shelter to refugees. They were built about a century ago by Christian refugees who arrived in Greece after the defeat of the Greek army in Turkey and the exchange of populations between Greece and Turkey imposed by the Treaty of Lausanne. The Muslim inhabitants of Thessaloniki were displaced to Turkey and the Christians of Turkey to Greece. Many thousands of newcomers arrived in Thessaloniki and settled in the houses of the former Muslim community in the upper city. However, because there were so many newcomers, they built more houses in every empty space up to and alongside the Byzantine-Ottoman walls of the city. Many of these houses are now abandoned and serve as refuge for new arrivals. The abandoned wall houses are relatively hidden but also provide direct access to the city centre.

Figure 17. Wall houses in the upper town of Thessaloniki often used as temporary shelter by people on the move.

From abandonment to arrival infrastructure

New arrivals in Greece are subject to a series of restrictions and are sometimes stripped of their rights, including the right to adequate housing. As such, abandonment and neglect are key migration policies used by the European Union and the Greek state. In response to the institutional policies of abandonment, newcomers have invented ways of overcoming this condition of abandonment by squatting abandoned train wagons and wall houses. Because of their transformative use by newcomers, these abandoned infrastructures have become part of the city's arrival infrastructure, wherein newcomers reorganise their own lives, claiming either the right to the city or the right to move on.

\# Sometimes squatting abandoned buildings is the only option for migrants to secure a roof over their heads. These squats become essential parts of the arrival infrastructure along migratory routes, transforming urban vacancy into a valuable resource.

\# Occupying buildings is not merely a survival strategy but a form of agency, where newcomers assert control over their housing and create spaces of autonomy within a system that often marginalises them.

\# Oftentimes, contemporary migration is connected to historical patterns of displacement and resettlement, underscoring how the arrival infrastructure is a more or less stable moment in a process of sedimentation.

\# The contrasting experiences of newcomers in remote camps and urban squats call into question the effectiveness of segregated and isolated arrival infrastructures established by governments and humanitarian organisations, underscoring the need for more inclusive and accessible alternatives.

HOUSING
Hosting newcomers in private homes in Brussels: remediating a politically constructed reception crisis

This story explores the grassroots response to the politically constructed reception crisis in Brussels, focusing on the practice of hosting newcomers in private homes. It delves into the origins of this movement that emerged during the 'Long Summer of Migration' in 2015 (see concept box 6), the subsequent challenges faced by asylum-seekers and the evolution of citizen-led initiatives like the Plateforme Citoyenne de Soutien aux Réfugiés. By examining the motivations, experiences, and impacts of private hosting, this account highlights both the solidarity and the complexities involved in providing shelter and support to those left unaccommodated by the state.

A manufactured reception crisis

During the Long 'Summer of Migration' in 2015, Belgium, like numerous other countries, witnessed a surge in arrivals of people fleeing from conflict zones. During that period, the Belgian federal government failed to accommodate or provide shelter for all newcomers, resulting in many of them being forced to live on the streets. This led activist groups to take up responsibility and build the iconic camp in Maximilian Park, right next to the intake centre of the Federal Agency for the Reception of Asylum-seekers (Fedasil). The camp was closed shortly after, but the network of supportive citizens grew into more organised, bottom-up arrival infrastructures, notably the volunteer-based Plateforme Citoyenne de Soutien aux Réfugiés (Plateforme Citoyenne), now active under the name BelRefugees.

Since 2015, Belgium has faced a series of recurring reception crises. This is due not only to increasingly hostile migration policies in Belgium and across Europe, but also to the Belgian state's crisis-driven approach. Rather than investing in permanent accommodation centres to address ongoing needs, the state opts to create emergency centres during peak times. However, these centres are often too few, too late, and are dismantled again as soon as possible. Due to the ongoing shortages this crisis-driven approach creates, the state even started to refuse male asylum-seekers the right to reception facilities in 2021.

After the initial reception crisis in 2015, a second occurred in 2017, when an increasing number of newcomers faced homelessness on the streets of Brussels. This time, the crisis predominantly involved people on the move to England following the dispersal of the Calais camps in France. Members of the Plateforme Citoyenne mobilised to provide emergency accommodation not only in shelters, but also in citizens' private homes. Approximately 6,000 citizens in and around Brussels stepped up to offer a room, a couch, or a mattress to those who would otherwise have been left on the streets.

In October 2021, Brussels faced its third reception failure within six years. Thousands of asylum-seekers and people on the move were left unaccommodated by the state, and hosts continue to fill this gap tirelessly. Some do so within the framework of BelRefugees, while others do so independently.

Hosting in private homes: beyond the provision of mere shelter.

Most citizen hosts offer not only a bed, but also food, some clothes, or other necessities, sometimes even money. Many also offer support with translations, paperwork, or looking up information, and thus build expertise on legal matters over the years. By channelling services and information to people who need it, these hosts do important arrival infrastructuring work.

Private hosting is therefore an extraordinary means of providing resources where the state fails to provide them. Many guests and hosts perform care and potentially forge strong bonds. A guest who moved on to England said, "I am happy to be in the UK because I receive shelter and a fast procedure, but if it was just about the people, I would have preferred to stay in Belgium because there was so much solidarity and I made so many friends" (Fieldnotes, Brussels 2022).

Often hosts and guests keep in contact for many years. Former guests then invite their former hosts to their new homes.

Nevertheless, this form of temporary shelter should not be romanticised. The private hosting is a remediation of a structural violation of the right to asylum and the right to housing. Furthermore, the host–guest relationship itself involves dependencies and hierarchies, and some newcomers have expressed that while they are grateful for being hosted, if they had a choice they would prefer the more independent situation of a state-organised shelter.

An alternative narrative that inspires a more hospitable world

Despite the challenges, the experiences of people who take part in this experimental and activist form of solidarity can provide meaningful insights for a more hospitable world. Hosting holds the potential to reshape how hosts live with and think about newcomers. It can be an active and everyday opportunity to destabilise dominant cultures that uphold narratives of exclusion.

One host explained that hosting served as a method to combat narratives that depict newcomers as dangerous: "I thought, OK, they are trying to make us believe we should be afraid of these people, and I don't want to, I don't want to succumb to it... so I thought, yeah, probably the only way not to accept it is to let them come here" (Interview, Brussels, January 2022).

Figure 18. Photo of a set-up in a private home to host newcomers.

Despite the exhaustive efforts of concerned citizens to fill the gaps in the state's arrival infrastructure, hosting a few individuals does not solve the bigger problem. In fact, this type of bottom-up infrastructuring work might even reinforce the status quo of state practices of exclusion by giving the impression that things are solved. Nevertheless, private hosting presents important alternative narratives and practices relating to arrival and migration.

By hosting newcomers in their homes, citizens engage in arrival infrastructuring, offering practical and emotional support that goes beyond providing mere shelter, including clothing, everyday care, and interpersonal bonds. However, it is important not to romanticise this practice or allow it to become a justification for the withdrawal of state services.

Private hosting of newcomers demonstrates the capacity of grassroots initiatives to fill gaps in the state-provided arrival infrastructure, such as asylum centres, showcasing the power of collective action and solidarity in response to institutional neglect.

Private hosting of newcomers is a way of remedying structural failures, addressing immediate needs while highlighting systemic violations of the rights to asylum and housing. It is important that it is complemented by advocacy for systemic changes to ensure that the responsibility for housing and care does not disproportionately fall on citizens.

Private hosting of newcomers not only aids newcomers but also transforms the hosts, reshaping their understanding of migration, challenging prejudices, shaping alternative narratives about migration and integration, and fostering empathy through personal relationships.

CONCEPT BOX 6

'The Long Summer of Migration'

'The Long Summer of Migration' (Kasparek and Speer, 2015) refers to the period during the summer of 2015 when a large number of refugees and migrants travelled through Europe, particularly along the Balkan route, seeking asylum and better living conditions due to conflict and war in their home countries. This term highlights the significant movement of people and the temporary suspension of strict border controls, which allowed many to cross into countries such as Germany and Austria.

During this time, there was a notable display of social solidarity and humanitarian efforts, with many European citizens and organisations providing aid and support to the migrants. The term 'Long Summer of Migration' stands in contrast to the more negative connotations of a 'migration crisis', emphasising the agency and resilience of the migrants as well as the collective response to their challenges. It also underscores that this was, in fact, more of a reception or accommodation crisis than a 'migration crisis', with governments failing to provide adequate shelter or support for the newcomers. As a result, many were forced to live on the streets, reflecting a systemic violation of the right to asylum and the right to housing.

Reference:
Kasparek, Bernard, and Marc Speer. 2015. 'Of Hope. Hungary and the Long Summer of Migration'. bordermonitoring.eu. Retrieved from https://bordermonitoring.eu/ungarn/2015/09/of-hope-en/

See the academic complement of this *Integration Otherwise Inspiration Kit*, the edited volume *Infrastructuring Arrival* (Arnaut, Beeckmans, and Meeus, 2026), in particular:
– Chapter 1 (Arnaut, Beeckmans, and Meeus, 2026)
– Chapter 7 (Shila Hadji Heydari Anaraki, 2026)

TOOL 7
VISUALISING NEWCOMERS' (INTERRUPTED) HOUSING TRAJECTORIES

MATERIALS: Paper, writing utensils.

TOOL SUMMARY: This tool helps illustrate the housing insecurity many newcomers face due to various barriers while also shedding light on the factors that positively influence their housing trajectories. It encourages you to map out these often-interrupted pathways, highlighting the frequent moves and sacrifices migrants make to secure shelter. This visualisation fosters a deeper understanding of and discussion about the challenges, obstacles, and key stakeholders that shape migrant housing experiences.

Housing trajectories are often disrupted by administrative barriers, policy gaps, xenophobic landlords, oversaturated housing markets, and other challenges. As a result, newcomers frequently have to find solutions on the go, often sacrificing 'secondary' needs such as privacy or comfort in exchange for basic shelter. This instability often means they lack secure, long-term housing, leading to frequent moves in search of a place to stay.

STEP 1: Use your own housing trajectory, or someone else's, either through talking to them specifically or because you have encountered them in your work.

STEP 2: To visualise this trajectory, draw a table with time stamps in the vertical column, and places in the horizontal line (see example below). Use a time scale that is appropriate for the situation: if the person moved every few days, then a weekly scale will work best; if it was every few months, a monthly scale will be better, etc.

STEP 3: Ask the person to tell you more about their housing history and draw a line to visualise their trajectory.

STEP 4: Add elements to that trajectory by asking more questions. For example: how did they find the first place they lived in? Who provided it to them, and how long did they stay there? Why did they then move? Were any organisations or institutions involved? Were they paying any rent? Did their legal status change during that time? How did their legal status influence their housing trajectory?

You can add this information to the chart itself.

You can do this exercise with several people, one on one, or in a group, to open the conversation about interrupted housing trajectories and housing insecurity, as well as the many obstacles and barriers newcomers face to find stable housing.

The following diagram shows a housing trajectory based on a fictitious person, as an example of how the tool can be used.

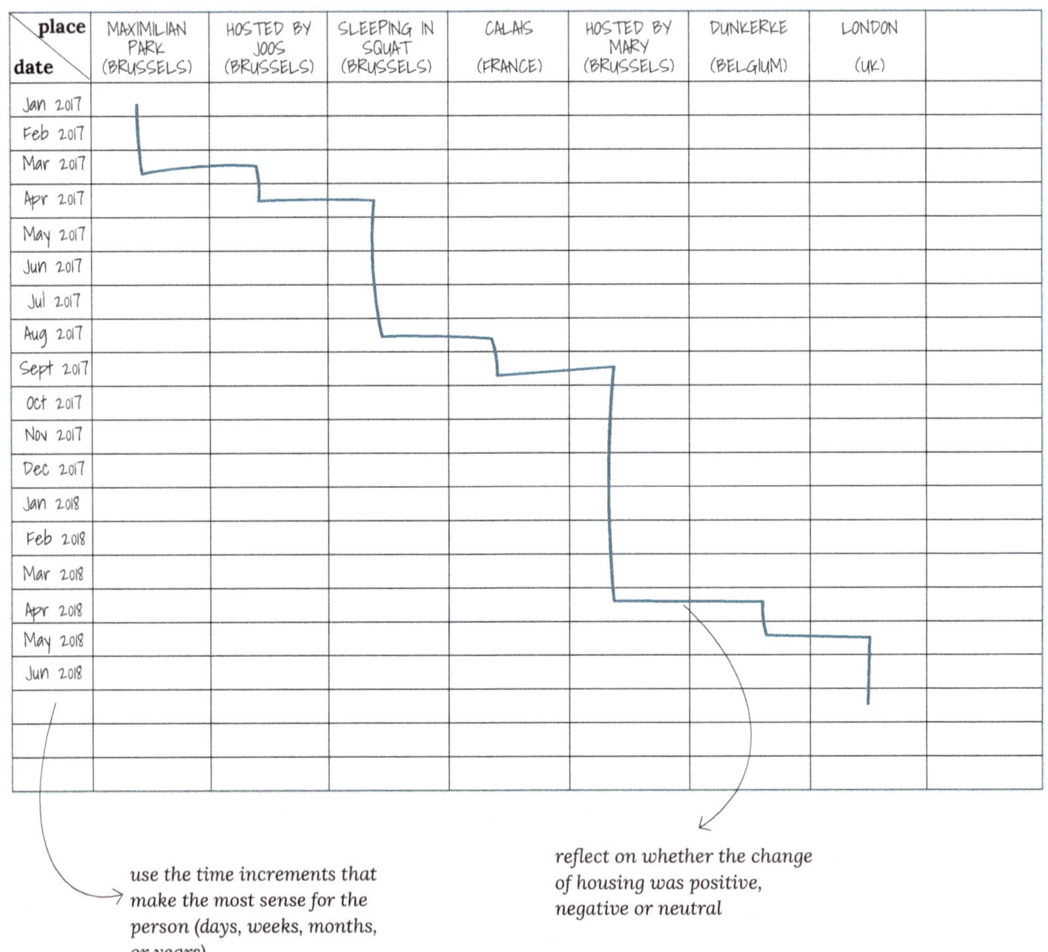

Figure 19. Diagram for visualising migrants' interrupted housing trajectories.

REFLECTION

Visualising housing trajectories reveals the housing instability and insecurity newcomers face, as well as the individuals and groups who either facilitate or hinder this process.

The diagram for this tool was inspired by Jørgen Carling's 'Migration History Chart'. See Carling, Jørgen. 2012. 'Collecting, Analysing and Presenting Migration Histories' in Carlos Vargas-Silva (ed.), *Handbook of Research Methods in Migration*. Cheltenham: Edward Elgar Publishing.

Student dormitories in Hungary: spaces of integration or segregation?

Hungary is widely recognised for its hostile migration policies and limited prospects for migrants' inclusion in society. In this context, non-state stakeholders play a crucial role in facilitating the arrival of newcomers. This story expands on the pivotal and challenging role of universities in providing accommodation and supporting the inclusion of newcomers in Budapest.

University housing as arrival infrastructure

In Hungary, a Foreign Ministry programme called the Stipendium Hungaricum allows students from certain pre-determined non-EU countries to study at a Hungarian university while receiving tuition-free education in English alongside a small stipend. The scholarship also provides a place in the student dormitories. Universities are thus an important arrival infrastructure in Hungary. Their role is not only to accept applications, select students, and provide the student status required for foreign residence in Hungary, but also to provide housing for these newcomers.

When choosing accommodation in Hungary, students have the choice between dormitories and the private rental market. Dormitories are covered by the scholarship, whereas housing on the private rental market is only partially subsidised. Private apartment rental thus requires more financial and social capital, but in return it provides more autonomy and personal space. In Budapest, dormitories mainly house first-year students, due to limited availability. In the first year, students often prefer to stay in dormitories because they offer more security and stability. As they gain experience and financial stability, sometimes taking a student job, they often move from dorms to private rentals.

Dorms as spaces of socialisation

Student dorms play an important role in newcomer-students' integration process in Hungary, bringing together many essential services and resources for arrival under one roof. Within the dormitories, university administrative services are easily accessible, sports facilities are often included, and they are essential spaces for socialising. It is common for friendships to form between roommates in the dorms. Often students request to be paired with someone from the same country or region, which creates a sense of comfort and a homelike atmosphere. Before departure, nationality-based social media platforms support this process. They connect newcomers with each other and with more senior students. Information about dormitory conditions, rental prices, and potential flatmates are available before arrival.

Spaces of 'integration' or 'segregation'?

Apart from roommates, student dormitories are also spaces where international connections are born. While international students easily create connections with other international students, relationships with Hungarian students are more difficult to establish. We identified two reasons for this difficulty. First, there is a spatial barrier. Most universities have floors reserved specifically for international students. As one newcomer-student explained, "And even in the dormitory, we have the floor for Hungarians, and other floors are for international students, so it is like we don't really mix. We don't have the opportunity to meet Hungarian students there" (Columbian student, Miskolc, January 2022).

Second, for students to feel included a more conscious effort is required from the stakeholders involved. In Budapest, management of one of the dorms has tried to set conditions and apply policies that create a more inclusive environment. For example, it abolished the nationality-based separation between the dorm's floors. However, the results of these efforts remain to be seen. At this dorm, the student organisation planned a three-day event called 'Dorm Days', involving fun activities designed to promote cross-cultural socialisation. Via a Facebook page and printed posters, they advertised the programme and invited students to participate in activities such as beer pong, disco night at a club, dog therapy sessions, a football championship, and other games. An international day was also organised. Yet the event was only advertised in Hungarian. According to one international student, "There was one event I really wanted to join, a dog therapy session. So, I postponed a meeting at the university and managed to change my shift in the workplace. I was the only international in the group when I got to the venue. They were speaking Hungarian, and I could not understand what was happening. It was so disappointing" (Georgian student, Budapest, May 2023).

Although the dorm management has made efforts to promote the inclusion of national and international students, they do not always have the desired impact. We found that Hungarian students often had less motivation to build ties with international students. This lack of motivation had mixed results in cross-cultural events. International students living in dormitories find themselves pulled in two directions simultaneously. On one hand, they feel pulled to 'integrate' into existing local structures, while on the other hand, they are directed into separate and parallel systems.

Universities are an important arrival infrastructure for international students.

The broader hostile migration environment in Hungary amplifies the importance of university infrastructures in providing stability and security to international students. Universities should particularly take care that Hungary's broader 'politics of disintegration' (see concept box 7 below) are not mirrored and made manifest within their own spaces and organisation (such as dormitories).

Inclusion initiatives, such as cross-cultural events, may fall short when they fail to account for language barriers or cultural accessibility, highlighting the need for more thoughtful planning and implementation.

Social media platforms that connect incoming students with peers and provide critical pre-arrival information demonstrate how the process of arrival begins well before physical relocation.

CONCEPT BOX 7

'Politics of disintegration'

The term 'politics of disintegration', as discussed by Collyer et al. (2019), refers to deliberate political and institutional strategies aimed at fragmenting or undermining established systems of integration and inclusion, particularly in the context of migration. Hence, what are sometimes framed as policies of integration in fact seek to create barriers for newcomers, fostering exclusion and disintegration rather than facilitating their inclusion in host societies.

This approach can involve restricting access to housing, education, and social services, or implementing measures that isolate migrants spatially, socially, and economically. In doing so, the 'politics of disintegration' not only hinder opportunities for migrants to build connections with local communities but also reinforce divisions and hierarchies, perpetuating segregation and marginalisation.

The 'politics of disintegration', as discussed by Collyer et al. (2019), align closely with the concept of 'welfare state bordering', as both involve the use of policies and practices to restrict migrants' access to social rights and services, creating exclusionary boundaries within welfare systems. A good example of 'welfare state bordering', described by (Bendixsen and Näre, 2024, 2693) as the "state-authorised practices of managing access to social rights based on residence, migrancy, and/or citizenship in a given socio-political order", is when access to social housing is made dependent on local bonding, for instance the requirement of having lived in the municipality for more than five years, thus excluding newcomers.

Reference:

Collyer, Michael, Sophie Hinger, and Reinhard Schweitzer. 2019. 'Politics of (Dis)Integration – An Introduction' in Sophie Hinger and Reinhard Schweitzer (eds.), *Politics of (Dis)Integration* (Cham: Springer).

Bendixsen, Synnøve, and Lena Näre. 2024. 'Welfare state bordering as a form of mobility and migration control. Journal of Ethnic and Migration Studies', 50(11), 2689–2706.

See the academic complement of this *Integration Otherwise Inspiration Kit*, the edited volume *Infrastructuring Arrival* (Arnaut, Beeckmans, and Meeus, 2026), in particular:
– Chapter 11 (Arnaut and Meeus, 2026)

HOUSING
Building managers in Parisian social housing: balancing hierarchical pressures and on-the-ground needs

In social housing, frontline workers like building managers play a crucial intermediary role between the state and tenants. However, economic pressures increasingly burden their role. This is evident in Paris, where overworked building managers can no longer support residents, often leading to situations where residents are unable to pay rent.

A short history: from social workers to building managers in Parisian foyers

Building managers are frontline workers who play a central role in the day-to-day running of the Parisian social housing for West African migrant workers, also called *foyers*. The prominence of this role dates back to the 1960s, when these professionals were recruited from the French Colonial Army and with the residents coming from former French colonies in West Africa. Between the 1990s and the early 2010s, their profiles became more diverse as they were more often recruited for their expertise, for instance knowledge of the French welfare system. Since then, many building managers had social work instead of military backgrounds. In the 2010s, the profile of these building managers shifted again to what it is currently (2024): professionals with backgrounds in real estate and accountancy. This latest shift reflects a larger shift in the use of the foyer buildings: from migrant housing to broader social housing, management of which is often outsourced to private firms, such as real estate developers. The position of building manager is now considered a stepping stone for career advancement in real estate management. This is an important shift, because initially, the role focused on addressing the facility needs of inhabitants while also handling management tasks such as rent collection and monitoring technical issues in housing units.

The shift in the business model of Parisian *foyers* – from accommodating migrant workers to providing individualised social housing for a diverse population – significantly alters the daily responsibilities of building managers. Previously, building managers were in charge of one building, in which they worked on a daily basis. Subsequently, job cuts have forced them to rotate between sites, dividing their time between several buildings over the course of a week or even a day. The actual onsite presence of building managers has drastically reduced, but the number of residents remains the same. Moreover, they tend to focus on the most lucrative activity, those upon which their superiors insist the most: rent collection. Inevitably, the number of hours dedicated to welfare assistance is reduced. Managers are then encouraged to 'redirect' inhabitants to municipal social services, as the social work component of their jobs is perceived by their superiors as less important than their management tasks. Furthermore, these management tasks are the only ones they can put into their activity monitoring software. Welfare assistance is therefore an 'extra' activity, to be carried out at the end of the working day when everything else has been done.

Resistance to becoming mere rent collectors

Despite the changing business model of the *foyers*, several of the managers who have been working in *foyers* for many years resist the changes to their daily tasks. They claim providing support for residents is one of the reasons why they like their jobs, and that the reduction in the time dedicated to this support has immediate consequences for their ability to collect rent.

An example of this is when, during the Covid-19 lockdown period, the jobs and therefore incomes of many residents were deeply disrupted, as the vast majority of social housing inhabitants work in restaurants and the construction sector. For those without fixed contracts, this period of uncertainty resulted in a wage cut or even the loss of all their income. Combined with professional problems, the Covid-19 period also saw the curtailment of social rights due to applications for benefits such as housing subsidies or even to renew residence permits being blocked. Exacerbated by the inaccessibility of public services, these administrative issues had a direct impact on residents' ability to pay their monthly rent.

In the eyes of many building managers, the Covid-19 period and the years that followed should have been a time of stronger social support for residents going through major professional and administrative disruptions, instead of further cuts. Some of them contested this development actively by keeping up their support even though it increased their workload. Moreover, the degradation of the housing conditions in some of the social housing estates led various managers to take subversive decisions, such as to stop collecting rent if the elevator was not working, arguing that residents were not receiving the service they were paying for.

Social support as an essential part of building management

For many building managers, social support is a crucial activity and has even a key role in the building management: being able to unblock a retirement application for a resident who cannot write in French ensures not only an income for the resident, but also rent payments for the manager. Without their support, residents can see administrative problems drag on, and managers face an increase in unpaid rent, for which they have to take responsibility.

TAKEAWAYS

Within social housing, frontline workers such as building managers serve as crucial intermediaries between the state and the tenants. This dual role often places them in an ambiguous position, balancing the responsibilities of both controlling and accommodating newcomers – a position they frequently find challenging but that often deserves appreciation.

Important infrastructuring work cannot always be assured within frameworks that are increasingly driven by economic interests. For instance, the social and administrative support that accompanies the provision of housing for migrants is often the first to disappear when frontline workers are overburdened or pressured to prioritise profit over care.

Despite institutional pressures, many frontline workers in the housing sector continue to advocate for tenant welfare, often taking on additional workload or resisting purely financial directives to ensure residents receive the necessary support.

This story underscores that housing is not merely about physical structures but also about creating environments that support dignity, stability, and the ability to navigate life's challenges.

> Further reading: For more information on the topic of building managers in Parisian *foyers* see: Guérin, Laura. 2022. '"On nous a dit clairement: 'vous n'êtes pas travailleur social'"', *Plein droit*, 132: 18–21.

2. BRIDGING

This chapter tackles infrastructuring practices that allow newcomers to connect to an existing service offering that is, for one reason or another, difficult to access. It is the work not of providing a service, but of providing a connection so that a service or information can be accessed. This is why we have called this form of infrastructuring work 'bridging', thereby also referring to an important concept in migration studies (see concept box 8 below).

It is also the work of translation (literally and figuratively) of government paperwork, making appointments for someone, etc. In addition to these forms of signposting, some service providers adapt their offering to reach out actively to potential service users, which allows more people to access the service.

CONCEPT BOX 8

'Bridging'

'Bridging' in migration studies refers to the process of creating social connections between individuals or groups from different backgrounds, fostering relationships that span cultural, ethnic, or social divides. Unlike 'bonding', which strengthens ties within homogenous groups, 'bridging' emphasises building inclusive networks that facilitate 'integration', social cohesion, and access to resources for migrants. 'Bridging' often occurs through shared activities, community organisations, or institutional support, enabling migrants to connect with host communities, access information, and navigate social systems more effectively. These connections are particularly significant in overcoming structural barriers, as they help migrants access employment, housing, and other opportunities that may otherwise remain inaccessible.

'Bridging' also plays a role in reducing prejudice and fostering mutual understanding between migrants and local populations. For instance, research by Putnam (2000) highlights the importance of 'bridging social capital' in promoting trust and collaboration in diverse societies, a concept that has been extensively applied in migration studies to understand the 'integration dynamics' of newcomers. However, Hickman et al. (2012) critique the notion of 'bridging social capital', arguing that it disproportionately places the responsibility for integration on migrants while neglecting the need for reciprocal adaptation by the majority society. Wessendorf and Phillimore (2019) further argue that, in the process of migrant settlement, the most useful relationships are not necessarily those with the majority society, but rather a combination of different types of connections with a diverse range of people, including both recent and long-established migrants.

References:
Hickman, Mary, Nicolai Mai, and Helen Crowley. 2012. *Migration and social cohesion in the UK* (London: Palgrave Macmillan).
Putnam, Robert D. 2000. *Bowling Alone: The Collapse and Revival of American Community* (New York: Simon & Schuster).
Wessendorf, Susanne, and Jenny Phillimore. 2019. 'New Migrants' Social Integration, Embedding and Emplaced Belonging in Superdiverse Contexts', *Sociology,* 53(1): 123–38.

2.1 THROUGH INFORMATION

Accessing useful information is often challenging for newcomers who are unfamiliar with the language or institutional context of the place they arrive in. Much infrastructuring work focuses on communicating the essential information required for the arrival process. Dedicated information points exist, whether physical – such as municipal centres – or online platforms like Facebook groups. However, information also circulates through many other contexts.

In some cases, as part of their services to newcomers, individuals use opportunities such as language classes to share other important information. Additionally, some people provide essential information because of their roles or positions. For instance, housing providers (landlords or others) often become key sources of information for newcomers. Similarly, spaces for essential services, like healthcare centres, also serve as important hubs for information exchange.

Sharing information often involves a trade-off between reach and personalisation. For example, a teacher in a small class can tailor information to the needs of individual students, but the reach is limited. Conversely, an official information point can communicate broadly to anyone passing by, but for some, processing the information may require additional guidance. In the process of bridging information, individuals can simultaneously act as enablers and gatekeepers, shaping how and to whom the information is communicated.

Creative English classes in a London borough: promoting service access through language courses

In this story, we explore the significant language and other barriers newcomers face when trying to access essential services. Our researcher in the London borough found that a lack of English proficiency or knowledge of available services can have severe consequences. We share the case of an innovative language programme, which integrates health engagement skills into language learning, helping people navigate emergency situations and access health services. The story also examines the broader implications of such initiatives, emphasising the dual role of language classes in building both linguistic and practical skills for service access. However, we also acknowledge the persistent challenges within health systems that are not always user-friendly, illustrating the ongoing need for supportive measures to aid non-English speakers.

Language and lack of knowledge as barriers to health services

Lacking knowledge of health services or the language skills to engage with them can have devastating consequences. In the London borough where our research was based, a community centre was running an informal English programme that helped address this issue for residents in the early stages of learning English. The community hub was run by a local charity and included a range of services that aimed to reduce social isolation and empower residents to participate in local life through activities such as volunteering and a low-cost community lunch. It was running one of the only social-sector English programmes in the borough at the time of the research.

An English curriculum with health engagement skills built in

Developed by a resident of the borough, the Creative English methodology used in the programme uses things like puppets, props, and role play to encourage participants to imagine different everyday scenarios and the English vocabulary needed to interact in them.

On one occasion, the lesson focused on calling emergency services. It started with a game where learners had to physically act out gestures to indicate emergencies such as 'Fire!' or 'Thief!' and their counterparts had to respond with the appropriate number to call for the emergency services in the UK – '999'. A second game involved the learners dividing into two groups. Each group would act out an incident and then all would be challenged to identify which of the two was the greater emergency. Later, the lesson featured a story about a mother and father who are babysitting a neighbour's child, who becomes ill, vomiting continuously.

Based on the emergency numbers learned earlier on in the session – including 999, 111 (non-emergency health advice), and 101 (non-emergency police services) – learners had to suggest which would be the correct number to call.

In groups, learners then role-played calling the non-emergency health advice helpline and asking for an interpreter to explain the problem in the scenario. In one group, a Syrian newcomer who was attending for the first time and had little confidence speaking English was selected to hold the baby and pretend to call and ask for an interpreter. Although she was assisted in the class by a friend who interpreted certain things, the lesson provided an opportunity for her to learn about the existence of the national helpline and the possibility of requesting an interpreter. In addition, it offered an opportunity to try saying the word 'interpreter' in order to practise the act of requesting such a service.

Since that time, a Creative English programme specifically focusing on English for healthcare engagement has been tested in the borough. When a member of the Supporting Migrants Network in the borough piloted the course in a different community hub, places on the course were filled almost immediately, illustrating how crucial these skills are seen to be.

The Creative English programme gives some pause for thought about the different functions that a support initiative can play, and the importance of building capacity among non-speakers of the local language to successfully navigate everyday service interactions as well as social occasions. As the lesson described above illustrates, navigating services requires both language and local know-how – knowing the numbers and functions of different services, and about the availability of interpretation when calling. Informal English lessons are one way in which important information about service availability and access can be communicated to learners whose social networks do not provide it.

But it is more complicated

The Creative English course provided a basic introduction to the idea and practice of health engagement. But health systems are not always designed in a user-centred way and in practice can still present many barriers to those trying to engage with them. Health helplines involve long recorded messages in English and a triaging process using a long series of recorded questions asked in English. This linguistic maze must be navigated before it is possible to ask an actual human being for an interpreter, and many beginner English speakers will not succeed without support.

A similar issue is that hospital correspondence explains diagnoses and gives instructions in English, which some recipients cannot read or fully understand – even when they try to use translation apps. Communication breakdowns can easily have serious consequences. In one case we encountered in the London research, a child with a serious health condition received no treatment for two years until the mother met an English speaker she felt comfortable asking for help to investigate the delay.

TAKEAWAYS

\# Navigating service access requires both language and local know-how – for instance, knowing the correct phone numbers and functions of different services, and about the availability of interpretation when calling.

\# Support initiatives can serve more than one purpose: a language class can build local language skills as well as the skills and knowledge to access services and interact socially. At the same time, it can also combat social isolation and help build social networks among learners.

\# Health systems, among other basic services, are not always designed in a user-centred way and can in practice still present many barriers to newcomers trying to engage with them.

> To design a service with this in mind, see **TOOL 4**: 'Identifying unexpected barriers to everyday life tasks' and **TOOL 8**: 'Visualising obstacles to service access' (you can also use those tools with this story in mind).

HOUSING
Migrant hotel managers in Westland as key intermediaries: connecting seasonal labourers to vital services

In the industrial agricultural region of Westland (the Netherlands), migrant labourers are often housed in specific hotels owned by employment agencies specialising in temporary and seasonal labour. The managers of these hotels play a crucial role in the lives of the residents. They offer useful information, connect residents to health services, and remain available 24 hours a day. At the same time, as personnel of the employment agencies, the hotel managers must protect the interests of their employers, which can produce ambivalent relationships and distrust with hotel residents. Migrant hotel managers are essential links to other arrival-related services for newcomers, but the relationships between managers and migrants are subject to the pressures of personal and professional obligations, often resulting in shifting loyalties and ambivalence

Arriving in a migrant hotel in Westland

In many arrival situations, individuals play a crucial yet ambivalent role in guiding newcomers to information and services, often operating in a grey area between formality and informality. In the case of housing facilities in Westland, hotel managers embody this ambivalence. Hotels are often the first place migrant workers arrive, making them the initial source of information on navigating their new environment.

Petru is one such hotel manager at a migrant hotel in Westland, where we stayed for six weeks during our fieldwork. Petru spends most of his shifts in the lobby, where there are a few tables and chairs, but most importantly the service desk and the office of the hotel manager(s). The desk is occupied 24/7 by Petru and his assistant managers, who alternate shifts. Petru, originally from Moldova, moved to Westland with his wife. His previous experience of working abroad and his command of English, Russian, and Romanian made him a suitable candidate for the job at the migrant hotel, which is owned by an employment agency. Petru and his wife live at the hotel. His wife works at a logistical centre for agricultural products with other migrant workers also living at the hotel. The other managers primarily speak Polish, enabling the management team to communicate with almost all the migrant workers staying at the hotel.

Signposting beyond the official role of the hotel manager

When we asked Petru about his daily and weekly tasks, he explained: "Every Sunday, the new people arrive, with the bus. And then we make the introduction here. About the hotel, the agency. We have to take care they have the right room. And then the rest of the week we are doing all kinds of things. Checking if there is nothing going wrong. No parties. And they come with problems and questions, and we can answer them. About the planning for work, about the transport [to work]. When they are sick, I tell them where to go. When they get here, they don't know anything. So they don't know where to go" (Petru, Westland, May 2022).

Petru is able to answer questions about healthcare, work, and public transport for connections to urban centres, which is important because the hotel is relatively remote and difficult to reach without private transportation. Given that he is employed by the employment agency, we asked whether he also connects newcomers to the support office at the agency. Petru responded, "No, that takes a lot of time and does not always solve the issue. If I have time to help someone, I avoid the support office" (Petru, Westland, May 2022).

Figure 20. Fruit and vegetable transportation in Westland.

An ambivalent relationship

Two residents of the hotel, Lucija and Sara, explained their relationship with the hotel manager. Lucija said, "We go there for any issue. Sometimes they help us, sometimes they don't. That time I broke my ankle, it was very difficult. The managers don't speak our language, so we had to talk in English. They arranged transport to the emergency room, but I waited a long time in the lobby and didn't understand what was going on. And the agency was not helping me; they wanted me to go back to work" (Lucija, Westland, April 2022).

Lucija and Sara often complain about the managers being too controlling. The same managers who might help one day can enter rooms unannounced the following day, to check that tenants are following the rules. During the peak of the energy crisis in 2022 and 2023, the managers put up signs in the lobby, kitchens, and rooms forbidding residents from using heating at night and limiting it to 17 degrees Celsius during the day. Lucija and Sara felt constricted and controlled in the hotel. At the same time, managers often look the other way when residents bring non-resident visitors, which is officially not allowed.

This inconsistency reflects the ambivalent position of the hotel managers. On one hand, they deliberately avoid the agency's support office to help residents with various arrival-related questions. On the other hand, they have a complicated relationship with residents, being both bound by agency rules and guided by personal boundaries.

Migrant housing facilities, such as migrant hotels for seasonal migrant labourers, act as a vital arrival infrastructure and critical entry points for newcomers, providing not only shelter but also initial guidance on navigating essential services like healthcare, transportation, and work. Hence, the story underscores the need to view housing not only as a necessity but also as a leverage point for improving the broader inclusion and well-being of migrant workers.

In many arrival contexts, some individuals play a crucial yet ambivalent role in guiding newcomers to information and services. In the case of the migrant hotels, the ambivalent role of hotel managers is shaped by the conflicting demands of their employer, residents, and personal boundaries and ethics, making them both enablers of support and enforcers of control.

Hotel managers with a migration background are uniquely positioned to act as cultural mediators, understanding both the residents' challenges and the institutional pressures they face.

Formal support structures, such as those offered by the employment agency in this story, often involve complex processes that some key intermediaries, like hotel managers, prefer to bypass to provide quicker and more effective solutions.

Migration does not start with the point of arrival. In fact, many newcomers have had long pre-arrival trajectories full obstacles and opportunities. Even before 'landing', arrival is infrastructured by multiple people, organisations, and institutions, including newcomers themselves. Understanding the interplay of these stakeholders and their significance within arrival processes can be very helpful for practitioners providing essential support.

Referring newcomers to other organisations in a private clinic in Istanbul: expanding access to services beyond healthcare

In an arrival context with inaccessible healthcare for migrants, one doctor at a clinic in Kumkapı, located in the Fatih neighbourhood of Istanbul, emerges as a key figure, providing not only essential medical services but also vital connections to broader support networks. By offering care with minimal identification requirements, he creates an accessible environment for migrant patients who often face language and cultural barriers, as well as economic challenges. Beyond treating immediate health concerns, the doctor actively refers patients to organisations that provide crucial resources that are not immediately accessible through formal arrival procedures. This story underscores the significance of arrival infrastructuring work by certain individuals, such as healthcare providers, who become reference points for newcomers, often working beyond their professional scope.

Inaccessible healthcare

The Covid-19 pandemic has exposed the fragilities of health systems and their insufficiencies, in particular with regard to migrant populations. In Turkey, since the substantial arrival of Syrian refugees in 2011, migrant clinics have been established in different parts of Istanbul to provide basic health services to different migrant and refugee groups. Yet they remain unfit for the treatment of a wide range of illnesses. Without health insurance, migrants are required to pay high fees for special tests and treatment in other hospitals in Turkey. In our research, we found that many migrants visited a private clinic in the arrival neighbourhood of Fatih – specifically in the locality of Kumkapı – to receive treatment at an affordable fee. The head doctor of the clinic we studied performs important arrival infrastructuring work by referring his patients to other migrant organisations for support beyond the scope of the clinic's services.

A clinic adapting its services to the needs of newcomers

The clinic has been active in the arrival neighbourhood of Fatih for many years. Unlike state or other private hospitals, the clinic requires very simple proof of identification, such as a passport, national ID card, driver's licence, or residence permit. The identification papers presented do not have to be up to date, meaning that migrants and refugees with expired residence permits or passports can still receive medical services in the clinic. It is always full and busy, with at least several children and many patients of different nationalities and ethnicities in the waiting room. The majority of patients are African and Uzbek women. The clinic provides a range of different services, from gynaecology and paediatrics to ophthalmology and orthopaedics. There is greatest demand for paediatric services and gynaecology/pregnancy follow-ups. The demand for gynaecological services is also due to the presence of migrant sex workers in the area. Previously the staff of the clinic studied the area to improve their service delivery by collecting data, providing workshops, and drafting reports regarding sexually transmitted diseases in the area.

The head of the clinic has an established reputation in migrant communities. An Uzbek newcomer woman who came to the clinic for the first time from a remote district and did not speak Turkish explained that she had come to see an Uzbek doctor, which she thought the head of clinic was. Although the doctor is not in fact of Uzbek nationality, he manages to communicate with his migrant patients in their language on a very basic level. That makes a big difference for migrant patients, since most private and state hospitals require migrants to hire interpreters or bring with them someone who speaks Turkish.

The clinic: an entry point for other services

The doctor not only provides medical care but in some instances has also referred his patients – migrant women – to other organisations. One recent case recounted to us involved an African woman with two children and a deceased husband, who was in an economically vulnerable position. The doctor gave her the address of an organisation that has a programme to support migrant women and even called the organisation to confirm his referral. In other instances, he also provided information and signposted patients to different institutions with services tailored to survivors of sexual and gender-based violence. The doctor is highly respected and trusted due to his care and extra-medical mediation.

TAKEAWAYS

In contexts of arrival where newcomers face many barriers to accessing services, those who manage to lower barriers quickly become reference points. A case in point are clinics that simplify identification requirements and demonstrate cultural sensitivity. They create an environment where newcomers feel safe seeking essential medical care and often serve as an important referral network for additional support services.

Healthcare professionals, particularly in newcomer-friendly clinics, often serve as essential intermediaries who bridge gaps between newcomers and broader support systems, going beyond their medical responsibilities.

The ability of healthcare providers to communicate in migrants' native languages, even at a basic level, significantly improves the patient experience, addressing one of the main barriers to service access.

2.2 THROUGH TRANSLATION

Access to information alone is often insufficient. Foreign institutional contexts require translation or decoding to make them accessible to newcomers. In this sense, translation should be understood not only as converting one language into another but also as making governmental and bureaucratic systems comprehensible to those unfamiliar with them. In our research, we found that the responsibility for making these frameworks understandable and accessible often falls heavily on newcomers themselves, as well as on bureaucrats, social workers, activists, and others.

While many institutions perform the essential task of publishing guides for newcomers in multiple languages, additional effort is often required for these guides to be effectively disseminated and made accessible through additional explanation and guidance to those who need them most. The role of making these guides accessible is sometimes taken on by more established migrants who act as 'brokers' or intermediaries in the arrival process. At other times, this 'brokering' (see concept box 9 below) is done by institutionalised cultural mediators or by volunteers and activists who accompany individuals through complex bureaucratic procedures.

Translation work, in this broader sense, is an essential aspect of bridging, as it facilitates newcomers' access to institutional frameworks, making systems and services comprehensible and actionable. By translating not just languages but also bureaucratic and cultural contexts, intermediaries – whether individuals or institutions – play a critical role in reducing barriers, fostering inclusion, and enabling meaningful participation in the host society. Their translation work this is an important arrival infrastructuring practice.

power imbalances. 'Brokering' is inherently connected to 'bridging', as 'brokers' facilitate connections between migrants and host institutions, helping to overcome cultural, linguistic, and institutional barriers and fostering integration into the wider society. Yet 'brokering' focuses on mediating access to resources and navigating institutional barriers for migrants through intermediaries or 'brokers', while 'bridging' emphasises creating social connections and fostering relationships between migrants and host communities.

'Brokering' is closely linked to 'welfare bricolage' (see concept box 4), as 'brokers' often creatively navigate and assemble fragmented welfare resources and networks to meet migrants' needs, compensating for gaps in formal systems.

Reference:
Faist, Thomas. 2014. 'Brokerage in Cross-Border Mobility: Social Mechanisms and the (Re)Production of Social Inequalities', *Social Inclusion*, 2(4): 38–52.

EDUCATION
Mediating between Roma parents and teachers in Nordstadt (Dortmund): overcoming mistrust in public authorities through translation work

Members of the Roma community from Romania and Bulgaria living in the arrival neighbourhood of Nordstadt, in the city of Dortmund, face specific challenges. Often burdened by a long history of discrimination, they frequently mistrust authorities, including educational institutions. As a result, many Roma children struggle with school attendance, highlighting the need for initiatives that foster understanding and communication between families and schools. One such initiative is the Vast Vasteste programme, which aims to bridge these gaps by pairing teachers with parents. This account highlights the experiences of Sara, who serves as a mediator between a Nordstadt school and the Roma community, and Caro, a teacher in the school. Together, they play a vital role in translating essential information between Roma parents and schools, fostering a more inclusive educational environment and raising awareness on both sides.

A long-standing history of discrimination

After the expansion of the EU in 2012 and the implementation of new freedom-of-movement policies, many people from the new member states of Romania and Bulgaria arrived in Germany. People from the Roma community concentrated in certain areas, and Nordstadt was one of them. Due to a long-standing history of discrimination, people from the Roma community often mistrust authorities, including schools. This often leads to school absences and a need to convince parents of the importance and benefit of attending school on a regular basis. The Roma mediation programme Vast Vasteste (translated as 'hand in hand') financed by the federal state of North Rhine-Westphalia aims to improve school access and attendance for Roma children. This initiative aims to enhance communication with parents in the Roma community by pairing a teacher with a community representative for each participating school. The mediator also functions as an interpreter, as most translation apps do not include the Romany language. With their command of Romany and their knowledge of both the school system and the community, Roma mediators form a bridge between the authorities and the community, thereby reducing mutual prejudices. In addition to providing support with everyday issues, along with signposting and translating, they highlight the importance of sending children to school every day by facilitating a welcoming atmosphere.

"You need eight arms": how a Roma mediator became the face of a primary school

During the pilot project for the programme, a one-week workshop offered the opportunity for mediators and teachers to get to know each other. It was in one of these workshops that Caro and Sara met. Caro is a teacher in a Nordstadt primary school and Sara is a Roma mediator. Building a relationship helped deepen their understanding of the needs of both the school and the Roma community, while improving collaboration in the school setting. Sara and Caro provide each other with mutual help and support, as well as a lasting friendship.

As the mediator, Sara has been able to open up the perspective of both the Roma community and the school. In this sense, Roma mediators balance two roles. For the Roma community, they are the 'face' of the school as an organisation. For the school administrators, the mediator is the 'face' of the Roma community. As a social worker from another school participating in the programme told us, a large part of mediation work involves establishing and maintaining trust.

As Caro explained, "This building [the school] is no longer (laughing) just an empty building that somewhat scares people and where lots of German people are running around, but um yes, it's also a building that has an open door" (Caro, primary school teacher, Dortmund, November 2022).

Because of Sara's dedication to building trust between the Roma community and the school, as a mediator she is highly regarded and sought after by the parents from the community. As Caro told us, "I came in the other day and [Sara] had a mobile phone to her ear, then a landline phone to her [other] ear and in between she was somehow handing out sheets of paper to parents who asked her questions. (laughing) I thought, God, you need eight arms" (Caro, primary school teacher, Dortmund, November 2022).

In her role as a Roma mediator, Sara forms a bridge between the school and Roma families. She, and others in her role, support them in many everyday issues, not only signposting parents to helpful resources, but also interpreting for them at the school's jobcentre.

Cultural mediation connecting different worlds

The story shows that long-standing discrimination means cultural mediation is sometimes needed to overcome barriers to inclusion. The Roma mediator is a role model integrated in both worlds – a government institution and the community. For both parties, the mediators become the 'face' of the other. In connecting both worlds, a start is made in reducing mutual prejudices and mistrust. The pilot project discussed in this story led to the more established programme Vast Vasteste.

TAKEAWAYS

A cultural mediator is more than just an interpreter. Their role is not only to translate from one language to another, but to effectively become a bridge between two cultures.

Cultural mediators play a critical role in establishing trust between marginalised communities and public institutions, for instance transforming schools from intimidating spaces into welcoming environments.

By representing both the institution and the community, cultural mediators contribute to dismantling stereotypes and reducing prejudice on both sides.

Small-scale initiatives and pilot programmes can evolve into established solutions for complex societal challenges. This example shows how investment in cultural mediation can lead to systemic improvements in inclusivity and accessibility for marginalised communities.

> Check **TOOL 27**: Barnga: a community-building exercise with a twist' for a useful tool to understand cultural barriers to dialogue and communication. Barnga is a game where participants play cards without knowing they are playing by different rules.

Practical support to see a doctor in London: the role of social contacts in overcoming language barriers to service access

A combination of barriers can prevent newcomers accessing services. Without the necessary local knowledge, language skills, IT skills, or social contacts to bridge these gaps, some individuals find themselves unable to engage with available support systems. Anghel, a middle-aged Romanian man, was living in a room in exchange for doing odd jobs when we interviewed him. He expressed concerns about the loss of his identity documents and shared that he was struggling with depression. Having lived without his antidepressant medication since arriving in the UK, he had turned to alcohol as a coping mechanism. When asked if he had seen a doctor, Anghel was unaware that he was eligible for free medical treatment. He spoke virtually no English and could only be interviewed with the assistance of a Romanian interpreter. Lacking social contacts to help him navigate healthcare services, Anghel had not received the support he needed, which he might otherwise have accessed years earlier. This story reflects our researcher's perspective during the process of supporting Anghel to resolve these challenges.

How we – willing strangers – helped Anghel navigate the process of general medical practice registration

When we met Anghel, he was not accessing health services, but we quickly recognised that simply telling him to register with a doctor would not solve the issue. He had limited English language knowledge and lacked the accepted forms of proof of address, which are sometimes required before registering a patient. To prevent Anghel approaching a doctor who would turn him away, we did some online research into local general practitioner practices and emailed around to find a local doctor who accepted patients without proof of address. We then took Anghel to register there. He followed us, looking overwhelmed, as we navigated a confusing array of reception areas within the practice and explained to a receptionist that he could not comply with their policy of registering online, because he is not IT literate. We sat with Anghel in the waiting room and filled in his English-language registration form, using Google Translate to ask him the questions and record the answers.

We handed in the form and asked the receptionist how Anghel could get an appointment without needing to call the practice. We knew he would not understand and be able to successfully navigate the recorded English-language options that are a feature of telephone appointment booking. Also, he would likely struggle to understand spoken English and make himself understood even if he was able to get through. We also pressed the clinic administrators for a way around online appointment bookings, which involved coming in person to the practice to ask for an appointment. Knowing that interpretation is usually available to National Health Service (NHS) practices, we asked how Anghel could obtain a Romanian interpreter for his appointment. Anticipating from our prior experience that stressed NHS receptionists might try to rebuff Anghel if he approached the practice for an appointment in person, we worried that he might become frustrated, upset, or angry, and consequently be barred from the practice (there are 'zero tolerance of abuse' signs in most practices). We therefore advised him to always be polite to the receptionists even if he felt frustrated, because he would get a better service this way. Having conveyed the various details of how to make an appointment slowly in simple English, we subsequently communicated to Anghel in Romanian, using Google Translate, in case he had not properly understood what we had said. The next time we saw Anghel, he was in high spirits. He had been seen by a doctor and was prescribed antidepressants. A few weeks later, a Romanian mutual acquaintance reported seeing him in a much better state and working in a local takeaway outlet near her home. While his mood had lifted through access to healthcare, his ability to obtain a formal job was aided by a similar accompaniment process to retrieve his identification papers from the Home Office.

The accompaniment function of social contacts

Afterward, Anghel told us that he could not have done it alone – "Lonely I couldn't do it," he said (Anghel, London, June 2022). What we learn from this story is that the everyday language skills, technical skills, and local know-how of others is an essential resource for newcomers when it comes to accessing services they are entitled to. While mainstream services are often designed to signpost people to services they need, they do not always recognise that seemingly simple processes, such as registering with a doctor, can involve multiple steps and require challenging linguistic, technical, and emotional skills from a newcomer who is living in difficult circumstances. Practical assistance from a family member, friend, service provider, or casual acquaintance is a valuable but time-consuming form of everyday arrival infrastructuring that helps newcomers with limited local language skills, IT skills, or local know-how to overcome the many barriers that they can face in accessing services.

\# Mainstream services do not always recognise that seemingly simple processes, such as registering with a doctor, can involve multiple steps and require challenging language, know-how, technical, and emotional skills from a newcomer.

\# Social contacts (like a family member, service provider, or casual acquaintance) often provide newcomers with essential assistance in navigating systems that are often inaccessible to those without language proficiency, digital literacy, or knowledge of local procedures, even though they are entitled to them.

\# While many systems are shifting to online platforms, not all individuals have the IT skills required to navigate them. Personal step-by-step guidance and practical assistance remains an indispensable resource.

\# Helping newcomers with essential steps, such as accessing healthcare or recovering identity documents, can have a ripple effect, improving both their mental well-being and employment opportunities.

TOOL 8
VISUALISING OBSTACLES TO SERVICE ACCESS

MATERIALS: Paper, writing utensils, your own or someone else's story about accessing a service (you can do the exercise alone or directly with them as a way of discussing their experience).

TOOL SUMMARY: This tool enables you to identify and understand the challenges newcomers face when attempting to access services. It involves mapping out the steps required to access a service and highlighting additional, often unforeseen, steps that complicate the process. The tool aims to reveal the discrepancy between official procedures and the actual, often arduous, experiences of newcomers.

What are the obstacles newcomers face when trying to access services? For newcomers who are not familiar with the context, seemingly simple procedures require a lot of effort. As a result, they either have to go through a stressful, complicated, and lengthy process or end up avoiding the service altogether.

STEP 1: Choose a service you are familiar with that is important in newcomers' arrival situations. On the horizontal axis of the diagram below, write all the steps needed to access this service. What is illustrated below is the procedure for seeing a doctor, like in the story of Anghel.

STEP 2: Thinking of your own experience or talking to a newcomer about theirs, fill in the vertical axis with additional steps encountered in the process before being able to reach the next step.

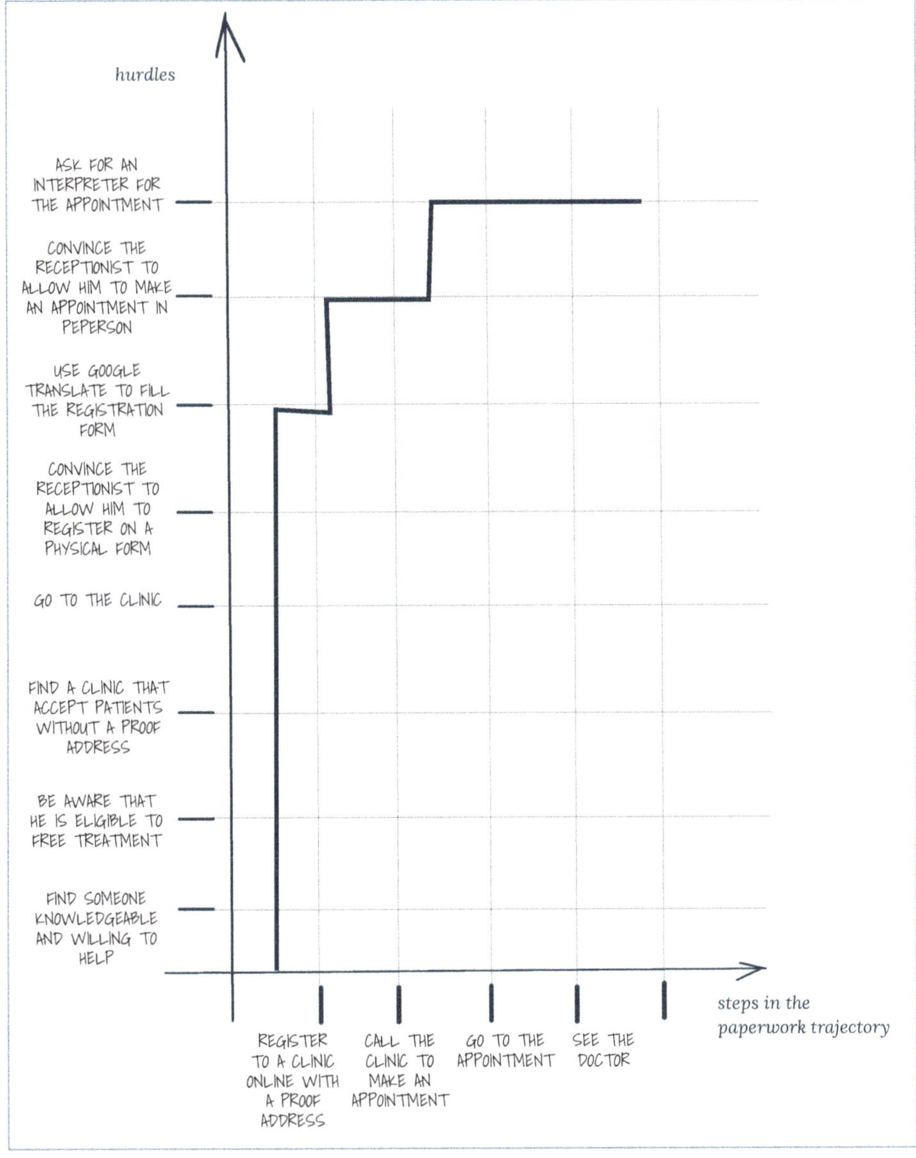

Figure 21. Diagram for visualising obstacles to serive acces

REFLECTION

This tool reveals how the trajectory of accessing a service is different from what is officially announced and sometimes becomes – almost literally – a mountain of obstacles to climb.

> CHECK **TOOL 4**: 'Identifying unexpected barriers to everyday life tasks'. That tool tackles the material barriers newcomers encounter in their everyday lives, but it can be also used in relation to this story, to explore the multiple language barriers resulting from not speaking the local language.

2.3 THROUGH ACTIVE OUTREACH BY EXISTING SERVICES

In many cases, to ensure access to their services, service providers establish mobile programmes to reach those they want to serve. These mobile services first identify the spaces that newcomers are using, and then actively publicise their activities in those spaces. In the first story, mobile services are provided by the municipality, which collaborates with a local NGO. In the second, mobile services are born from a need on the ground and implemented by activists.

HEALTHCARE

Mobile medical services cruising from occupation to occupation in Brussels: bridging healthcare gaps across the city

> In Brussels, asylum-seekers rejected or not accommodated by the state reception services often find themselves without stable accommodation and disconnected from essential services. Many rely on temporary shelters or 'sleep rough' on the streets or in parks, navigating a fragmented social support system that makes accessing help difficult. In this story, we recount the emergence of various mobile services that actively reach out to these individuals, providing food, medical care, and information directly in their temporary locations. These initiatives aim to ease the burden on vulnerable newcomers by shifting the responsibility of service accessibility to the organisations, ensuring support reaches those in need.

A failing reception system

Since October 2021, the Belgian government no longer systematically provides accommodation to asylum-seeking newcomers. With the federal agency for asylum giving priority to families, women, the elderly, and children, the people not given accommodation are – with a few exceptions – single men. Having lodged their asylum request at the intake centre in Brussels, they are asked to leave the reception centre and wait – often for several months – until a place is made available in an asylum accommodation centre.

In the meantime, the men have to rely on very limited temporary shelter. The options for temporary accommodation include shelters run by non-governmental organisations, the homes of friends or family, and private citizens who become hosts by temporarily opening their doors to newcomers. If these options are not available, these newcomer-men commonly turn to informally occupied vacant buildings in the city, often called 'squats', or have no choice but to 'sleep rough'.

These squats are dispersed throughout the city and are temporary in nature due to regular evictions and their general poor conditions. Hence, the men are forced to move from one place to the next. Apart from the non-governmental shelters, most places do not offer officially organised social infrastructure such as legal, medical, or well-being support. Many squats lack basic amenities such as water, electricity, toilets, or kitchens.

Navigating the maze of social services

Many of these men have been on the move across Europe, navigating across countries, experiencing violence from border authorities and neglect. Having arrived in Brussels, they do not find rest and a sense of security. Rather, they experience continued exclusion, further neglect, and displacement, and more-over, because of having to move across the city to find shelter, risk being cut off from necessary information, basic services, and care.

Humanitarian agencies and social centres offering food, showers, information, and health services to homeless people can be found in various places across Brussels. However, some people do not know about the existence of these services. Once they find out about them, ticketing systems, long waiting lists or queues, and the distances to be travelled form extra barriers to accessing these services.

Service providers on the move

In response to this observation, a range of grassroots mobile services have emerged, actively seeking out and visiting newcomers in their temporary dwellings. Examples of these services include volunteers who cook and deliver food to occupied buildings, squats, and those sleeping rough; outreach teams distributing blankets, tents, and information; first aid and medical services; and even a mobile team providing haircuts and showers in a mobile 'washing truck'.

The case of Brussels shows that when the work of arrival infrastructuring is left solely to the newcomer, they face many barriers and miss out on opportunities. The mobile service providers in Brussels demonstrate that when residents and local organisations directly reach out to newcomers and take an active role in infrastructuring arrival, fewer newcomers are excluded. They do not wait for service users to find them, but instead make their infrastructure mobile and actively reach out to their users. In so doing, they shift the responsibility for locating services and travelling across the city from the newcomers to the organisations themselves.

\# In large cities, services for newcomers often exist but are geographically dispersed and poorly advertised, leading many to remain unaware of their availability. Mobile services address this gap by actively seeking out individuals in need, shifting the responsibility for locating and accessing support from newcomers to the organisations themselves. In this way, the arrival infrastructuring work does not fall solely on newcomers.

\# Waiting for service users to approach fixed points of assistance excludes many who lack the knowledge, mobility, or capacity to travel. Mobile service providers demonstrate that proactive outreach is essential for reducing exclusion and increasing service accessibility.

\# Migration policies that result in the spatial dispersal or displacement of newcomers – whether intentionally or not – intensify their vulnerability. Mobile services are an effective response to the spatial dispersal of newcomers. By moving between locations such as squats, parks, and shelters, these initiatives help connect dispersed beneficiaries to essential resources like food, medical care, and legal aid.

\# Mobile services that combine practical support (such as food and shelter) with information and care (like health services and legal aid) provide a more holistic response to the interconnected needs of newcomers in vulnerable situations.

EMPLOYMENT

Mobile information points for EU migrant workers in and beyond Westland: broadening the reach of existing outreach services

This story describes intersecting challenges faced by EU migrant workers in The Hague, particularly during a consultation hour held by HelpInEU, where volunteers provide crucial support on issues like housing and employment. In this story, we provide a glimpse into the consultation sessions of individuals like Pjotr and Marek to illustrate the interconnectedness of health and work-related problems. In response to these challenges, a mobile information point was established to connect migrants with essential services, making support more accessible. This initiative emphasises the importance of addressing the fragmentation that can occur in service provision, a barrier many newcomers experience.

An emotional consultation hour

On a cold January evening in 2021, a queue forms outside a neighbourhood centre in The Hague's Transvaal district. Three Polish-speaking volunteers from HelpInEU (an NGO offering integration support in The Hague for European migrants) hold their biweekly consultation hour. Some volunteers have first-hand experience as EU migrant workers in the Netherlands, while others have legal backgrounds and learned Polish later in life. Both kinds of expertise are needed to help Polish and other Central and Eastern European newcomers in the area seeking free advice on housing, working, health, language, or education issues in The Hague.

One of the people looking for advice is Pjotr, who got seriously injured at a construction worksite. His employment was one of 'false self-employment' – this is a situation in which people are officially classified as self-employed but are, in reality, working under conditions similar to regular employees. This arrangement is often used by employers to circumvent employment rights, taxes, or employer obligations, such as providing benefits or paying social security contributions. In the case of Pjotr, it meant that his employer was not paying insurance money and as a result he was not entitled to paid sick leave for the time he needed to recover. This consequently caused problems with his housing.

Another consultation visitor, Marek, came in for the second time in a month. Due to some unfortunate circumstances with his old job, as well as what he described as "my own stupid actions", he had incurred serious debt. During his previous visit, the volunteers referred him to organisations for financial support, who could not however help him because he needed a registered address but was unhoused at that time. Soon after this rejection, he was able to get an official address registration at a homeless shelter, meaning he could start getting financial help, which would also help his other issues. Understandably, Marek got emotional at the end of the consultation and the volunteers tried to console him. Seeing his ongoing distress, they also referred him to migrant organisations offering mental health support.

That evening in January, most of the questions from visitors concerned physical and mental health, and labour. The stories of Pjotr and Marek and many others we encountered highlight the common interrelation of labour and physical/mental health challenges among EU migrant workers in the Netherlands. In most of the cases we studied, issues in both these domains often affect other areas of life as well.

Fragmented networks of support

The drop-in centre's location in the Transvaal district is strategic, given its high population of EU migrant workers living in precarious, often informal or illegal housing. The nearby square of Kaapseplein is a gathering spot where EU migrants await transportation to work in Westland's greenhouses, either on formal contracts or as informal day labourers. The presence of many vans and cars from employment agencies at this location is a manifestation of the most important infrastructural absence for EU migrant labour in Westland: housing. Of the 12,000 migrant workers employed in the greenhouse sector, only 4,500 are actually housed in Westland. As a result, employment agencies and other intermediaries offer substandard housing in the surrounding urban areas, such as The Hague. Over time, neighbourhoods of The Hague with cheap private housing, such as Transvaal, have become a major arrival infrastructure for EU migrant workers. In already deprived neighbourhoods, the precarious housing and working conditions lead to multiple challenges. Due to language problems, the fact that many of them are not officially registered, limited knowledge of their rights or duties as working residents in the Netherlands, and long working hours in physically demanding industries, EU migrant workers in The Hague are particularly vulnerable to exploitation, homelessness, or social isolation and have difficulties in finding help to solve these issues. Recognising these challenges, organisations like HelpInEU have established support networks over the years, although these networks remain spatially and socially fragmented.

Connecting arrival infrastructures spatially and socially

The municipality recognised the problems faced by a growing group of EU migrant workers in the city and the impact this has had on neighbourhoods such as Transvaal. Collaborating with existing stakeholders in the arrival infrastructure, like HelpInEU, the municipality set two goals: first, to ensure that existing and emerging support infrastructures connect, and second, to prioritise access for harder-to-reach groups of people. In 2023, two years after our first visit to the drop-in consultation centre, we were invited to attend the opening of a mobile information point. The van, intentionally devoid of municipal logos so as to be more approachable, features icons and some words in different languages to indicate that anyone can drop in for free information on work, health, education, legal advice, or housing. The municipal team of multilingual practitioners from different cultural and migration backgrounds connect people to existing support networks, but also to official services such as legal aid, language schools, health facilities, and municipal offices. Crucially, the van moves between different informal spaces of the arrival infrastructure, like Polish or Bulgarian shops, schoolyards, or squares and parks where migrant workers spend time or have set up tents for shelter. Both spatially and socially, mobile information teams connect the fragmented formal and informal landscape of the arrival infrastructure and reach out to more diverse newcomers.

\# In contexts where migrant workers live disconnected from key resources and services, mobile information points, for instance, can make a big difference.

\# Locating support initiatives in spaces such as markets, shops, or parks that are frequented by newcomers helps overcome spatial and social barriers to service access.

\# In contexts where institutional services are not attuned to the diverse needs of a specific group of newcomers and/or when there are social and spatial barriers to accessing existing services, arrival infrastructuring work risks being fragmented. Yet when municipalities collaborate with grassroots organisations, they can better identify gaps in support and expand access to underserved groups.

\# 'False self-employment' deprives migrant workers of essential protections, such as sick leave or insurance, often leaving them unable to recover from injuries or illnesses without severe financial and housing consequences.

TOOL 9
MAPPING SERVICE GAPS AND OUTREACH POTENTIAL

MATERIALS: A printed map of the area you work in, coloured markers, stickers, pins (optional).

TOOL SUMMARY: This tool helps service providers identify areas where mobile services might be needed. By mapping out where service users come from, it highlights potential gaps in service coverage and areas with transportation barriers. It aims to improve outreach and ensure services are accessible to all newcomers.

For those who are working on providing a service, it can be difficult to identify the spaces where a mobile service might be needed. This tool makes it possible, as a first step, to map out the reach of a service to identify potential gaps.

To get an overview of the services that are still lacking, disconnected or difficult to access, it is important to identify where services are made available and who they reach out to.

STEP 1: Preparation
In your offices, the reception area or inside the office, hang a big map of the city or area you work in.

STEP 2: Mapping
Every time someone uses your service, ask them to put a pin or a sticker on the area where they are coming from. It does not need to be exact, to continue to protect their privacy.

Alternatively, if there are barriers to that, you can make a private map with your internal data, without hanging it on a wall. This depends on your needs for this tool: do you want it to be a collective participatory exercise, or is it more appropriate as an internal organisational exercise?

STEP 3: Analysis
After a while, once you have a significant number of locations on your map, you can begin the analysis:

What is present?

- Are the areas your beneficiaries come from close to or a long way from your service? Are they able to access your service on foot, or are there transportation barriers to them reaching you? Are there areas with stickers outside the limits of the map?
- If there is a cluster of stickers in a distant area, what could explain it? Is there a similar service in that area that is less well known, or does it reflect a 'ser-

vice desert'? If so, it could mean that this area has potential for establishing a mobile service.

What is not present?

- Are there areas that are known as arrival infrastructures, but that have no stickers on them? What could explain that? Are there similar services to yours there, which means the need is covered, or is there a gap because people living or working there are unable to come to you? Do barriers like language, cultural differences, or lack of trust prevent users from accessing the service? This area could also be a good candidate for a targeted mobile service.
- Are there nearby areas that do not have any stickers? Is this because there is no need for your service, or because your service is not well known? If so, outreach activities might be required.

In The Hague, service providers identified the need for support in specific spaces where migrants gather.

This tool can also be used to map the offline reach of your service provision. To do this, consider asking clients to share where they heard about your service. Was it online? If so, where?

REFLECTION
By looking at the geographic origin of service users, this tool offers a first indication of access to a service, with the aim of evaluating the relevance of a mobile service in that context.

> CHECK **TOOL 24** IN PART II FOR EXAMPLE: 'Choosing an outreach strategy: open call or word of mouth?'.

> SEE ALSO **TOOL 1**: 'Am I in an arrival infrastructure?'

3. COMING TOGETHER

This chapter focuses on arrival infrastructuring work that brings people together, creates communities, fosters communities, and creates opportunities for socialising, peer-to-peer support, and solidarity. In this chapter, we share stories from our research that illustrate how the act of coming together infrastructures arrival. By coming together, information can circulate among newcomers and feelings of belonging blossom through shared linguistic, national, or regional backgrounds, as well as through common interests, everyday life activities, and shared political projects. We explore these aspects through stories divided into three sections: navigating the arrival situation, fostering belonging, and enabling collective action.

Coming together often serves not only as a means of socialising but also as a way to exchange knowledge and advice on navigating the arrival situation more easily. This is the case in our accounts of markets in Istanbul, the restaurants of La Chapelle in Paris, and the temporary stays in abandoned train wagons of Thessaloniki.

Frequently, coming together helps foster feelings of belonging in the place of arrival. It combats not only loneliness but also alienation – the feeling of being unwanted in a place. A sense of belonging can emerge as a 'side effect' of an activity, as seen in our stories of volunteering by newcomers in London or working by agricultural labourers in Belgium and the Netherlands. Combatting loneliness can also be the explicit goal of initiatives, such as the Polka community centre in The Hague, founded to support Polish newcomers.

In some cases, people intentionally build on shared experiences or identities to form communities or organised groups working towards a common purpose, requiring deliberate efforts to achieve specific goals. This can happen within institutional frameworks, such as in Karditsa, where an informal council of asylum-seekers was established to support individuals with their applications and to advocate politically for their rights. Similarly, we observed instances of coming together with a specific aim among informal networks of political activists, such as during the occupation of a government building in Brussels.

In eight stories, this chapter explores the vital role of infrastructuring work in fostering community among newcomers, highlighting how collective gatherings facilitate socialisation, peer support, and the amplification of solidarity.

3.1 TO BETTER NAVIGATE THE ARRIVAL SITUATION

In many arrival situations, newcomers face hostile environments, from exclusionary policies to maladapted or fragmented service provision to anti-migrant sentiment. Communal activities and spaces play a significant part in supporting newcomers' arrival. Through three distinct narratives, this subsection illustrates how newcomers carve out time for themselves, empower each other, and provide practical assistance through socialisation and shared experiences, despite extremely limiting circumstances. In Istanbul, Central Asian domestic workers gather in Aksaray on their one day off to exchange vital information and support each other. In Thessaloniki, newcomers use abandoned train wagons for temporary shelter and to foster a sense of community and mutual aid. In La Chapelle, Paris, Sudanese restaurants and cafés serve as essential hubs for recently arrived migrants, navigating the complexities of co-national solidarity. These stories underscore how the practice of coming together infrastructures arrival, through alleviating loneliness, sharing knowledge, and forging valuable connections.

ESSENTIAL DOCUMENTS
Sudanese restaurants in Paris: sharing knowledge among co-nationals and beyond

This story explores how newcomers infrastructure arrival in La Chapelle, Paris, highlighting Sudanese restaurants and cafés as hubs for recently arrived migrants. These establishments provide crucial support and information, helping newcomers navigate their new environment. However, the story also delves into the complexities of co-national solidarity, where both established and more recently arrived newcomers weigh the risks and benefits of sharing personal information. Additionally, it shows that support often extends beyond ethnic lines, with diverse relationships forming through a shared goal of building solidarity with newcomers experiencing precarious conditions.

Solidarity in the streets of an arrival neighbourhood in Paris: the opportunity of chance encounters

The story of Sudanese restaurants in La Chapelle, an area in Paris that is important for Sudanese and East African migrants in general, reveals the dynamics that come into play in networks of co-national newcomers. La Chapelle is home to several Sudanese shops and restaurants where Sudanese migrants infrastructure their arrival. In the context of a dispersion policy adopted by the French state, in which informal camps (the most famous being those in the northern districts of Paris and in Calais) are dismantled regularly and inhabitants forcibly dispersed across several regions, La Chapelle serves as a stable neighbourhood where newcomers know they can find support. Solidarity between Sudanese co-nationals, often from established newcomers to more recently arrived newcomers, manifests in several ways. Upon arrival in Paris, Zakaria, a Sudanese man, was supported by a fellow national to find an organisation specialising in asylum-seeker assistance: "When I first came to Paris in 2007, I found a Sudanese guy in the street and he drove me to France Terre d'Asile [NGO]. Now it is me who drives Sudanese I meet there, imagine!" (Interview with Zakaria, [City], [Month] [Year]...).

Restaurant and cafés as knowledge-sharing spaces

Restaurants and cafés in La Chapelle are essential in the process of sharing knowledge between more established migrants and newer arrivals. Informal conversations are crucial for learning how to apply for asylum and other administrative procedures related to family reunification or procedures to acquire French nationality. For example, we came across a man quizzing others on questions to pass the compulsory language exam to access French citizenship. It is important to note, however, that co-national solidarity also comes with some limitations. For Sudanese newcomers in Paris, for example, there is a constant tension between getting close to other co-nationals and keeping a distance. There is always the potential danger of being exposed as an 'illegal' migrant, becoming the subject of a counter-investigation that threatens their asylum status, being reported for association with a political movement considered problematic in Sudan, or having very intimate aspects of their private lives revealed (for instance, some individuals fled their families due to violence or armed disputes). Therefore, for Sudanese newcomers in the La Chapelle restaurants, there is a constant management of familiarisation: they have to reveal enough information about their lives to be able to be trusted and get the necessary support, but not too much as to risk being rejected.

Figure 22. One of many Sudanese restaurants in the north of Paris.

Solidarity crossing the bounds of national borders

Another important element of the dynamics of the neighbourhood is that the solidarity described above is, despite appearances, not just extended to co-nationals. Indeed, even in a neighbourhood such as La Chapelle, known to be a key arrival neighbourhood for Sudanese and other East Africans, very diverse relationships arise that are not exclusively based on national or ethnic background. Many people report receiving support from volunteers and other more established newcomers who are not co-nationals. Some of the commercial partners of the restaurants in the neighbourhood are from Mauritania or Iraq. In addition, the Sudanese restaurants were important for the densely populated migrant camps in the north of Paris in 2015–2017 because their owners provided material help, free food, and administrative information to the inhabitants. As such, these Sudanese restaurants extend their influence beyond the borders of the neighbourhood and become crucial for the production and maintenance of the wider arrival infrastructure of Paris.

TAKEAWAYS

\# Beyond their economic function, commercial spaces in arrival neighbourhoods such as restaurants or cafés often serve as informal hubs for socialisation, knowledge exchange, and mutual assistance. Being there unlocks crucial information for navigating arrival conditions.

\# Newcomers often receive support from more established migrants, and then 'return the favour' to recently arrived newcomers once they are well established in a place. Therefore, long-standing migrants often take on the role of mentors, extending the cycle of assistance they themselves benefited from when they first arrived and perpetuating a culture of support.

\# Solidarity among people from the same background is both common and visible, yet it brings with it inherent challenges related to privacy and the potential reproduction of dynamics that some newcomers sought to escape through migration. Consequently, newcomers must strike a delicate balance: seeking support while safeguarding personal information, as the advantages of co-national solidarity can be offset by risks of exposure, mistrust, and personal vulnerability.

\# Although not immediately visible, solidarity extends beyond people from the same national or ethnic background, as new relations are continuously created throughout the arrival process.

Coming together in abandoned train wagons in Thessaloniki: transforming desolate spaces into hubs of solidarity for people on the move

> The following story describes the transformation of abandoned train wagons in Thessaloniki into a vital refuge for undocumented migrants, providing not only shelter but also a space for socialisation and mutual support. In this desolate environment, people on the move to other destinations in Europe, like Hussein and Karar, form friendships and share experiences, helping each other navigate the challenges of their journeys. These gatherings foster a sense of community, allowing them to exchange advice and cope with feelings of fear and isolation. Ultimately, the train wagons serve as an 'oasis', where the act of coming together infrastructures arrival by sustaining mental health and enabling newcomers to envision alternative futures together.

An 'oasis' to rest while travelling

The area of abandoned train wagons on the western side of Thessaloniki, in Greece, is a place of self-organised temporary accommodation and a relatively safe space to rest and recover for undocumented people on the move. At the same time, and perhaps most importantly, it is also a place for meeting and gathering, networking and creating new friendships, and developing practices of mutual support. Within these temporary shelters, newcomers also share worries and reimagine and redesign their plans to cross the Balkan countries next on their migration journeys.

Mutual support and solidarity in abandoned train wagons

In the area of abandoned train wagons in Thessaloniki, people oftentimes meet, form friendships, and then continue their journey together. Take for example the case of Hussein from Palestine. He lived for several months in the abandoned train wagons. Later he participated in solidarity groups providing food and first aid to people on the move.

He explained: "The very interesting point in the long migrants' journey to Europe is that they come in contact with other people on the move, establish friendships and relationships of solidarity. For example, here in the train wagons during the food distribution, many people have met, have come in contact, even from different countries, with different cultural backgrounds. I have even met people who, even when from the same country, considered themselves enemies, but now here in the train wagons, they come together, support each other, and form small groups to move to the next countries" (Interview with Hussein, Thessaloniki, November 2021).

Karar from Iraq had a similar perspective on the solidarity formed among newcomers in the abandoned train wagons. After one month of staying in the train wagons, he describes the living conditions as follows: "We sleep seven people here. Some nights some can't sleep, they are usually newcomers, and they have nightmares, then the rest of us try to calm them down. We need to support each other, otherwise it's very difficult" (Interview with Karar, Thessaloniki, January 2022).

A space for direction in the middle of loss

The journey of undocumented people on the move is full of danger, threats, multiple disorientations, and feelings of failure, frustration, and disempowerment. People on the move are constantly exposed to weather extremes. In the winter they endure cold temperatures, rain, and snow. In the summer, high temperatures are an additional risk, especially given that survival resources like food and drinking water can be hard to come by.

In addition, people on the move face xenophobic attacks from local people and the constant threat of arrest by border guards, police patrols, and Frontex. Consequently, during their journey undocumented people on the move constantly experience feelings of fear, insecurity, and melancholy. For this reason, meeting places like the abandoned train wagons in Thessaloniki are crucial. These spaces allow them to get to know each other and develop practices of mutual support and care, so that on the one hand they can face and cope with the various physical, social, and personal obstacles, and on the other hand plan the next steps in their migratory trajectory together. In a world that feels devoid of future opportunities, new possibilities and directions emerge when people come together to share their anxieties and dreams, allowing them to redefine their paths.

TAKEAWAYS

Abandoned urban spaces, initially symbols of neglect, are sometimes transformed into spaces of solidarity, showing how people on the move reclaim and reimagine desolate environments for survival and solidarity.

Migrant journeys often involve being exposed to threats and loneliness for long periods of time. Along these journeys, shared temporary shelters not only provide a roof but also become 'oases' to feel safe, meet fellow people on the move, share feelings and develop mutual support practices that help people navigate logistical, emotional, and social challenges, creating a collective buffer against isolation and despair.

Sharing experiences of hardships and traumas can become a source of support in spaces where people on the move can gather safely.

In the abandoned train wagons, coming together infrastructures arrival by sustaining mental health and imagining alternative futures together.

EMPLOYMENT
A day off for Central Asian domestic workers in Istanbul: sharing knowledge on how to navigate challenging working conditions

In this story, we show the significance of day-off activities for live-in Central Asian domestic workers in Istanbul, who use this time not just for leisure but also for socialisation and support. By gathering in Aksaray, located in the arrival neighbourhood of Fatih, these women share vital information and advice on navigating their challenging working conditions, and reconnect over shared cultural backgrounds. This account illustrates how these communal activities help alleviate feelings of loneliness and homesickness, while also empowering newcomers to regain some control over their lives. Overall, it underscores the important role of spaces for connection and support within the arrival infrastructure.

One day off per week

For domestic migrant workers and caretakers who live in at their employer's house, a day off is not just an ordinary leisure day where they can rest from their work. For live-in workers who have limited autonomy in the private households where they are employed, it is a space for socialisation, connectivity, and recreation that is particularly crucial. Some Central Asian live-in domestic workers in Istanbul arrange their day off collectively in order to meet up on the same day in Aksaray.

Many Central Asian labour migrants working and living in different parts of Istanbul visit the arrival area to shop and send remittances, to gather in cafés and restaurants, and to socialise. Live-in domestic workers arrange their trips to the neighbourhood on their day off, which is usually a weekday. Suray, an Uzbek domestic worker in her sixties, visits Aksaray and the neighbouring Kumkapı on Thursdays — when the neighbourhood open-air bazaar is held — to buy clothes for her grandchildren and send them via shipping offices nearby. She usually comes to the bazaar with her friends and hangs out with them in the Uzbek cafés afterward. Similarly, Dilyara (a Turkmen domestic worker and care-giver in her fifties) and her relatives and friends specifically arrange Fridays as their days off in order to browse in the famous high-end Fındıkzade Friday bazaar. Their choice of visiting days and days off are thus determined by the opening hours of certain commercial infrastructures like bazaars, shipping offices, and cafés in the area.

A time to build connections and share advice

Suray and Dilyara go to these bazaars with friends, yet they do not necessarily buy goods or clothes each time they visit the area. They come to exchange information, send money home, and visit the migrant clinic to address health issues, among other activities. These migrant domestic workers also go there to reconnect with their friends, share the latest news from their home countries, learn about updates on any migration-related issues, and advise on different strategies for dealing with the precarious conditions of work and migrant life. Many newly arrived migrant domestic workers learn to negotiate their working conditions from experienced migrant women at their gatherings on days off. For example, Suray advised her newly arrived cousin to use a subtle 'threat to quit' strategy when tensions were rising with her employers.

Dilyara left a job in Izmir and came back to Istanbul because of these day-off gatherings with relatives and other migrant women: "I don't have anyone in Izmir. The weather is nice, people are great there, but I couldn't do it. I come here [to Aksaray] every Friday and blow off [a week's] steam. In Izmir, I earned well and had nice employers, better than in Istanbul. But on my days off I was going out and was sitting in the park alone. I didn't have any acquaintances and a place like Aksaray in Izmir. My niece was working in Antep, she also left her job there and came to Istanbul" (Interview with Dilyara, Istanbul, January 2021). A day off for Dilyara was not only about finding leisure time; it was also a way to alleviate her homesickness and loneliness and connect to "her people".

Networking and bonding with other migrant domestic workers through mundane activities like shopping and sharing food is important not only in the arrival process in Turkey but also for coping with long-lasting emotional pressure such as longing and depression, as well as the various types of harassment, violations, and abuse that undocumented domestic migrant women face. Many migrant women consolidate these network ties on their days off by spending them collectively in Aksaray. Hence, a day off is an important arena for regaining some control over their lives, times, and space.

Newcomers often experience intense and challenging working conditions, such as those of live-in domestic workers who spend their days and nights at their employer's house. Therefore, for live-in domestic workers, a day off is not merely a break from work, it is a critical opportunity for socialisation, emotional support, and regaining autonomy over their time and space.

Places where migrant workers can meet and spend free time are an important aspect of the arrival infrastructure. The time spent together with friends and acquaintances has a key infrastructuring role in mitigating loneliness and homesickness and creating a support system among migrant workers.

Day-off gatherings allow experienced migrant workers to mentor newcomers, offering practical advice on navigating precarious working conditions and life as a migrant.

Commercial spaces such as bazaars, cafés, and shipping offices act as informal hubs for community building, reinforcing the importance of accessible and culturally relevant infrastructure in arrival areas. The ability to form and maintain social networks in arrival areas influences migrants' decisions to remain in specific cities.

TOOL 10
MAPPING (THE LACK OF) SAFE AND CAREFREE TIME-SPACES

MATERIALS: Paper, writing utensils, someone to talk to who is going through a stressful period (optional).

TOOL SUMMARY: Using this tool, you will identify moments and places where individuals, especially newcomers, can recharge, connect, and regain control over their lives. By mapping out a typical week, it highlights the availability and quality of restful times and spaces. This tool aims to help you understand the limited safe and carefree spaces for newcomers and the feelings of exhaustion and anxiety that this sometimes causes.

Everyone is in need of moments and places of respite and rest to recharge and allow us, literally or figuratively, to continue our route forward. In those times and spaces, we can reset and regain a sense of control over our lives. Free time is, moreover, essential to be able to come together, share knowledge, and get some perspective on the overwhelming aspects of arrival. However, newcomers generally have a lack of safe and carefree time-spaces. Gaining an insight into this might help you better understand their feelings and decisions, some of which might seem contradictory at first glance.

STEP 1: Draw a rough table representing the seven days of the week or use the blank template below. Think of a typical week for you. Fill in when and where you feel you are able to recover from the stress of everyday life, indicating where that takes place, the nature of the activity, and who is involved in it.

STEP 2: Look at your week: do you have enough time to rest? Is there a time when you had more, or less, time to recharge? How was it different from now?

STEP 3: To do a comparative exercise, fill in the same table for a person you know who is undergoing a stressful period, such as arriving to a new country, or look at the one filled in for a live-in domestic worker in Istanbul from the story above.

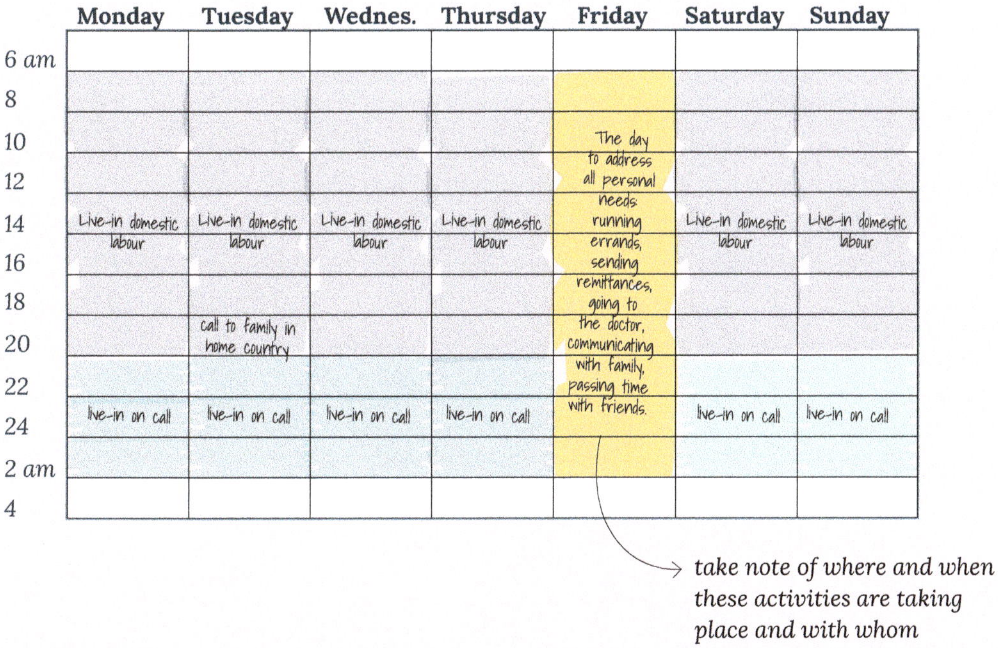

	Monday	Tuesday	Wednes.	Thursday	Friday	Saturday	Sunday
6 am							
8					The day to address all personal needs: running errands, sending remittances, going to the doctor, communicating with family, passing time with friends.		
10							
12							
14	Live-in domestic labour	Live-in domestic labour	Live-in domestic labour	Live-in domestic labour		Live-in domestic labour	Live-in domestic labour
16							
18							
20		call to family in home country					
22							
24	live-in on call	live-in on call	live-in on call	live-in on call		live-in on call	live-in on call
2 am							
4							

take note of where and when these activities are taking place and with whom

Figure 23. Diagram for mapping lack of safe and carefree time-spaces filled in based on the example from the story.

Your safe and carefree timespaces

	Monday	Tuesday	Wednes.	Thursday	Friday	Saturday	Sunday
6 am							
8							
10							
12							
14							
16							
18							
20							
22							
24							
2 am							
4							

Safe and carefree timespaces of a person undergoing a stressful period (as arriving could be)

	Monday	Tuesday	Wednes.	Thursday	Friday	Saturday	Sunday
6 am							
8							
10							
12							
14							
16							
18							
20							
22							
24							
2 am							
4							

Figure 24. Diagram for mapping lack of safe and carefree time-spaces

REFLECTION

This tool may help you understand how limited safe and carefree time-spaces are for some newcomers in your context. This lack of safe and carefree spaces might also cause feelings of exhaustion and anxiety and in turn a disinterest in some activities that are proposed.

3.2 TO CREATE FEELINGS OF BELONGING

In this subsection we share three stories that demonstrate how newcomers come together to build connections, skills, and confidence in their new environments. Through coming together with other new arrivals, established migrants, and people working in the arrival infrastructure, by means of volunteering, workplace interactions, and community-building efforts, newcomers can also foster feelings of belonging.

In London, the experiences of two newcomers volunteering at a food distribution service in a community hub demonstrate how such activities can be a crucial form of infrastructuring work for newcomers. In Belgium and the Netherlands, migrant workers in the agricultural sector navigate challenging labour conditions and cultural differences to form supportive networks. These workplaces become vital spaces for socialising, exchanging resources, and building reciprocal friendships across linguistic and ethnic backgrounds, despite the inherent difficulties. Lastly, the Polka community initiative in The Hague provides a safe haven for Polish women facing isolation and mental health challenges. Founded by a Polish woman, this centre offers language cafés, workshops, and social events, supporting participants in building connections, improving self-esteem, and combatting loneliness. Such community centres play a pivotal role in creating opportunities for social encounters and fostering a renewed sense of community among newcomers.

ESSENTIAL MATERIAL SUPPORT
Volunteering at a community hub in London: building connections, skills, and confidence

The stories of two women who volunteered at a food distribution service in a community hub in London illustrate how volunteering can be an important form of infrastructuring work on the part of newcomers. The food distribution service is run by a charity with support from the local council, and operates mainly through the efforts of volunteers who reflect the diversity of the borough. Staff and volunteers include people from different walks of life, including both first- and later-generation migrants.

Volunteering as a stepping stone for future employment

When she first arrived in the London borough we based our research on, Ferial, a woman from a country in Eastern Europe, volunteered at an organisation which targeted services towards people of her language and nationality. However, she quickly felt that remaining within an ethnically focused context might be a disadvantage. Ferial already had an advanced education and work experience in her home country, and did not particularly need the forms of support on offer. She thought volunteering at a place with English-speaking people would be more useful for her and might be a way of using skills she had gained working in a large ICT company in her country of origin. Hence, she began volunteering at a food distribution service within a local community hub. After a year of volunteering, she was successful in interviewing for employment at the charity that ran the service. She saw this trajectory as being a direct result of her decision to volunteer in a service that formed part of the wider community.

Figure 25. An example of a London food provision hub often used by newcomers.

Volunteering to improve language skills

Volunteering seemed to play a different role for another woman, Miriana, from another part of Eastern Europe. Miriana was not very confident in her English when she first began volunteering for the same food distribution service and was accompanied by a family member who interpreted for her. However, we noticed that volunteering seemed to have an empowering effect on Miriana. After initially showing insecurity, self-doubt, and self-consciousness, Miriana very quickly transformed into a confident and gregarious volunteer, quick to smile or hug people, share home-made food, or take the initiative to solve problems. Her increased confidence, friendliness, and East European language skills were an asset to the charity, which struggled at times to communicate with certain guests of the service who speak little or no English. Having started out as someone who needed assistance in order to participate in a team, Miriana soon became a support to others and contributed unique and valuable skills that strengthened the service in its provision to people from Miriana's home country. Whilst she never talked explicitly about this trajectory, it was obvious that volunteering made a significant difference to Miriana's confidence, and one of Miriana's family members shared with us how glad they were that she had started volunteering, as she looked so happy whenever she worked at the service.

Volunteering as important infrastructuring work

These two stories show different aspects of the infrastructuring power of volunteering. For Ferial, volunteering led directly to a future employment opportunity when a vacancy became available at the same charity. The act of volunteering also provided an environment for everyday English language practice, and provided relevant work experience that would enhance her prospects when interviewed. For Miriana, volunteering also provided English language practice, but the most evident effect of becoming part of a local service to others, and part of a team of others doing the same, was on her confidence and happiness. It is worth noting that the food distribution service did not have a deliberate, targeted service to build individuals' skills, confidence, or sense of belonging. Rather, these were simply the positive 'side effects' of the confluence of individual migrants' desire to participate and the availability of volunteering opportunities for local residents.

TAKEAWAYS

Accessing local activities or labour markets is not always possible for newcomers who experience language – and other – barriers. Volunteering can be an accessible opportunity with unexpected, positive 'side effects': it connects newcomers to local groups and can increase self-confidence and well-being, enhance language proficiency through practice, and open future trajectories to employment.

Volunteering enables newcomers to shift from being recipients of support to active contributors, enhancing their agency and creating mutual benefits for both migrants and local communities.

Newcomers' unique skills and experiences enrich the (volunteering) services they contribute to, such as their ability to communicate with guests in their native language, strengthening the support provided by the organisation.

Fostering relationships through agricultural work in Belgium and the Netherlands: work as a vital place for socialising across languages and origins

This story explores the experiences of migrant workers in the agricultural sectors of Belgium and the Netherlands, focusing on the workplace as somewhere established and recently arrived newcomers infrastructure arrival by coming together in various ways. Despite challenging labour conditions and cultural differences, these agricultural sites facilitate important exchanges of support, language, and resources among workers from different backgrounds. This account illustrates how such interactions are not always easy, but can produce valuable reciprocal friendships and material exchanges across linguistic and ethnic backgrounds.

Newcomers – old and new – in the strawberry fields

"Of course I miss the other Turkish women… But the Polish women… Yes, the young girls don't work as hard, they smoke, loud music. But when they go back in a couple of weeks, I miss them all year. They will hug me when they get back" (Interview with Fatma, Zepperen, August 2022).

We sit in the shadow underneath the raised strawberry beds of a plantation in Haspengouw while Fatma, the first of her family to move from Turkey, talks to us about her relationships and interactions with other pickers. Her statement reflects how tensions and solidarity among workers coexist. She started working at this strawberry plantation 28 years ago, along with a larger group of Turkish women, all neighbours in Genk, Belgium. Over time, the other women had children and grandchildren who started earning money, or they simply got too old and were physically unable to do this demanding work. When the EU enlarged, the farmers started hiring Polish workers, a transition Fatma witnessed closely during her almost three decades of working at this farm.

Building meaningful relationships under precarious working conditions

In an arrival situation that draws newcomers in through labour, agricultural worksites become crucial places to build relationships with others who have just arrived, or older newcomers like Fatma. These worksites are 'superdiverse' (see concept box 10 below) – meaning a very high level of diversity exists in the area, not just in terms of ethnicity or nationality, but also with regard to language, culture, religion, and social backgrounds. Labour conditions are often unstable and precarious because many workers have temporary contracts and face high pressure at work. This situation is made worse by farmers' biased preferences for hiring based on factors like gender, ethnicity, religion, and migration history.

These characteristics of agricultural labour often cause tensions amongst workers. In this case, Fatma mentions her discontent with the 'quality' of the work the younger Polish women perform. The girls' smoking breaks, loud music, and, according to Fatma, slow speed of working will also affect her performance and the general mood of the farmer. At the same time, by working with these women every season, every day of the week, she has developed amicable connections with them, making work more bearable. In the greenhouses of Westland, an agricultural region in the Netherlands, it is even quite common for friendships or romantic relationships to develop at work or in the housing facilities, across ethnic and linguistic boundaries.

Figure 26. Fostering relationships with colleagues at an agricultural worksite in the Haspengouw.

Besides material and linguistic exchanges, the practical exchanges are perhaps most significant in these worksites. In a tomato packaging factory in Westland, Doina and Aylan met each other from among one thousand employees. Both want to spend the rest of their lives in the Netherlands, but do not want to get stuck in the factory. Doina worked as a nurse in Moldova and hopes to resume this type of work in the Netherlands. Aylan studied history and languages and hopes to start her career in education there. Since neither of their diplomas are recognised in the Netherlands, they need to go through a long trajectory of taking new courses, most importantly one to prove their proficiency in the Dutch language. Bound by the same dreams and struggles, they study for their Dutch exams during their lunch breaks. These exchanges reveal how much infrastructuring work is performed by migrant workers in the worksites, from friendship to material exchanges, across linguistic and ethnic backgrounds.

Infrastructuring at work: exchanging materials, language, and support

The building of relationships does not merely have to do with interpersonal feelings of companionship or friendship. It also comes up in material and immaterial exchanges. Food, gloves, raincoats – all necessary in harvest work – are exchanged between and across groups of workers. Language is another domain of exchange and socialisation. Although many migrant workers do not speak the same language, people find ways of communicating and teach each other important words in their own language. In the greenhouses of Westland, language exchanges have led to the creation of a hybrid language spoken amongst colleagues from diverse linguistic backgrounds: "I speak all the languages of the greenhouse, except Dutch," a Croatian worker joked when she spoke about the other languages she has learned to communicate with while working at this greenhouse (Informal conversation Marija, Maasdijk, June 2022). The lingua franca was not Dutch or English, but a new language with elements of Polish, Romanian, Russian, and Turkish.

TAKEAWAY

Agricultural worksites are often 'superdiverse' spaces (see concept box 10 below) where workers from different ethnic, linguistic, and cultural backgrounds come together. These interactions, despite their challenges, foster meaningful connections and mutual learning.

Labour conditions of migrant workers in agriculture are often precarious, characterised by temporary contracts and unequal treatment based on gender, ethnicity, and migration history. However, migrant workers still manage to build solidarity, navigating tensions to form friendships and support networks that make the work more bearable.

Although workplaces can be spaces of tensions, often caused by the characteristics of the labour itself, they are also spaces of crucial infrastructuring work deployed through reciprocal friendship and material exchanges, across linguistic and ethnic backgrounds.

'Superdiversity'

The notion of 'superdiversity', originally coined by Vertovec (2007), is used to describe a new condition of societal complexification that has emerged as a consequence of intensifying and intermeshing migration – a diversification of diversity, so to speak. A substantial scholarly literature now exists on how this new condition of diversity has affected cities in Europe. Since the Second World War, European cities, due to their aggregation of services and opportunities, have attracted immigrants. This happened first during the 1950s to early 1970s with guest workers, often via bilateral government agreements with other European and North African countries and sometimes former colonies. More recently, since the early 1990s to 2000s, as a result of the opening up of the EU's borders and accelerating globalisation, new immigrant groups have arrived in Europe from an increasing number of countries of origin (often without specific historical or colonial links), driven by a wide range of different reasons (economic, political, ecologic, etc.) and following less linear migration trajectories.

'Superdiversity' thus describes the complex and dynamic nature of contemporary diversity that goes beyond traditional categories of ethnicity or nationality. It reflects a multidimensional understanding of diversity, shaped by factors such as country of origin, ethnicity, legal status (for example citizen, asylum-seeker, refugee), gender, age, language, religious practices, socio-economic status, and migration history and networks. The concept underscores how these dimensions intersect, creating highly nuanced patterns of diversity that challenge simplistic categorisations. Superdiversity also captures the fluidity of identities and interactions in increasingly globalised urban environments, emphasising the need for context-sensitive approaches to understanding and dealing with diversity.

Building further on the notion of 'superdiversity', scholars now speak of 'superdiverse neighbourhoods' or 'superdiverse streets'. 'Superdiverse streets', as explored in the work of Susanne Hall (2015) and others, are urban spaces defined by an unprecedented range and depth of diversity. Often they are part of historical arrival neighbourhoods where more established migrants have been infrastructuring the arrival of more recently arrived migrants. 'Superdiverse neighbourhoods', as discussed by Wessendorf (2014), bring together residents from multiple countries and ethnicities, speaking a variety of languages and embodying diverse cultural, religious, and socio-economic backgrounds. The social dynamics within such neighbourhoods are complex, shaped by overlapping and intersecting differences that require navigation across multiple linguistic, cultural, and social divides.

In 'superdiverse neighbourhoods', diversity is often normalised in dense social networks, shaping everyday interactions. However, 'superdiverse neighbourhoods' also reflect broader societal patterns, sometimes mirroring social inequalities or spatial segregation. At the same time, they often act as vibrant hubs of cultural exchange, creativity, and social innovation. Yet, alongside their potential for fostering connection, they can also become arenas of tension, with competition over resources, representation, and recognition. More recently, we also find 'superdiverse spaces' outside cities, such as agricultural worksites where migrant labourers of different origins, genders, and ages work together.

In summary, 'superdiversity' and 'superdiverse neighbourhoods' provide critical frameworks for understanding how migration and globalisation re-shape urban landscapes. They highlight the need for new policies, practices, and research methodologies that move beyond binary or static views of diversity to capture its dynamic and layered nature.

References:

Vertovec, Steven. 2007. 'Super-diversity and Its Implications', *Ethnic and Racial Studies*, 30(6): 1024–54.

Hall, Susanne. 2015. 'Super-diverse Street: A "Trans-ethnography" Across Migrant Localities', *Ethnic and Racial Studies*, 38(1): 22–37.

Wessendorf, Susanne. 2014. *Commonplace Diversity: Social Interactions in a Super-Diverse Context* (London: Palgrave Macmillan).

LANGUAGE
Community-building initiative for Polish women in The Hague: creating a safe space for encounter, exchange, and combatting loneliness and depression

The following story focuses on the Polka community initiative in The Hague, which supports Polish women facing isolation and mental health challenges. Founded by a Polish woman living in The Hague, the centre provides a safe space for socialising, learning, and sharing experiences, helping women in arrival contexts build connections and improve their self-esteem. Activities include language cafés (rather informal gathering spaces where people meet to practise and improve their language skills through conversation), workshops, and social events, fostering a sense of community among participants. Places like this community centre that infrastructure arrival opportunities for social encounter and exchange over practical, everyday, and more serious matters can become spaces to re-find a sense of community.

"Are you a Polish woman and do you live in The Hague?"

"Jesteś Polką mieszkającą w Hadze?" ("Are you a Polish woman and do you live in The Hague?"). The flyer on the front door of the neighbourhood centre invites all Polish women in the area to visit if they want to learn more about living in the Netherlands, take an interesting course, or simply meet "other interesting women" (as quoted on the flyer, November 2021).

When we spoke with Anna, the founder of Polka, about her reasons for creating the initiative, she mentioned the extreme isolation many Polish women in The Hague experience. Even though the group of Polish women in The Hague is extremely varied in terms of work status, migration history, level of education, and family status, many of them experience similar hardships. Separated from their families and often reluctant to share their hardships, many find themselves stuck in unstable jobs or reliant on sickness benefits after years of physical labour. Factors such as dependency on their partners and a small social circle primarily consisting of other Polish newcomers – especially when prolonged over the years – contribute to low self-esteem, loneliness, and depression. "So I thought, we need a place where they can meet and support each other, helping with all kinds of questions and problems. Can we create such a safe space to help them from their own cultural context and language? I founded Polka to provide a space where they can build new social contacts, improve their self-esteem, get the right information and tools to improve skills, and grow their self-reliance and overall resilience" (Interview with Anna, The Hague, November 2021).

A safe space for multiple exchanges

A few months later, we witnessed first-hand the impact of such a space. Every Friday evening, Polish women gather at the community centre. Here, Polka organises a variety of activities: a book club, yoga and salsa classes, consultations, information sessions by local and national government services in Polish, courses on financial independence, stress management workshops, information about the Dutch school system, and sessions with a Polish-speaking labour union representative. Around Christmas, they host an open dinner for Polish migrants in The Hague who have nowhere to go at Christmas.

Although language is one of their focus areas, they initially lacked the resources for Dutch language activities. As Anna explained to us: "Many women are scared to learn Dutch even after living here for a long time, too insecure and afraid to make mistakes. They might start official courses but are too afraid or unable to speak it in everyday life, also because of the limitations due to the nature of their work" (Interview with Anna, The Hague, November 2021). To address this, they set up a biweekly language café where Polish women could discuss everyday topics like their neighbourhood, hobbies, food, and carnival. More than just practising Dutch, it became a space for mutual exchange and learning, often filled with humour but sometimes tinged with sadness over shared or individual hardships.

The language cafés began attracting more people, including Polish men from The Hague. Jakub, for example, started attending regularly. He became one of the most loyal participants. He had lived alone in The Hague for a long time and had been sick for a while, but tried to stay well with healthy food, exercise, reading, and movies. The Polish women adopted him like an uncle, and even though he was mostly quiet during the sessions, he visibly enjoyed the company. After the cafés, he often approached us with a twinkle in his eyes to share an interesting book he had read or a new video he had seen on YouTube. More than anything else, Polka became a space where he re-found a sense of community and dignity.

The multiplying effect of successful community building

All these activities are made possible by volunteers. When Polka began in 2018, the volunteers were Polish women who were already confident in their place in the local community, both within and outside Polish circles. As Polka grew, more women joined the activities, saw improvements in their social health and confidence, developed skills, and eventually became volunteers themselves. This created a multiplying effect, boosting the self-esteem and skills of individuals and expanding Polka's reach in The Hague and beyond. They have now opened a second centre in another neighbourhood in The Hague, yet remain dependent on unstable funding.

TAKEAWAYS

Migrant women often face isolation, low self-esteem, and depression due to prolonged exposure to unstable working conditions, separation from family, and limited social support networks. These challenges highlight the need for targeted interventions that address both practical and emotional well-being.

Creating safe, culturally sensitive spaces for encounter and exchange allows women to share experiences, build social connections, and improve their mental health. These spaces act as vital parts of the arrival infrastructure that foster community, belonging, and mutual support.

Language cafés, which offer informal settings to practise a new language without fear of judgement, play a dual role. They improve language skills while simultaneously becoming spaces of emotional support, humour, and shared learning. These exchanges help participants regain their self-confidence and feel more included.

Volunteers play a crucial role in sustaining and expanding community-building initiatives. Often we can speak about a 'multiplier effect' where participants transition into volunteers, creating a self-sustaining cycle of empowerment.

Women in migration contexts often face gendered vulnerabilities, such as economic dependence, while often being reluctant to share their hardships. Community-building initiatives can help address these challenges by building trust and offering a culturally relevant support system.

3.3 TO CREATE COMMUNITY

So far in this chapter we have discussed how newcomers come together to support their arrival and foster meaningful connections in their new environments. In this subsection, we tell two stories that show how collective efforts and shared experiences can help build strong community ties among newcomers and established residents.

In Karditsa, Greece, the municipality's project to provide housing and services for newcomers led to the formation of an informal council of asylum-seekers. This initiative allowed newcomers to voice their concerns and participate in decision-making, strengthening community ties and facilitating joint advocacy for shared needs. Despite challenges, this approach promoted inclusion and empowered both newcomers and established residents to work together to address housing and service provision.

Our story in Brussels recounts the occupation of a federal building by unhoused asylum-seekers and activists who together created a unique space for community building amid dire living conditions. During the two-week siege by the police, the occupants forged strong bonds through shared daily routines and activities, from cooking and cleaning to playing games and organising language lessons. This intense shared experience also fostered empowerment and created lasting networks that continued beyond their eviction, enabling asylum-seekers to advocate for their rights and maintain solidarity amidst uncertainty.

In both stories, a shared goal between newcomers and established residents (whether municipal employees, volunteers, or activists) supports the empowerment, inclusion, and ultimately the arrival infrastructuring of newcomers.

SOLIDARITY
Informal council of asylum-seekers in Karditsa: strengthening community ties and joining forces in advocacy for shared needs

In the small central Greek city of Karditsa, the municipality launched a project to provide housing and services for newcomers, aiming to foster inclusion and community. The hosting organisation expanded its role to include various initiatives, but faced challenges in effectively representing diverse newcomer desires. To improve representation, the municipality collaborated with newcomers to set up an informal council, allowing newcomers to voice their concerns and participate in decision-making. Although not without its challenges, this approach helped strengthen community ties and facilitated joint advocacy for wide ranging issues important to both newcomers and established residents.

A new method: an action plan for the provision of adequate services

In 2017, the municipality of Karditsa enrolled in the Emergency Support to Integration and Accommodation (ESTIA) funding project, which is managed by UNHCR. While the primary aim of the project was to provide accommodation for newcomers and help them access essential services and infrastructure, the implementing organisation, ANKA (a development partner of the municipality), took on initiatives that extended well beyond its original mission. ANKA implemented various 'integration' efforts in collaboration with local, regional, national, and international organisations, both public and private. The project's goal was to promote peaceful coexistence between the local community and the newcomer populations.

According to the project team, the success of the integration initiatives was based upon three interrelated processes. First, they established frequent communication with representatives from the newcomer population in Karditsa. The employees of ANKA held monthly meetings with these representatives. In those meetings, which were often held outside the premises of the organisation (mainly in cafés around the city, accompanied by refreshments, the participants discussed their views, thoughts, and concerns, and had the opportunity to suggest more effective planning and implementation of actions based on the cultural specificities and habits of each community. Second, an Urban Working Group (sponsored by the municipality of Karditsa) was established, in which representatives of different local organisations dealing with the provision of services to newcomers participated on a regular basis in order to investigate how the services provided could be improved. Those meetings were informed by the views, thoughts, and concerns of newcomers, as expressed during the above-discussed monthly meetings between ANKA and newcomers' representatives. Third, for each area of intervention (education, healthcare, accommodation, etc.), a specific reference person (focal person) – a member of the project team – was appointed, who had under their supervision the overall action plan for their area of responsibility.

Implementation on the ground

After the initial implementation of the project, representatives of different newcomer groups raised several issues about the process. One representative expressed uncertainty about how effective these meetings were in addressing the diverse needs of the group and voiced concerns about the potential erosion of trust with intermediaries: "at a certain point we had to deal with requests or suggestions which were at least incompatible, if not contradictory... Such situations, apart from being extremely time consuming, also undermine trust ... and trust is very important and hard to achieve" (Interview with Agni, Karditsa, June 2022).

This situation posed a significant challenge both in terms of the efficiency and effectiveness of the outreach and representation process.

The establishment of an informal council

When exploring alternative ways to enhance newcomer representation in decision-making processes, the organising team identified two key barriers to establishing an association that would unite and represent newcomers. First, the length of stay for newcomers varies based on asylum decision-making processes. Second, establishing a formal association involves complex bureaucratic procedures. Therefore, in consultation with the newcomer community, an informal council was formed. This approach aimed to ensure broad representation.

News of the launch of the informal council was disseminated both by its core members and by members of the host organisation to the different newcomer groups. An explicit goal was shared with all participants, that of preparing regular briefings and updates to track the process. Although not all groups were equally represented, the operation of the council was still considered successful by many participants. During regular sessions with social workers, most newcomers declared that they felt informed about the issues raised by other newcomers and confirmed they had been invited to participate in the informal council meetings if they were interested. In addition, whenever ANKA put out a call for community volunteers, the participation of newcomers was particularly high. Furthermore, several newcomers became members of the Greek Forum of Migrants (a formal organisation based in Athens), expanding their social network outside the city. Membership of the Forum allowed them to also participate as members of the Migrant and Refugee Integration Councils (a formal collective body of the Athens' municipality).

In summary, the informal council facilitated joint advocacy related to common needs, in a more concrete, realistic, and clear manner. Many of the requests made by newcomers were addressed either with the help of ANKA or internally within the migrant community. Prioritising the recognition and inclusion of the diverse interests of newcomers gave members of the informal council a shared identity and goal, opening the door for continued collaboration.

TAKEAWAYS

Sometimes newcomers create their own platforms to develop a shared objective or community, despite their diverse backgrounds, through the establishment of informal councils or collectives.

Some organisations (like ANKA in this story) play a vital role in arrival infrastructuring as intermediaries, connecting the voices of newcomers with decision-makers. However, maintaining trust requires consistent communication, managing conflicting requests, and ensuring transparency in decision-making processes.

Creating participatory structures that give newcomers a direct voice in decision-making in newcomer organisations is important. Such initiatives help bridge the gap between diverse newcomer needs and the institutional frameworks designed to support them.

Active involvement of newcomers in local newcomer organisations, for instance through volunteering, improves both the quality and relevance of services. Community participation also strengthens ties among newcomers and between them and local residents.

Successful arrival infrastructuring practices bring together diverse stakeholders, from local authorities and NGOs to newcomers themselves. This story highlights that 'integration' is not solely the responsibility of newcomers but requires active collaboration among a variety of stakeholders.

Arrival infrastructuring work, especially when organised across different groups of stakeholders, might carry the risk of misrepresentation. Exploring various ways of coming together and being represented might contribute to addressing this issue.

HOUSING

Occupying a government building in Brussels: engaging in political mobilisation and creating community amid dire living conditions

This story starts at a federal building in Brussels that became the site of an occupation by 70 homeless asylum-seekers and 20 activists, who found themselves under siege by the police for two weeks. During the siege, the occupants forged a strong sense of community, sharing daily routines and engaging in activities that ranged from cooking and cleaning to playing games and organising language lessons. This intense togetherness not only fostered empowerment but also created lasting networks that continued beyond their eventual eviction from the building, as the group continued to organise communal events and support each other in building temporary shelters. Even in the face of police oppression, the relationships established in collective mobilisations enable asylum-seekers to advocate for their rights and maintain a sense of solidarity amidst uncertainty.

A growing community and sense of empowerment within an occupation under siege

In the spring of 2023, as part of a series of occupations and evictions of buildings in Brussels, a collective called 'Stop the Reception Crisis' occupied a federal government building. Shortly after 70 homeless asylum-seekers and around 20 activists had entered the building, the occupants were put under siege by the federal police for the entire period of their occupation. During the two weeks of that occupation, local activists and newcomers were able to forge an important network for newcomers, who experience a heightened risk of exposure to police oppression and violence.

Figure 27. An activist occupation of a federal government building in Brussels advocating for the rights of newcomers.

Negotiations between activists and the federal police resulted in limited numbers of people, goods, medications, and food being allowed to enter and exit the building at specific times of the day. However, due to the circumstances, the group of people present in the building remained relatively constant. Being bound together around the clock facilitated enough time for meetings where all the relevant information could be translated into the various languages spoken by the occupants. This extended togetherness also nurtured care and constructive exchanges aiming for a well-organised space and shared daily routines, alongside thorough preparations of protest actions involving participants inside and outside the building. Everyday endeavours evolved from essential activities like eating or cleaning, to more social engagements such as playing games, dancing together, and even organising language-learning sessions. This communal experience, despite the violent exclusion from state services that lay at the base of it, offered activists and (activist) newcomers alike a unique living situation where community life and empowering mobilisations converged.

Figure 28. Newcomers organising leisure activities in Brussels.

A lasting sense of community

The empowering as well as bonding character of the community lasted beyond the occupation itself. When the occupants were evicted from the building, all of the asylum-seekers were provided with places in two provisional shelters in Brussels, where they awaited their transfer to an official asylum centre. During this period, communal activities continued. Some activists organised game days and festive evenings in parks or at their homes, and some invited newcomers to public debates around the issue of homelessness. When it became clear that the food in some of the temporary shelters was not suitable for the needs of the inhabitants, especially during Ramadan, the occupants organised a festive iftar. Even after the protection-seekers were moved to asylum centres across the country, many continued to join in with support events and protest actions in Brussels.

Furthermore, in situations where inhabitants from former occupations experienced police and other forms of oppression and were not able to voice their concerns in their new environments, the community of the former occupation was of utmost importance. This was the case in one of the temporary shelters in Brussels, where some asylum-seekers experienced violence from an employee of the organisation running the shelter. He threatened the inhabitants by saying things like "you are worth nothing", "I can make sure that you will not be transferred to an asylum centre", and other oppressive talk. The inhabitants addressed this with the employee's superior, who waved the situation off. Next, they called one of the activists who had lived in the occupied building with them. The asylum-seekers knew that the activist advocated for the rights and good treatment of asylum-seekers and trusted that he would stand by their side in such a situation. Video footage supported their claim, and soon after the employee was removed from his position.

Meaningful networks versus service dependency

Temporary occupations with political objectives, or 'political squats', in Brussels not only exert pressure on the federal government to provide shelter and social services to homeless asylum-seekers, they also foster community building and friendships among local activists and the newcomers due to the harsh conditions in which they are forged. The two-week siege of the occupied building that forced activists and (activist) newcomers to live together intensively enhanced their experience of community building and empowerment. It also created a meaningful network of people beyond the period of the occupation. To a lesser extent, we observed similar effects in temporary occupations in Brussels, despite those involved not being stuck in the building. Communal activities (for example basketball matches, shared dinners, or other leisure activities) and political mobilisations for newcomer rights, in which a mix of locals and homeless newcomers participated, fostered long-term relations that transcended the mere fulfilment of basic needs and service dependencies between those involved.

TAKEAWAYS

Occupations with a political purpose create opportunities for asylum-seekers and activists to forge strong bonds and empower each other. These spaces enable newcomers to become active participants in advocating for their rights, such as their entitlement to asylum accommodation.

Temporary occupations function as more than survival strategies; they are platforms for political mobilisation. By combining direct action with communal living, these spaces challenge systemic neglect and bring attention to issues affecting asylum-seekers like homelessness, police violence, and inadequate asylum services.

Solidarity-based networks created during (political) occupations act as safety nets for asylum-seekers. These networks empower newcomers to confront abuse, seek justice, and navigate systems that often marginalise them. Networks formed in temporary occupations can thus become a source of long-term support, advocacy, and empowerment, transcending to a considerable degree the physical and temporal boundaries of the initial occupation.

Political occupations serve as direct challenges to systemic failures. They expose the harsh realities of police oppression, inadequate shelter systems, and exclusionary policies, while simultaneously offering a vision of collective empowerment, action, and community-driven solutions. This underscores the transformative potential of grassroots action.

> For more details on the reception crisis in Brussels, see another story in this volume: Reframing the 'refugee crisis' in Brussels as a 'reception crisis' in Belgium: holding the government accountable for violating the right to asylum (p. 167).

4. CLAIMING

In this chapter we address three types of claims that play an important role in infrastructuring arrival: claims for space, for rights (to asylum, to housing, to the city, to access resources, etc.), and for a voice in the public debate on migration and integration and to weigh in on dominant narratives. The arrival infrastructuring practices discussed in this chapter range from less overtly political claims, for example a space in social housing, to intensely political ones, for example a political mobilisation against the Belgian asylum policy which no longer provides asylum accommodation to single men. In most cases, claiming is an act of resistance against the often marginalised spatial, social, and 'discursive' position that many newcomers hold due to processes of discrimination because of their legal status, race, ethnicity, gender, sexuality, etc. Very often, newcomers are supported in their claims by political activists, activist scholars, and activist citizens. Claiming is a form of infrastructuring practice that makes the bridge to 'doing integration otherwise' in the second part of this Kit.

4.1 RIGHTS

In the context of tightening regulations and exclusionary policies, efforts to claim rights for and by newcomers are numerous. Strategies often used for claiming rights that are not being fulfilled but to which people are entitled include (a combination of) protest, occupations, lobbying, advocating, coalition-building, and other forms of arrival infrastructuring work. Sometimes claiming rights also involves questioning national citizenship and how it determines differing access to rights. Hence, claiming rights is very often about addressing systemic forms of discrimination and structural barriers for newcomers. In the following story, you will read about opposing housing discrimination in Dortmund.

HOUSING
Housing support for newcomers in Nordstadt (Dortmund): addressing housing exploitation, instability, and discrimination

This story sheds light on how newcomers and others infrastructure arrival through housing provision. In the case of Nordstadt, an arrival neighbourhood in Dortmund, many newcomers face serious barriers to finding affordable and decent housing, which forces them to turn to informal housing solutions. In addition, newcomers sometimes face discrimination for not following the housekeeping practices imposed by the local municipality. In the following account, we share how local stakeholders intervene to address these challenges.

Turning to informal solutions in a tightening housing market

The rental housing market in Germany has become oversaturated in recent decades. Often discrimination on the housing market in the rest of the city pushes newcomers to more accessible and affordable housing options in arrival neighbourhoods. The pressure to accept anything that provides a roof over one's head has increased in recent years. This situation leads households to the informal segment of the housing market, which is part of a larger shadow economy of activities that occur outside of government regulation and taxation. In this informal housing market, substandard housing is mediated by brokers for a fee, sometimes combined with precarious work arrangements. Often newcomers pay a brokerage fee in their countries of origin before leaving, in exchange for housing and work arrangements upon arrival. Once they arrive in Nordstadt, these arrangements commonly turn out to be very precarious, if they are fulfilled at all: the housing conditions are poor and the work only temporarily. Thus, newcomers remain dependent on their broker for mediation with landlords, paperwork issues, interpretation issues, etc.

From supporting tenants...

A central aim of local organisations working in Nordstadt is to prevent people from becoming stuck in these exploitative arrangements. Tenant support and advice ranges from presenting their own organisation as a contact point for all sorts of everyday issues, to actively supporting newcomers in housing-related issues, such as negotiations with landlords, and providing tenants with knowledge about their rights. For instance, they organise tenants' meetings and negotiate with providers by proxy. To involve the tenants' association or a lawyer in these negotiations, the municipality sometimes requires "days of dialogue, research, and documentation work," says Patrick, who works at a local organisation working on housing. He shared with us that property rights and finding out who is responsible for each housing unit can be quite complicated. For him, it is essential to ask, "What are the structures that lead to housing conditions becoming so precarious in some cases?" (Interview with Patrick, Dortmund, January 2022). Having knowledge about ownership structures turned out to be the basis for helping people in precarious housing conditions.

... to the right to housing: adding a political component

In relation to precarious housing conditions, newcomers are often asked to bear the burden of aligning with local norms of good housekeeping practices; if they do not, they risk being discriminated against. For example, for some new arrivals, the municipal household waste policies were not obvious. This led to an excess of waste present around the homes of these newcomers, which in turn resulted in characterisations of these groups as 'unhousable' by sensationalist media. In response, organisations collaborated in changing the perception about newcomers' household practices and insisted on their right to housing in affordable and decent conditions. Thus, local organisations organised public actions to change the focus from the newcomers to the structures that produce precarious housing conditions, while at the same time supporting newcomers in following the recycling regulations.

Embedding local initiatives in broader housing actions

The local organisation working on housing issues in Nordstadt also participated in the annual Europe-wide 'housing action days'. Within this framework, a local event was organised in the neighbourhood involving several organisations from the surrounding area. The event shed light on increasing rents, on housing discrimination and access barriers for migrants on the housing market, and on the financially driven housing economy and the consequences thereof. Additionally, campaigns were organised to highlight the precarious housing conditions that were framed in mainstream media as being to do with the 'improper' household practices of certain migrant groups.

TAKEAWAYS

\# Against the backdrop of a structural shortage of affordable housing, infrastructuring work also includes supporting newcomers so that they do not get stuck in exploitative and discriminatory housing arrangements.

\# Collaboration between tenants' associations, municipalities, and legal experts strengthens the ability to address housing exploitation and support residents in precarious housing conditions effectively.

\# Infrastructuring work in the domain of housing can have various dimensions: efforts to uphold the right to housing involve not only providing direct support for individuals, but also addressing broader policy issues through advocacy and public campaigns. The latter is crucial in shifting the focus away from individual newcomers' responsibilities and negatively perceived household practices, towards the systemic factors that produce precarious housing conditions.

\# Participation in larger initiatives, like the Europe-wide housing action days, amplifies local issues and connects them to global housing rights struggles.

\# Arrival neighbourhoods like Nordstadt highlight the dual role of these spaces as accessible entry points for newcomers and hubs of vulnerability requiring targeted interventions.

TOOL 11
MAPPING ROLES AND RELATIONS IN SOCIAL ACTIVISM

MATERIALS: Paper, writing utensils.

TOOL SUMMARY: This tool aims to help you identify and understand the different roles individuals and organisations play in driving social change. By recognising these roles and their interconnections, you can better position your own efforts and see how they complement others working towards the same cause. This tool encourages reflection on personal and organisational roles and relations within social activism, as well as the methods used to foster a more cohesive and effective social movement.

Many of the stories within this Kit showcase people (including newcomers) bringing about, through small or bigger actions, social change for newcomers. Each in their own local contexts, they take on different, often complementary roles.

While there are different ways to see those roles, we propose here a reading of social activism through four different roles:

<table>
<tr><td>

The advocate:

Advocates are those who focus on pushing to change laws and practices of those in power. They do the work of reforming the system

</td><td>

The supporter:

Supporters act on a personal level: they volunteer in organisations they believe in, they support people in need, in short, they are "engaged citizens"

</td></tr>
<tr><td>

The rebel:

Rebels create noise and a mess around the causes they find unfair. Their voice is loud, and they disrupt the status quo to provoke social change

</td><td>

The organiser:

Organisers bring people together to create wider movements: they set up systems so people can work collectively for social change

</td></tr>
</table>

Figure 29. Diagram for mapping roles and relations in social activism.

STEP 1: Do you recognise yourself in any of the roles described above? If so, is it one role, or a hybrid of several roles?

STEP 2: Do you recognise any organisations or people who are working on similar things as you, but who take on different roles and use different methods? Where would you position them? You can write their names in the four corners in the diagram above or even on the lines separating roles.

STEP 3: What are the relationships between the people and organisations you have added to the diagram? You can draw a circle around those who work together and trace dotted lines between those who do not. You can add your own analysis of the relationships between them, based on their values, approaches, methods, geographic location, the specific topic they work on, and more.

REFLECTION

Often in social activism, all four of the roles are fulfilled by different people and some people fulfil multiple roles. This tool is a helpful way to start positioning the work of the many people and organisations that are working for the same cause in relation to each other. This can help you to see how their roles are all complementary, even though they may each use very different methods to enact social change, as well as which roles might be lacking in your imitative.

> FURTHER READING: This tool is inspired by Bill Moyer's 'Four Roles of Social Activism': https://wagingnonviolence.org/2016/02/bill-moyer-four-roles-of-social-change/.

4.2 SPACE

The role of migrants in shaping cities is often overlooked. Newcomers, like everyone else, appropriate living spaces, move through the city according to specific desires, transform their neighbourhoods, and make homes with the means available to them. In this subsection, we present three stories that give examples of different ways in which migrants claim space and in doing so infrastructure their arrival. In Paris, migrant residents of social housing claim their right to host non-residents, often friends and family, by changing the locks and sharing their keys. In Katerini, leisure activities in public spaces give migrant women a sense of belonging and visibility in a new environment, claiming their right to a 'normal' everyday life. Finally, in a London borough, unhoused individuals (newcomers and UK nationals) transform public infrastructures into temporary shelters, claiming their right to subsist while facing constant risk. In all of the stories, we see how newcomers transform space by claiming their right to address their needs, pursue goals, and move on to the life they wish to achieve.

CONCEPT BOX 11

'Migrants as city-makers'

Migrants are essential 'city-makers', actively shaping urban spaces through their spatial, social, cultural, and economic contributions. Glick Schiller and Simsek-Çağlar (2010) conceptualise migrants as place-makers forging spaces of belonging and influence while navigating and challenging structural constraints. Through their practices and networks, migrants contribute to the vitality of urban life, often despite exclusionary policies.

Beeckmans (2025) builds on this perspective, highlighting how migrants circulate place-making practices 'from below' and how these impact cities. As such, she sheds light on the 'physical place-making' of migrants in cities adding to a rich scholarship that explores instances of migrants' 'social place-making'(Pemberton and Phillimore 2018). Migrants' place-making practices are deeply intertwined with 'home-making' practices, especially in contexts of displacement and precarious housing. In *Making Home(s) in Displacement* (Beeckmans et al. 2022), 'home-making' is presented as a critical spatial practice that reveals how migrants actively reimagine constrained spaces as lived and meaningful homes, challenging institutional narratives that reduce them to passive occupants.

Most scholars emphasise that migrants negotiate citizenship through physical place-making, i.e. by appropriating and adapting urban infrastructures, a process which is conceptualised by Lemanski (2019) as 'infrastructural citizenship', thus recognising the politicised nature of urban infrastructure. Together, these scholars demonstrate that migrants are agents of urban transformation, challenging dominant narratives that render them marginal or passive.

References:

Beeckmans, Luce, Alessandra Gola, Amrita Singh, and Hilde Heynen, eds. 2022. *Making Home(s) in Displacement: Critical Reflections on a Spatial Practice* (Leuven: Leuven University Press).

Beeckmans, Luce. 2025. 'Mobile urbanism from below: Afro-Christian churches as place-makers and scale-makers in European midsized cities', *Urban Studies*, published online in 2025.

Glick Schiller, Nina, and Ayse Simsek-Çağlar. 2011. *Locating migration: rescaling cities and migrants* (Ithaca: Cornell University Press).

Lemanski, Charlotte. 2019. *Citizenship and infrastructure: practices and identities of citizens and the state* (London: Routledge).

Pemberton, Simon, and Jenny Phillimore. 2018. 'Migrant place-making in super-diverse neighbourhoods: Moving beyond ethno-national approaches', *Urban Studies*, 55(4): 733–50.

HOUSING

Passing down one's room in Parisian social housing: claiming space in a rigid institutional housing system

In Paris, a specific form social housing for West African migrant workers, also called *foyers*, is currently being transformed into more general social housing. This transformation has a direct impact on the current residents, limiting their ability to use the space as they have in the past. In this story we focus on the limitations the transformation has imposed on residents' social and spatial practices, particularly hosting friends and family, and the various ways they are reclaiming the *foyers*.

An exclusionary renovation programme

One of the main goals of transforming the collective housing typology of the *foyers* into individual social housing units is to offer residents studios in place of the former dormitories with communal bathroom facilities and kitchens. For the public authorities and building managers, the individual space offered by a studio guarantees a basic standard of housing. When residents move in, they are now given a furnished studio with a small kitchen and bathroom. The building managers give them a non-duplicable key, a copy of which is kept by the manager in order to be able to access the accommodation in case of emergency or for occasional repairs to utilities when the resident is not home.

However, since the creation of the *foyers* in the 1960s, migrant residents have used their spaces there to offer hospitality. This includes preparing and sharing food with friends and family, as well as offering temporary lodging during housing shortages. To compensate for the lack of housing and to accommodate undocumented migrants, prior to the renovations the residents of the *foyers* dormitories took in informal residents. The transformation of *foyers* into more standardised social housing units and the advent of the single-key studio apartment complicates these hospitality practices, particularly by restricting access to accommodation. Indeed, as the dormitories were shared by many residents, those living informally could always find someone to open the door. Today, there is only one official resident per housing unit, so if that person is at work, the dwelling is inaccessible to informal inhabitants.

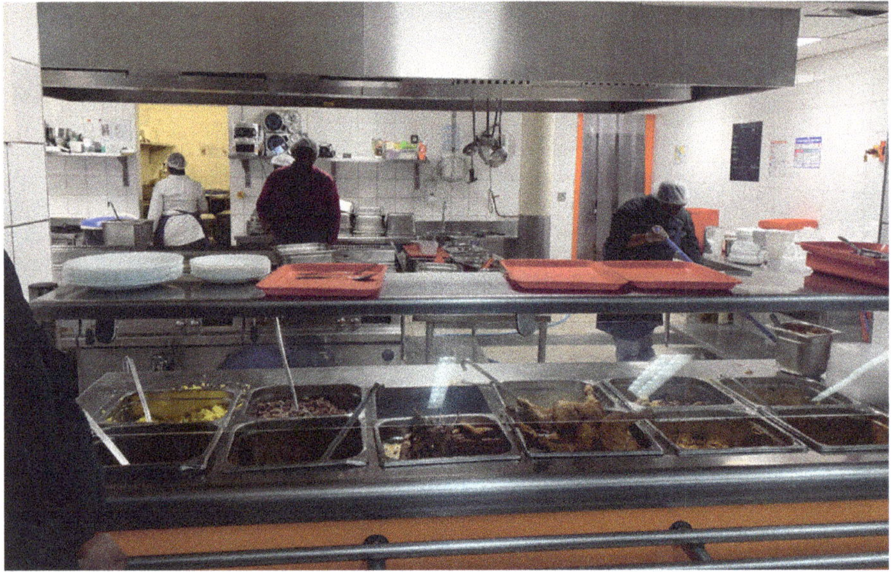

Figure 30. Collective space usage in the *foyer* prior to renovations that reduced such spaces.

Informal solutions to lack of shelter

The transformation of the *foyers* into social housing has added new limitations to the lives of migrant residents, especially those who are residing there informally. Many of the residents we talked to expressed resistance to the single-key access restrictions that make it harder for informal guests to come and go. However, while the main goal of transforming the *foyers* was to reduce or even eliminate these accommodation practices, residents have been successful in negotiating policy changes.

On a day-to-day basis in the shared accommodation, a number of do-it-yourself solutions have been developed to cope with the single-key constraint. The letterboxes installed at the residence entrances appeared to offer a working solution to the problem. The small, easily duplicated keys to the letterboxes were distributed to all residents, who could then deposit the non-duplicable key to their studio in their letterbox. Thus, if the letterbox is empty, it means that the resident is at home in their studio; if the key is in the box, it means that no one is there. This solution is frequently used by residents who are hosting relatives, and so the information has gradually spread both inside and outside the *foyers*. As a result, burglaries following the opening of letterboxes became more common. The key as a symbol of home protection then lost its effectiveness, and this strategy aiming to circumvent the rule of non-duplication became problematic.

Consequently, a second strategy was adopted by many residents. To make a studio accessible to all its occupants (both formal and informal), while at the same time protecting the home from intruders, the locks had to be changed for one with a new, easily reproducible key. While this second strategy improves the autonomy of residents, it contradicts the regulations governing daily life in the building.

Unintended consequences and repercussions

However, this strategy is not without its consequences. Although no eviction has so far been motivated by this breaking of the rules, several building managers have decided not to give priority to inhabitants who have changed their lock. When the manager has a copy of the original key, repairs can be carried out even when the occupant is not present, but when the lock has been changed, the resident's presence is required, reducing the time available for repairs. This means that while the inhabitants may have appropriated their studios – through claiming the right to close it with their own keys – this leads to the management reducing level of the practical care and maintenance they receive.

TAKEAWAYS

\# Migrants' practices of hospitality – such as sharing their housing units with friends and family, sometimes undocumented – serve as a form of resistance against exclusionary housing policies that aim to standardise and privatise space.

\# Social housing residents' creative solutions, such as letterbox key-sharing and changing locks, illustrate how migrants exercise spatial agency to reclaim autonomy in times of restrictive housing policies, even as these strategies are met with institutional pushback.

\# Migrants negotiate their 'infrastructural citizenship' (see concept box 11 above) by adapting their housing to fit their needs, demonstrating that social housing is shaped not just by policy but also by everyday home-making practices of residents.

\# Claiming space can have differential risks for those involved in the arrival infrastructure.

Friday meetings of newcomer women in public parks in Katerini: everyday convivial claiming of public space in the city

In this story, we share how having low-threshold spaces to gather with individuals undergoing similar life transitions can be a useful step to infrastructuring one's arrival. A Greek NGO in Katerini offers newcomers this opportunity through organising skill-building classes, social events, and guided weekly trips to the local city centre park. Through these activities, newcomers can feel more at ease navigating the city and life in general in Katerini. Spending free time in public spaces, especially with the guidance of more established and local residents, can also be a way of claiming the right to a 'normal' life and visible position in the city.

A weekly gathering for migrant women

In Katerini, the NGO Perichoresis ran courses to improve integration outcomes for newcomers (classes in English, Greek, and computer literacy) in a rented space in the city centre. In addition to providing decent accommodation and services to all beneficiaries, the organisation also ran gender-specific programmes. One example of this is the organisation of social gatherings for women newcomers, who reported feeling a lack of social connection and empowerment in the city.

The women's gatherings took place at the NGO's offices and involved group excursions to the city market on Fridays. At the office, the gatherings included activities such as music, games, and discussions about everyday issues, often concerning family, everyday life in the city, and challenges finding accommodation, employment, and basic necessities. One of Perichoresis' employees emphasised the importance of these gatherings for women. She mentioned that it is an opportunity for newly arrived women lacking established social connections to meet and socialise. Newcomer women shared their reluctance to leave the house, citing their unfamiliarity with local cultural norms and a fear of appearing different. At the gatherings, they could exchange ideas and thoughts while also playing various games to have fun. The employee also told us that many women reported that these gatherings were the best day of the week for them. The gatherings were convivial, usually with tea, coffee, juice, and some snacks. Sometimes the participants would bring sweets and homemade dishes to share. "They feel very happy if they can also contribute something and share it with everyone else," the employee added (Interview with Jane, Katerini, June 2022).

Collective excursions to the public park

When these gatherings took the form of an excursion, the women went to Katerini's central park. This park already serves as a meeting point for locals and hosts numerous events, cafés, and social events. During these outings, the newcomers would stroll around the park, meet other mothers, and experience a common social practice popular with many local residents.

Through these group excursions, the park became an important space where newcomers could learn about and become involved in daily life in Katerini. These excursions to the park, therefore, not only foster social interaction but also contribute to the overall well-being and sense of belonging among newcomers.

Figure 31. A group excursion to a park in Katerini for newcomer women.

Appropriating the city and becoming visible

Migrant women's gatherings and trips to the park are not merely activities for leisure or relaxation. Indeed, apart from facing issues related to finding housing, employment, and securing basic necessities, some newcomers feel uncomfortable appearing in public as they fear being perceived as different. The weekly outings to Katerini park served as a means for these migrant women to become involved in the local community, exchange experiences and ideas, and feel a sense of belonging. Therefore, this initiative serves as an example of how solidarity and support can create environments where new residents feel welcomed and acknowledged.

\# Participating in everyday social practices – like strolling, socialising, and watching children playing public parks – allows newcomers to engage in a sense of 'normal' life, challenging narratives that frame them as perpetual outsiders. Spending free time in public parks for collective activities thus enables newcomers to experience autonomy, gain confidence, and develop agency in navigating their new environment.

\# Some newcomers feel uncomfortable appearing in public as they fear being perceived as 'different'. Some organisations conduct key infrastructuring work by supporting them in navigating the tension between becoming visible in public spaces and managing fears of appearing 'different'. By claiming space collectively, migrant women, for instance, gradually reclaim their right to visibility without isolation.

\# It is important to recognise the gendered dimensions of the arrival infrastructure. The need for guided gatherings and excursions in this story highlights the importance of gender-sensitive support structures in helping migrant women overcome social and cultural barriers to participation in public life.

HOUSING

Repurposing abandoned buildings and public spaces in a London borough: claiming inhospitable spaces as shelter.

Claiming spaces for shelter when you have no safety net

Experiences of homelessness and rough sleeping were prevalent among both British-born and migrant residents in the London borough. Both groups had experience repurposing unexpected places as shelter while destitute, as they slept in parks, in carparks, under bridges, in church or library doorways, or on night buses, for example. Some stories were heart-rending, others heart-warming. One victim of human trafficking, prior to arrival in the borough, slept in the canteen of the business premises where she was forced to provide bonded labour as a cleaner, only to subsequently be arrested and detained by the Home Office in a raid. In contrast, during the Covid-19 pandemic, another migrant from within the EU built himself a makeshift house out of found materials in an industrial area in East London. He recalled being alone but happy there, "just me and God" (Interview with Anghel, London, March 2022).

Repurposing abandoned buildings and public spaces for shelter

Dominik, an Eastern European interviewee, revealed to us that for years he had found temporary shelter in housing provided by the council that had been vacated as part of regeneration projects in the borough. He got the idea to occupy these vacant council housing units at a time when he had lost his job and could not pay his rent. He saw his neighbours moving out one day and noticed that their flat was left empty, so he decided to move in. Over the course of several years, he lived in different units within three different apartment blocks that had been vacated in the borough. Sometimes this provided a (relatively) comfortable environment, particularly during periods when the electricity and water in a building were still connected. He fondly recalled finding a flat that was left with the microwave and fridge still in place, and food in the cupboards. In that flat, he was able to change the lock and live securely for an extended period.

Similarly, Avinash, a homeless East Asian migrant, spoke of a "good" place for rough sleeping in a neighbouring borough. The building was safe from petty crime because it was near the police station, it had a roofed section that protected him from the elements, and there was a homeless support centre nearby where he could get tea, coffee, and a shower in the morning. He contrasted this to another neighbouring borough where he had lived, where he said that homeless people cannot survive because there is nowhere to sleep, hide, or shower.

The risks of claiming inhospitable spaces

Yet repurposed spaces are often inhospitable. At times, Dominik was forced to live in unsecured, sometimes "apocalyptic" flats, and was assaulted on more than one occasion. In one case, he was robbed of the bag containing his documents, which led to him losing his job as he could no longer prove his right to work. His jaw was also permanently damaged after being attacked by more than 10 teenagers with knives and a bat. "An abandoned building is like a jungle, there are no rules," he said (Interview with Dominik, London, June 2022).

Migrant residents living in public spaces tended to have similar experiences of theft, loss of documents, and assault, as well as being regularly harassed by police or security guards. Busy areas, such as town centres and retail areas, receive a daily cleaning and litter-picking service as part of the borough's street cleaning service. This can result in rough sleepers' belongings being 'cleaned up' by a cleaning crew unless they carry all their items at all times.

Forms of policing, patrolling, and regulation are also often used to enforce norms of accepted behaviour, and prevent activities such as drinking alcohol, spitting, urinating, or begging in defined public areas. Yet, for rough sleepers, there is no private place to drink alcohol. To drink, one must conceal the alcohol in soft drink bottles or move to an area with lower levels of surveillance. When publicly accessible toilets are closed at night, bodily functions must still be attended to. Danut, a Romanian resident, had been forced to move on from his place of shelter under a railway bridge because there was evidence of urination/defecation in the vicinity.

\# Physical urban infrastructure can be repurposed as forms of shelter by newcomers seeking shelter in the absence of formal support, individually as well as collectively. These solutions, while necessary, underscore the urgent need for inclusive policies that address systemic housing inequalities.

\# Sleeping rough or in abandoned building or public spaces is a common survival strategy of . While these spaces provide temporary shelter, they also expose people to uncontrolled threats and further marginalisation. Their role in arrival infrastructuring should not be romanticised.

\# Newcomers' occupation of vacant urban infrastructure, such as abandoned housing or underutilised spaces, reflects both their response to exclusion and an assertion of spatial agency – transforming urban voids into makeshift homes or shelters.

\# The policing and regulation of public space – through street cleaning, surveillance, or behavioural norms – exacerbate the challenges faced by rough sleepers, as survival practices like drinking, resting, or attending to bodily needs become criminalised.

> See also the stories about reusing abandoned infrastructure in Thessaloniki (p. 80) and Brussels (p. 148).

4.3 A VOICE

Dominant narratives about migration and integration often perpetuate harmful stereotypes and justify discriminatory border and integration policies. This section tackles the way these discourses are experienced, transformed, and countered by newcomers and their allies, as this can also be considered as an important form of infrastructuring work. By claiming 'discursive space', hence a voice in the public debate, newcomers, in collaboration with others, aim to weigh in on the dominant narratives by which they are often marginalised and sometimes even criminalised. In Brussels the voice-claiming was to an important degree a work of reframing and weighing in on mainstream migration and integration narratives, while in Thessaloniki and Hungary it was to a large extent a matter of questioning the categorisation and labelling of newcomers, which is often experienced as dehumanising by migrants.

HOUSING

Reframing the 'refugee crisis' in Brussels as a 'reception crisis' in Belgium: holding the government accountable for violating the right to asylum

Throughout the year 2023, amid mobilisations against the systematic refusal of asylum-seeking men at the Belgian federal intake centre for asylum in Brussels, a collective called 'Stop the Reception Crisis' gained recognition. The term 'reception crisis' in the collective's name suggests a deliberate departure from the more conventionally used 'refugee crisis'. This intentional word choice reflects a larger public debate over migration reception policies. By advancing the term 'reception crisis', the collective aimed to highlight the root cause of the problem, namely the government's decision to no longer handle asylum-requests from male asylum-seeking newcomers and exclude them from asylum accommodation. In this story, we examine how the dominant narrative of 'refugee crisis' was constructed, nurtured, brought into action, and resisted by the counter-narrative of 'reception crisis'.

'Refugee crisis' or 'reception crisis'?

In 2023, the Belgian State Secretary for Asylum and Migration announced that, due to a lack of asylum accommodation, asylum-seeking men were excluded from access to state shelter, even though this is in violation of Belgian and international law. In practice this measure had been in effect for years already, but the formal declaration underlines that restrictive asylum polices are becoming normalised.

The practice of excluding men from state shelter created harsh realities of homeless, unwelcomed, and uncared-for people in Brussels' streets. Simultaneously, images of unhoused asylum-seekers in the media legitimised further restrictive and exclusive migration measures as they play into a visual and verbal perspective that depicts migration as an uncontrollable and unceasing flow of people flooding into the country. On the basis of this constructed narrative, the federal government and broader public laid the current collapse of the reception system with the asylum-seekers themselves and depicted it as a 'refugee crisis'.

By contrast, support organisations in the field criticise Belgian's adverse asylum policies and have mobilised in a variety of ways to counter this narrative that puts the responsibility out of the hands of the government. One of the important players has been the above-mentioned 'Stop the Reception Crisis' collective. It has been mobilising against the violation of newcomers' right to asylum through a series of protest actions that hold the government accountable for its responsibilities.

An occupation that effectively challenged the 'refugee crisis' narrative

Of paramount importance was the occupation of a government building. Together with a group of 70 homeless asylum-seeking men, the collective strategically chose to occupy the empty National Crisis Centre, which was being renovated and was about to be re-opened. This building was not only of symbolical value – its name and function signified a crisis which was argued to have been caused, rather than tackled, by the national government – but also permitted the activists to negotiate their presence in the building directly with the national government as it was the legal entity responsible for the building.

A group of activist lawyers (Progress Lawyers) and the collective built their case against an eviction on the previous convictions of the federal government for no longer accepting asylum applications from men. At the time, the government had been condemned more than 8,000 times nationally and internationally for neglecting to provide shelter and social services to asylum-seeking men. A lawyer we spoke to called this "a turning point in the history of Belgian's democracy" (Fieldnotes, Brussels, December 2022, translated from French to English by the authors). However, these condemnations had not had any direct consequences for the government, as it did not pay fines, nor change anything about its hostile and unlawful practices.

Holding the government accountable for its actions

Moreover, the government's subsequent convictions proved to be useful for the litigation against the federal government during the occupation of the National Crisis Centre. Based on its failure to respect the rule of law, the lawyers demanded that the federal government, in event of eviction, guarantee shelter and social services for the entire group of occupying asylum-seekers, from day one until the end of their asylum procedure. The judge ruled in favour of this demand and the occupants departed the building with the prospect of immediate shelter and a sense of empowerment. Hence, by safeguarding court-confirmed rights, the media coverage of the 'Stop the Reception Crisis' occupation countered narratives and practices that locate responsibility for the misfunctioning reception system with newcomers and successfully pushed for the opening of new asylum accommodation in the city, among other places in hotels.

TAKEAWAYS

\# The deliberate shift from 'refugee crisis' to 'reception crisis' challenges dominant narratives that blame asylum-seekers for systemic failings. Counter-narratives like 'reception crisis' reveal government neglect or failure as policy choices rather than inevitable outcomes. Therefore, offering alternative discourses and terminology play a pivotal role in shaping public perception and policy debates on migration.

\# Highlighting the lived realities of excluded asylum-seekers (homelessness, lack of care) brings public focus to the human cost of restrictive policies. Such actions counter dehumanising media portrayals that perpetuate stereotypes of asylum-seekers as a 'threat'.

\# Media coverage of asylum-seekers' struggles can amplify both harmful narratives (migration as an 'overflowing crisis') and counter-narratives (highlighting state failures). Activists' strategic use of media during protests and legal actions can shift public opinion and demand accountability.

\# The judiciary's role in safeguarding asylum rights underscores the importance of legal advocacy in countering governmental neglect.

\# Collaboration between grassroots collectives, lawyers, and advocacy groups in the strategic occupation of government-owned properties illustrates the power of forming broader coalitions in the face of challenging policies. Their infrastructuring work also fostered solidarity among the stakeholders involved.

TOOL 12
ANALYSING DISCOURSES AND THEIR IMPACTS

MATERIALS: Relevant texts such as newspapers or policy briefs, paper, writing utensils.

TOOL SUMMARY: This tool helps you to critically examine how language shapes our understanding of integration and migration. By analysing word choices, metaphors, and assumptions in texts or speeches, you can identify dominant discourses and their implications. This tool also guides you in formulating alternative discourses to promote more inclusive and supportive narratives.

Integration and migration are much-discussed and highly debated topics in many countries. Analysing how a discourse on integration or migration is constructed and what its impact is, can be difficult because it is often so prevalent that it becomes hard to get any distance from it. But by paying close attention to a text or speech, we can see when it makes logical jumps, when it uses euphemisms (a milder term used in place of another one), which metaphors or images it evokes, which assumptions it makes about people or society, and more. Being aware of this allows us to position ourselves towards it and avoid multiplying exclusionary discourses.

STEP 1: Choose a text presenting a mainstream discourse about integration or migration, such as a newspaper article, a speech by a politician, or a policy brief.

STEP 2: First, highlight the main arguments the text is making and choose two or three of these arguments to analyse in more depth.

STEP 3: For each argument, use the below main discourse analysis questions:

1) Choice of words: Which words related to integration or migration are used? Are there synonyms that could have been used? If so, what is the impact of using these specific words? How many times are these words used (you can for example highlight every occurrence in the text).

2) Characters: Look out for the words 'I', 'us', 'you', 'them': who are they referring to? What kind of groups are being formed by those words? Who is represented in a good light, and who are the 'bad' people in the argument?

3) Assumptions: What is being assumed about the groups you have identified? Is there anything that is not explicitly said, but that you nonetheless read as a certain judgement or negative connotation or perception?

4) Alternative discourse: Can you formulate an alternative to the discourse you are analysing? What would be a different or opposite way to think about this situation? This allows for two things:
   - First, you can get some distance from the discourse you are reviewing and understand that the arguments are a choice, not necessarily a 'truth'.
   - Second, if you disagree with the discourse in the text, you can formulate or align with an alternative discourse.

REFLECTION

This tool proposes a method of becoming 'unfamiliar' with discourses about integration and migration that we take for granted and that we hear a lot. Analysing a discourse allows us to become more sensitive to its recurrence (we can notice when we hear it again), therefore allowing us to identify it as a dominant discourse. From there, if we need it, we can start critically analysing it and perhaps formulating an alternative discourse.

> FURTHER READING: This tool was inspired by Gasper, Des. 2022. '"Making Strange": Discourse Analysis Tools for Teaching Critical Development Studies', *Progress in Development Studies*, 22(3): 288–304.

From 'migrants', 'asylum-seekers', and 'refugees' to 'people on the move' in Thessaloniki: resisting government labelling of people

In the European Union's legal framework and rhetoric, there are several distinct categories used to refer to newcomers, such as 'asylum-seekers', 'refugees', 'economic migrants', 'irregular migrants', 'illegal migrants', and other terms, each with its own specific rights and degrees of protection. This labelling of people is part of the EU's and national governments' strategy of controlling and channelling, but also criminalising and stigmatising newcomers. In recent years, the term 'people on the move' has emerged to counter the above categorisations. It is mainly activists' groups and grassroots humanitarian organisations that use this term, especially when they are referring to transit countries, as in the case of Greece.

'People on the move' and 'travellers'

The first time that we heard the term 'people on the move', we were walking with a volunteer from an international medical team in the area of the abandoned train wagons in the western part of the Greek city of Thessaloniki. The volunteer explained to us how 'people on move' use the wagons as temporary shelters. When we asked why he prefers this term over 'migrants' or 'refugees', he explained that his team prefers not to separate people according to the EU's and Greek authorities' categorisations. They prefer to see all people who are travelling as 'travellers' and 'people on the move'.

The right to travel

In 2016, a protest action called 'No Border Camp' took place in the state-run Softex Camp in the outskirts of Thessaloniki. Children raised a banner with the slogan 'The Right To Travel'. This was a pretty provocative banner that had obviously been prepared by European activists. Instead of 'refugees welcome', as was written on many banners at that time, the new slogan underscored the idea that everybody can be a traveller regardless of their passport and country of origin, thus dissolving the government-created distinction between privileged and unprivileged migration.

Who has the right to travel?

A young man from Casablanca (Morocco) was working in Casablanca airport and every day he saw people coming and going, arriving and departing the city. He was not facing any significant financial or other problems in his life. At that time, he was 24 years old and he also had the desire to travel, to get to know other places, exactly like the tourists he saw arriving at the airport every day. However, his passport did not allow him to travel freely in Europe. Despite this, he decided to start the long journey, first flying to Istanbul and then walking to Greece with other 'people on the move', simply because he wanted to claim 'the right to travel'.

Inventing new vocabularies

The three mini-stories above demonstrate that the desire of each person to move goes beyond their institutional categorisations. In the European context, which follows the Geneva Convention on refugees, the ideal scenario for any newcomer is to obtain refugee status. Thus, newcomers claim their right and struggle to become legally recognised refugees. However, in some cases, certain newcomers prefer to remain undocumented in the first EU country in which they arrive, because of EU migration policy like the Dublin Convention, which stipulates that once registered as an asylum-seeker they have to remain there until their request is formally processed by the government of that state. If they try and move on to another country after having been registered in the arrival country, other countries have the right to deny them asylum and send them back to the arrival country. This is known to happen in countries like Greece, when newcomers prefer to apply for asylum in a northern European country. Consequently, the process of someone's journey passes not only through physical, social, and political borders, but also through the multiple institutional borders of identification, acceptance, or rejection. Each of these border and institutional encounters comes with the potential of another categorisation controlling mobility and other rights. Thus, the proposed term 'people on the move' is an attempt to reclaim terminology and make sure it unites rather than separates people.

TAKEAWAYS

\# The term 'people on the move' resists state-imposed categories that often stigmatise and even criminalise migrants (such as 'illegals'). Using alternative and less stigmatising terms in everyday language reflects a broader push to humanise migration narratives. The term 'people on the move' also dismantles the distinction between those deemed 'privileged' (for example 'tourists') and 'unprivileged' (for example 'migrants' or 'refugees'), emphasising the universal right to mobility regardless of nationality or socio-economic status.

\# Migration journeys are shaped as much by institutional barriers — categorisation, bureaucracy, and legal frameworks — as by physical borders, adding layers of complexity to the movement of people.

\# EU policies like the Dublin Convention (assigning asylum claims to the first country of entry) create systemic obstacles for those seeking to move within the EU, leading to paradoxical situations where individuals avoid legal recognition to preserve their freedom of movement.

\# Grassroots organisations play a crucial role in shifting migration discourse, creating new vocabularies that reflect solidarity and inclusion while pushing back against restrictive national and EU policies.

Rejecting the word 'migrant' in a shrinking civic space: the balancing act of civil society organisations in Hungary

> In Hungary, the term 'migrant' has evolved from a technical term to a symbol of national threat, especially since 2015 under Viktor Orbán's government. This shift means civil society organisations like Menedék have to navigate a complex landscape where the word 'migrant' is heavily stigmatised. As a result, many institutions and individuals, including international students, avoid using the term to escape negative connotations. This 'de-migrantisation' highlights how people adapt their identities in response to a hostile sociopolitical environment. Despite these challenges, civil society organisations continue to play a crucial role in advocating for migrants and challenging restrictive government narratives.

'Migrants': from technical term to symbol of national threat

In 1995, when the association was established, its founders made the conscious decision to name it Menedék, meaning 'Hungarian Association for Migrants'. At the time, and until 2015, this was a fairly uncontroversial choice and a concise expression of its goals. Prior to 2015, the term 'migrant' was relatively unknown to the general public and was often considered jargon. However, since 2015, when Viktor Orbán came into power in Hungary, the word 'migrant' has gained a new connotation. Since then, there has been a tireless and continuous one-way political campaign in Hungary that opposes and stigmatises migration and discusses it in a conceptual framework of fear, contested national sovereignty, and conflict (or even war) between civilisations. The message, according to Prime Minister Orbán, is that migration is bad and must be stopped.

To understand the macro social-economic climate towards migration in Hungary, it is essential to note that the current political regime links the terms 'migrant' or 'migration' with ('illegal') border-crossing, non-Christian, non-European, non-white 'intruders', criminality, and thus threat.

Avoiding the word 'migrant'

As a consequence, institutions such as universities and most importantly migrant students often refrain from using terms like 'migrant' or 'migration' because of the negative connotations. The latter refer to themselves mostly as 'international students', which allows them to separate and remove themselves from the country's political context. It is an independent denominator that only refers to their specific status and that has a clearly defined time limit (because they will finish their studies at some point). A recent publication on the Stipendium Hungaricum international scholarship programme uses the term 'participants in international talent mobility' to avoid using any term that is related to 'migration'.

It is important to emphasise that the Hungarian government has been developing the Stipendium Hungaricum international scholarship programme and dismantling the asylum system in parallel. Although international students usually do not consider themselves refugees, many of them often mention similar push factors to those that asylum-seekers talk about. In addition, many students have similar aspirations and often do not consider Hungary a place where they would like to settle down, but more as a point of entry into the EU. This has not gone unnoticed by some politicians, who have started to depict Hungary's Stipendium Hungaricum international scholarship programme as an unofficial migration channel that is in their view importing migrants into Hungary.

How to talk about migration then?

The government's rhetoric on integration and migration also impacts the international students coming from countries such as Syria, Ethiopia, Algeria, Mongolia, Nigeria, Malaysia, Egypt, Kazakhstan, Russia, Ukraine, and Kyrgyzstan, among others. International students are increasingly refusing the 'migrant' self-identification. Therefore, 'de-migrantisation', or the omitting of the 'migrant' identification in communication about the Stipendium Hungaricum, is in their interest as well. Moreover, due to the political climate, doing research on any form of migration, like international student mobility, has become a sensitive issue. In this environment, an interview request may confuse students and stakeholders may be reluctant to get involved. However, while carrying out our research, it was difficult to avoid using the word 'migrant'. This created a set of issues, such as self-identification and reflection on our own categorisations and the politically complex and fraught migration context in Hungary.

Another source of tension that affected the fieldwork is Menedék's own approach to the government's framing and appropriation of the terms 'migrant' and 'migration'. The organisation deliberately refuses to accept the discursive turn, and continues to use the terms 'migrants' and 'migration' according to their original (or in the Hungarian context, past) meaning. It gives the association's advocacy and activist staff an opportunity to challenge and influence the political and public discourse on migration and also signals resilience against political pressure. However, the association's staff and volunteers who work in providing services often find it an additional burden. Due to the association's name, as well as its references to migration in a neutral or even positive context, partner institutions or service users are sometimes reluctant to cooperate. This conflict, and the discomfort it creates, could be circumvented by avoiding the contested terminology during everyday interactions, and accepting the partners' or service users' self-identification. Creating a supportive environment in which the appropriate meaning of these terms is explained is essential. However, it is not always possible because of the temporary nature of the interactions and the goals the association aims to achieve in supporting newcomers.

Government-driven fear campaigns can create an environment where migration is framed as inherently dangerous, influencing public perceptions and personal strategies for self-presentation.

The negative framing of migration has led individuals to distance themselves from the term 'migrant' and adopt alternative terms such as 'international student' to avoid stigma and political connotations.

The process of 'de-migrantisation', or rejecting the 'migrant' label, demonstrates how individuals adapt their identities in response to hostile sociopolitical environments.

Hungary's shrinking civic space not only limits discussions on migration but also hinders civil society's ability to challenge and reshape these narratives. Despite these constraints, civil society organisations remain crucial counterpoints to government rhetoric, offering alternative spaces for dialogue, advocacy, and support while contesting restrictive policies and narratives.

TOOL 13
EXAMINING THE LABELLING OF NEWCOMERS

MATERIALS: Computer or smartphone, writing utensils.

TOOL SUMMARY: This tool encourages you to evaluate how certain identifying terms, or labels, are applied to some people and not others, a process which is referred to as 'categorisation'. Words like 'migrant', 'expat', 'immigrant', and 'newcomer' are characterised by specific imagery. However, the connection between the label and the visual description is often forged by specific public narratives and is often inaccurate and reductive. In this exercise, you can explore your own biases as well as how certain biases are produced and reproduced in the public (visual) discourse.

STEP 1: Choose your favourite search engine and enter one of the labels found in the box below. Look for images in the search engine.

> *'Migrant', 'expat', 'asylum-seeker', 'immigrant', 'newcomer', 'person on the move, 'illegal migrant', 'political migrant', 'traveller', 'undocumented migrant', 'tourist', 'economic migrant', 'environmental migrant', 'international student', 'migrant worker', 'refugee', 'foreigner', 'naturalised citizen', 'unaccompanied minor', 'irregular migrant'.*

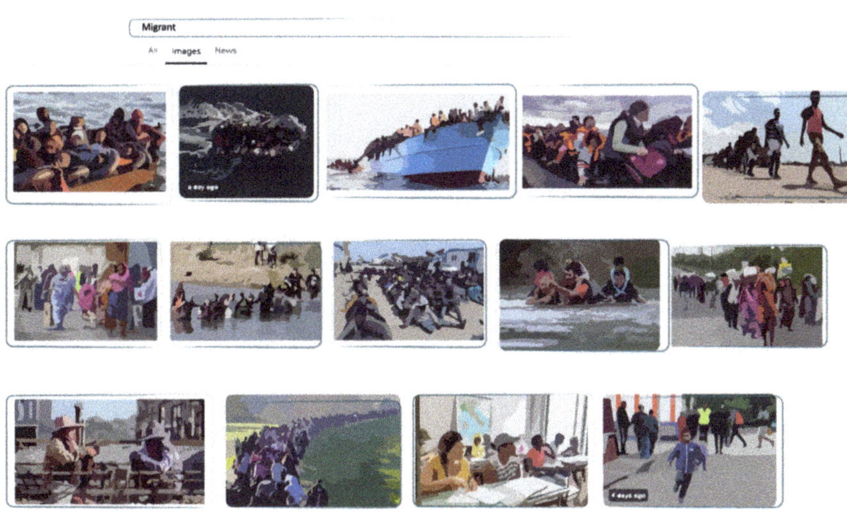

Figure 32. Diagram 1 for examining the labelling of newcomers

STEP 2: Repeat the exercise with another label.

Figure 33. Diagram 2 for examining the labelling of newcomers

REFLECTION

This exercise is an opportunity to review which biases we have internalised (for example that women with a scarf are 'migrants'). It also informs us about the dominant perceptions connected with labels (for instance, 'migrants' are almost 100% linked in search engines to people crossing the sea on boats). Being more aware of this can help us to not reproduce stigmatising and other exclusionary practices.

> SEE ALSO **TOOL 4**: 'Identifying unexpected barriers to everyday life tasks' (p. 63).

REFLECTION AND ADVICE

The stories you have read in Part I 'Seeing Integration Otherwise', showing how arrival is being infrastructured and integration is happening in several cities in Europe, were all observed, noticed, or lived directly by our researchers. For them to 'see' integration otherwise, they had a specific type of gaze on the world: the ethnographic gaze. Ethnography often consists of conducting interviews, organising focus groups and participant observation, which means spending time in a place to learn more about its people and functioning. Ethnographers thus often have to balance being full participants in activities with also observing what is happening and reflecting on it. In ethnographic research, self-reflection on what the research does and how people react to the arrival of the researcher is an important part of the research. Sometimes researchers acquire knowledge by participating in activities. For example, a researcher noticed gaps in healthcare services for newcomers while she was supporting a newcomer in obtaining a prescription for his usual antidepressants. It is this experience of volunteering which allowed her to reflect on obstacles to service access.

In addition to the stories and tools provided on the previous pages, which enable you to see arrival infrastructuring in your context, we now share with you some practical reflections and advice coming directly from our researchers. The advice in this section is thus based on the ethnographic fieldwork experience of our researchers, who share some reflections on how they were able 'to see integration otherwise'. They share their advice on opening up your gaze by: (a) spending time on the ground; (b) getting in touch with a diverse set of stakeholders; (c) nurturing an open and patient approach; and (c) developing reflexivity. In all of this, it is important to recognise that what we observe is always situated and cannot be simply generalised.

A.   SPENDING TIME ON THE GROUND

Spending time 'on the ground' is essential to understanding how arrival is infrastructured in everyday life. Surveys are not enough to give an understanding of how people do this work day-to-day. What can be helpful is to visit organisations that are on the frontline, spend time in a waiting room, observe a normal day in an administration, walk around in an arrival neighbourhood, follow grassroots organisations for a day, or sit for a few hours in a business offering services to newcomers (like a barber's or a print shop).

"By happening to be hanging around in the library one day, I saw
how caringly the security guards comforted a rough sleeper
who was crying after being beaten up the night before. I was
therefore able to see nuance, that security can also provide
an infrastructure of care or kindness in informal ways"

"Sitting in the waiting room of the health clinic, estate agencies, shops,
hotels, and staff rooms: opening conversations with people in the waiting
room, talking with shopkeepers, and observing their interactions with
customers, sitting and drinking tea, and sometimes smoking with clinic
workers opened up conversations as well"

While ethnography implies spending a lot of time (often many months or years) making observations and learning about a place, many people do not have that amount of time when they are seeking to understand a certain aspect of society. However, it is still possible to have similar 'results' in a shorter time by systematically taking stock of what you already know. For example, think of your workplace as a learning environment. What do you see in your everyday life that teaches you about arrival, integration, and migration?

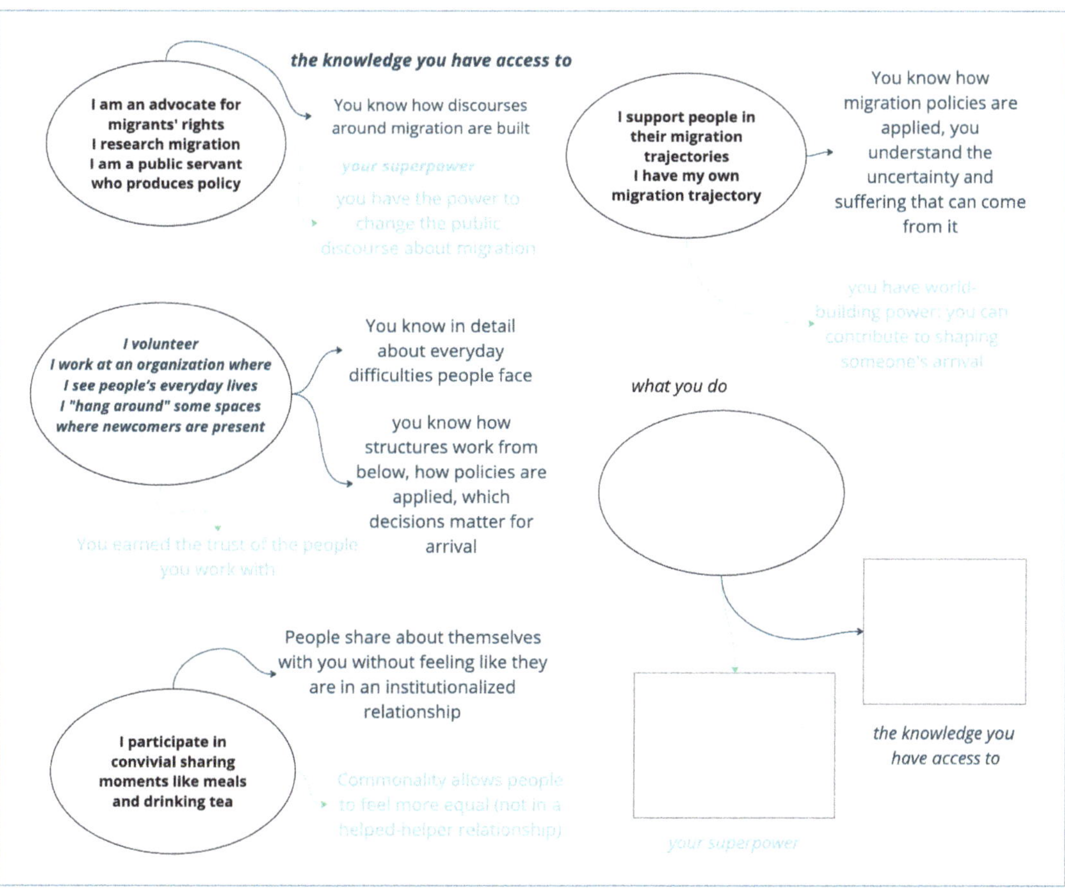

Figure 34. Diagram for evaluating your own infrastructuring work.

Reflection: In the diagram above, which we developed in a collective workshop with all our fieldwork researchers, every bubble represents a different role that people or organisations play when they are taking part in arrival infrastructuring. It shows what you can learn from the role you play at work, in your organising, or in your volunteering. Even just by being there, you are seeing and learning a lot.

Use this diagram to locate yourself in the wider arrival infrastructure in your context: in which bubble do you recognise yourself? Of course, it is possible that you play more than one role. Related to your role(s), the sketch shows what kind of knowledge you have access to by being in that position. You can add elements to the diagram by identifying other types of infrastructuring work that you do, or by identifying other types of knowledge to which you have access through your position.

Importantly, this exercise also helps you to see if taking on other roles (even temporarily) would allow you to glimpse another perspective than the one you usually see. For example, if you work in a municipal office and would like to know more, consider jumping to another circle, like volunteering for half a day at an organisation in the neighbourhood you serve.

While you 'hang around' and observe everyday interactions, it is important to be transparent about your intentions. Not only is it an ethical practice to disclose your objectives, but it also opens up new doors for you and gives legitimacy to your presence. When you are a recognised presence, people know who you are and are more comfortable sharing their own observations about the situation, especially on sensitive subjects such as migration, but they can also opt to not share if they do not want to.

B.   GETTING IN TOUCH WITH A DIVERSE SET OF STAKEHOLDERS

Observation alone is not enough to understand arrival infrastructuring work, as your gaze will always be limited. Bringing in the point of view of others is therefore very useful in completing yours.

First, connect to a diverse set of stakeholders. Look around you and evaluate who you have regular contact with. Who is missing from this group? Think of people whose stories you have read about in this Kit, like newcomers, social workers, policymakers, public servants, shop owners, activists, and others. Meet with those you do not usually have contact with to understand their point of view on the questions that interest you. Sometimes newcomers prefer to remain invisible. To still access their point of view, you can contact frontline workers who are in touch with them on a daily basis and are able to convey their lived experience to you. Remember that people are experts on their own lives, and that those who have a lived experience with certain issues will have insights you might not have heard before.

> "A big challenge for us was to find newcomers who would be willing to talk to us. My advice would be to search for local NGOs and previously established migrants [who could put you in touch with recent newcomers]. [In short] find the persons who are key stakeholders in the field. Language [barriers] and translation were a challenge too. Building trust is a challenge and with limited time – bringing a translator with you [from the beginning] is better"
>
> —RESEARCHER FROM THE KARDITSA/KATERINI SITE, DECEMBER 2023.

It is also important to connect with other organisations, whether similar or complementary to the one you work at. This allows you to learn from your peers in other organisations. You can achieve this by organising information meetings where you learn from each other, by volunteering at another organisation for a short period, or by shadowing someone whose work or life you are interested in. You can also check whether there are networks or regular meetings for people working in your domain (housing, food security, healthcare, etc.) or in the area you are working on (at the local scale, the regional scale, or the national scale). For coalition-building tips, read our story 'A network of organisations in a London borough: counteracting fragmentation in newcomer support' on p. 241 about the research-based action taken in London.

To identify people to engage with, you can use the diagram on p. 198. Identify the roles with which you are not familiar at all and consider talking to someone who is in that role, which will give you a more complete idea of arrival in your context. To join a network of peers, make a list of people who play a role similar to yours and check if those networks exist or initiate one.

When doing this, make sure you are aware of power relations within networks. Information is not shared in the same way with those who are equal to us and those who have power over us. When you are working with people who are marginalised or are counting on you to access a service, it is normal for them to choose what to share and what not to share. As far as possible, create spaces where horizontal relationships are welcomed and where hierarchical power relations are reduced. This means, for example, letting go of the model of charity and creating more mutual relationships of support and solidarity (see for example our story 'Volunteering in exchange for material support in Katerini: from charity to dignity and autonomy' on p. 135). In a more one-time gesture, you can create spaces of conviviality where everyone's culture is equal, rotating for example between different traditional meals or beverages that can be offered by people around the table.

"[We worked on] creating an environment where the other is not the other anymore, but we created somehow an equal relation, which makes it easier for the other to express and to activate [memories] to express themselves. Concretely that meant cooking together"

—RESEARCHER FROM THE THESSALONIKI SITE, DECEMBER 2023.

C. NURTURING AN OPEN AND PATIENT APPROACH

Learning new things requires an open mind: being willing to take on new perspectives, including ideas that contradict our pre-formed interpretation of the world. Some stories in this book might provoke some questioning of the knowledge you previously held. This is because our researchers also adopted this attitude of being ready to be surprised. To get a similar effect from your own endeavour to understand arrival, you have to be willing to go out of your comfort zone, follow leads even to a dead end, and be open to the unexpected.

> "Don't be too quick to think something will not be a good use of your time, because by doing it you may discover something unexpected"
>
> —RESEARCHER FROM THE LONDON SITE, DECEMBER 2023.

One of the prerequisites for being open to new discoveries is being conscious of the preconceived ideas you have about integration, migration, and newcomers. You can use tool 13 (p. 177) on labelling newcomers to remember the kinds of categorisations of newcomers that are often used in the public discourse. In general, once we confront these labels and prejudices with reality, they no longer hold up. So, what are the categories that are relevant to describe the situation around you?

"Look beyond the national categories of people, beyond ethnic boundaries and beyond certain categorisations of people as 'Hard working Poles', 'Eastern Europeans', 'Swift working women with soft hands', 'Freeloaders'. Understanding the different positions [of people] also requires time. There are specific vulnerabilities that are difficult to recognise and address [unless you take the time] to understand the different backgrounds and different needs [of people]. Start seeing migrant workers not as victims but [as having] creativity. Involve them in your programmes" (Researcher from the Haspengouw/Westland site, December 2023).

D. DEVELOPING REFLEXIVITY

Reflexivity is essential in any work, and even more in contexts of diversity, integration, and migration. By identifying your own position in society, your biases, your background, and your history, you can better identify your blind spots and act from a place of self-awareness, whether you are trying to understand a situation or taking action with others.

Reflecting on your own perspective

Yourself: When was the first time your encountered migration in your life? When was the first time you encountered migration or integration questions in your work? Did it change anything in the way you think about migration or integration? Do you (or your family) have a migration history? If so, how do you label yourself, and why? (See tool 13: ' Examining the labelling of newcomers'.) Have you identified any biases or judgements in the way you think about migration or integration? How did you work to change them? Did any story you read in this book surprise you?

Where you work: What is the purpose of the organisation in which you work? Which people are you reaching, and which are you not? Who is invisible to you? Who has power in the organisation you work in? Who do you have power over in your work?

The knowledge you have access to: Which information about newcomers, integration, and migration do you have access to? What is the source of that information? What are your potential blind spots and what information do you not have access to? Is there any way to get that information from elsewhere?

As newcomers working with newcomers

Reflecting on your own migration trajectory can be helpful in engaging deeply in the process of understanding other people's trajectories. You can use many of the tools in this book to explore your own migration history as a way to know yourself better.

Being a newcomer who works with newcomers means you have the added value of having gone through some of the experiences of the people you work with. However, it also means you have to be careful about projecting too much and identifying your story with others: this can lead you to both make assumptions and be vulnerable to difficult emotions in your work.

DOING INTEGRATION OTHERWISE

INTRODUCTION: TAKING ACTION

Part II 'Doing Integration Otherwise' reflects on our own contributions to 'doing integration otherwise' and aims to inspire you to take action yourself. There are various ways of 'doing otherwise', as demonstrated by the many people and organisations already engaging in the alternative infrastructuring practices discussed in Part I. You can also become part of this 'doing integration otherwise' and thus activate yourself.

Drawing from what we call 'platform-building' within our research trajectory, Part II of this Kit offers inspirational stories and tools to support you in making a meaningful contribution to 'integration otherwise'. ReROOT 'platforms' brought together arrival infrastructure stakeholders and served as spaces for initiating, facilitating, moderating, and supporting small yet impactful steps towards positive transformation of the arrival infrastructure.

Through the co-creation of platforms or the strengthening of existing platforms, we aimed to explore and support alternative ways of 'doing integration otherwise' and plant the seeds for long-term transformative approaches to integration that move beyond conventional organisational and institutional norms and routines. As such, 'platform-building' was a logical follow-up step to the ethnographic research conducted in the first phase that allowed us to see how integration is already being carried out otherwise on the ground.

Both the process of platform-building itself (co-voicing: overcoming fragmentation, navigating uncertainties, and seeking publicity) and its outcomes (becoming otherwise: transformative actions through infrastructuring work) were equally important. The platforms were designed as spaces where arrival infrastructure stakeholders could interact, reflect on their shared and diverse roles in arrival infrastructuring practices, explore potential interventions, and implement them.

Platform-building as a form of taking action is inherently contextual and cannot follow a one-size-fits-all approach. Instead, what we aim to do is to provide inspiration to develop and test tailored approaches for taking action. Setting up actions in your own context will therefore always require adapting formats to suit your specific site and focus area. This section details the nine platforms that emerged from ReROOT's platform-building experiences across different sites.

In the following, the platforms or actions are grouped into three chapters, each representing a common aim: awareness-raising, coalition-building, and empowering. While each platform arose from unique, layered processes, we hope that by nuancedly discussing their overarching objectives and the diverse methods used to realise them through stories, tools, and takeaways, we can inspire you to create new platforms in other contexts.

1. AWARENESS-RAISING

Actions can be set up to raise awareness about pressing migration and integration issues among a broader public. By publicly bringing together diverse local groups around specific topics, the ultimate goal is often to change narratives about migration and integration, put pressure on policymakers, and raise (public) awareness about newcomers' trajectories and situations.

Highlighting sensitive issues often involves addressing complex topics such as rights violations, claims for spaces, lack of resources, and the invisibility of these issues. When this is the case, the involvement of various people and organisations is crucial, and the methods of taking action can vary significantly depending on the local context.

The following stories offer various approaches from our own experiences. Some aim to bring specific groups of stakeholders together to build constructive dialogue, while others seek to reach as many people as possible. Some are more dialogical, while others aim to politicise more radically. In all cases, exposing these issues goes hand in hand with other objectives, such as giving a voice, co-creating, joining forces, and protesting.

EDUCATION
A public event in Nordstadt (Dortmund): raising awareness about school place shortages

In Nordstadt (Dortmund), our researchers, together with local stakeholders, chose to take action in the form of a public event to raise awareness about the shortage of school places, a significant issue affecting both local residents and migrant newcomers. The event featured 400 school chairs set up on a central square in the neighbourhood to symbolise the number of children without school places. The shortages are partly due to misunderstandings about the temporary nature of migration and has been exacerbated by recent arrivals from Ukraine. The event aimed to highlight the impact of this issue on families and to prompt discussions among stakeholders and policymakers about potential solutions.

Figure 35. 400 school chairs arranged in a public square to raise awareness about the lack of school places in Nordstadt.

Why put 400 chairs in a public square?

Since the so-called 'asylum crisis', the attention paid to arrival neighbourhoods has increased in Germany. The area of Nordstadt in Dortmund is known as an arrival neighbourhood, serving the entire region and beyond. On the one hand, it is recognised as a place where support structures and resources are concentrated. On the other hand, the public concern about its presumed attractiveness for newcomers makes the area and its infrastructures of interest to policymakers. As a result, arrival processes in Nordstadt are highly regulated through various initiatives – among them a municipal advice centre, integration agents, and the municipal integration policy entitled 'Overall Newcomer Strategy'.

Within this framework, newcomers face many challenges in Nordstadt: the maze of paperwork, the categorisation of migrant groups, and exploitative work and living arrangements. From these emerges a structural problem, also shared with local residents, that often has an amplified impact on migrant newcomers: the shortage of places in services for children and youngsters. The shortage of school places is, in the first place, a problem in itself. Approximately 400 children – a number that is constantly in flux – in Dortmund are not attending primary school because they do not have a place at a school. One of the reasons for the under-provision of school places is the incorrect assumption about the temporary nature of migration processes that was made during the school development planning process, further exacerbated by the arrival of people from Ukraine in 2023. For a long time, it was assumed that migration flows from Romania and Bulgaria would be only temporary. However, since 2012, Nordstadt, as a well-established arrival neighbourhood, has faced continuous arrivals.

The high pressure on the school system leads to opaque allocation practices that often go around the official waiting list system, resulting in particular in the exclusion of the most vulnerable groups. School place shortages have a further problematic implication: schools are important anchor points in arrival neighbourhoods as they mediate access to other resources and support services, for example by offering advice about paperwork. This leads to exclusion not only from education itself but also from the additional resources and support services that schools provide or mediate for migrant families. It further jeopardises the chances of education and social mobility for the children excluded from school. The city of Dortmund is putting in place some strategies to combat this, among them a bus service, a project to reuse old school buildings, and a building programme for schools and childcare.

Despite the seriousness of this structural gap in the educational service supply, there has been relatively limited media coverage of the issue. The significance of the shortage of school places, its impact on newcomers' families, and its absence from the public debate formed our main starting points for taking action. With the aim of raising awareness of these topics, we organised a public event where 400 school chairs were set up on a central square in Nordstadt.

Organising the public event: the tricky process of identifying stakeholders and getting them involved.

The main objective of our action was to raise awareness about the issue of school place shortages. Further aims were to bring together stakeholders affected by the issue, make the stories of the affected families visible, and show appreciation for those stakeholders dealing with the issue in their daily work. The idea of setting up chairs on a central square and using a visual performance to highlight the issue arose quite spontaneously and early on in the process. Immediately afterwards, it became important to identify which other stakeholders should be involved and how, and to ensure effective media coverage of the event.

We engaged with different groups as collaborators and/or participants. Those who collaborated in the event's organisation and realisation were service providers and stakeholders already involved in infrastructuring work. These stakeholders can be divided into two groups. The first group represented those confronted with and making an effort to tackle the gap in school provision in their daily work, for example teachers and social workers. The second group involved collaborators from the administrative realm, for instance public servants, the school authority, the youth welfare service authority, and related departments. They supported the event by providing the school chairs, giving a speech, creating posters and installations, being present with a booth, serving food, approaching families and children for participation, sharing information about and the announcement of the event (e.g. on social media), and organising a march to the square on the day of the event. We invited policymakers and local politicians to attend the event. Journalists also had an active part in the media coverage. Participants included schoolchildren and their families – the action in particular intended to target those experiencing and affected by the school shortage. Further participants on the event day were passers-by, students, families and children, scholars, teachers, and social workers who were not directly involved.

Given the objective of the action and the variety of stakeholders involved, a crucial element of the process was to plan an effective way of approaching each group. We first reached out to grassroots organisations, informing them about the ambition of the event. To involve institutional stakeholders, it was important to respect institutional hierarchies to ensure we were approaching the authorities properly. Institutional hierarchies are not always evident from the outside and therefore we developed the practice of asking potential institutional participants whether another department or official should be included first, or whether we were unknowingly leaving anyone out who should be approached.

Producing a draft description of the intervention in the early planning stages was very helpful both to focus and agree on its aims internally and to start approaching potential stakeholders. The idea was initially discussed informally with a limited number of potential stakeholders to get an impression of its feasibility. Next, we set up and chaired two preparatory meetings which served to bring potential stakeholders together and gather ideas for the action in a flexible online format. At this stage, it proved essential to balance co-creation by the cooperation partners and stick to a coherent programme on the day of the event. On the one hand, it was crucial to include stakeholders' ideas in planning the action. People doing important arrival infrastructuring work in Nordstadt were invited to set up booths where they could create posters with messages and put on activities for children. On the other hand, it was also important to ensure the coherence of the programme and thus clearly communicate this need to co-creators. This meant that some proposals were declined if they distracted from the main message of the event.

The main event took place at Nordmarkt, a central square in Nordstadt. In the morning, the booths were set up, followed by the 400 chairs. Children enrolled in the nearby school each brought their own chair, which gave teachers the occasion to talk to them about migration, integration, and school place shortages. Speeches given by the chairman of the working group for child- and youth-related services, a local service provider, and the district mayor pointed to the shortages in child- and youth-related infrastructures and their consequences.

The speeches were followed by informal gatherings on the square and visitors touring the booths of social organisations presenting their work, before people gathered again for a Q&A with the mayor of Dortmund. Press and media were invited to the event so that it could reach a wider audience.

Media coverage was a key aspect from the beginning of the process. The documentation of the event was later used to produce two videos, one for an academic audience and the other for a broader public. The production of convincing visual materials proved particularly effective to further shed light on the topic of school place shortages.

Figure 36. Local media coverage of the Nordstadt school chairs action.

Challenges and ethical concerns

We tried to raise awareness about a critical topic while also setting the scene for a constructive dialogue among diverse stakeholders. This highlighted an important ethical issue related to how our different personal and professional backgrounds have an influence on our perspectives and capacity for engagement. The topic of school place shortages has political implications that have to be carefully addressed, both to ensure the involvement of political stakeholders and to facilitate the participation of organisations that often depend on public funds. In this sense, an explicit choice was made to avoid finger-pointing towards political stakeholders and to opt for a 'neutral' way of addressing the topic of school place shortages. For instance, the project description and the flyer reflected this policy and was carefully reviewed by representatives of the city council to ensure the facts were presented neutrally, for example the number of missing school places. This rendered the involvement of policymakers less politically charged and, in particular, it enabled 'street-level bureaucrats' (see concept box 4 on p. 57) from state-run organisations (such as schools or childcare facilities) to participate in the event. Explicit finger-pointing could have placed the organisers and participants in an awkward position in relation to their employers. Such choices, however, remain controversial. It could be argued that reducing the political nature of the event permits the curtailing of political responsibilities. It is difficult to assess what approach would have been more beneficial from a long-term perspective, but it was our choice to follow a constructive path.

Further ethical concerns involved the impossibility of fully foreseeing what smaller actions the event would evoke, as well as their consequences. In an open public event, the way the topic was taken up and discussed could hardly be predicted. For instance, when interacting with families, the mayor asked to collect the names of those who did not have a school place and later provided one to them. This move could lead to a misleading interpretation of the problem: it could give the impression that the dimension of the problem was not structural, and this choice offered a solution to some but of course left out all those families who were not at the event. Similarly, the extent of exposure of the participants had to be carefully considered: can you give a voice to newcomers without risking their overexposure?

The main obstacles to implementing this event related to the inability to ensure the participation of some stakeholders. Some decision- and policymakers, despite declaring their support, did not participate in the initiative. In one case, the reason for not taking part was due to explicit pressure from within the participant's institution. It was also very hard to involve policymakers from supra-local levels. Local organisations could not always guarantee their presence, often because of their intense workload. This was the case for employees of childcare facilities, for example. Likewise, the primary school that eventually provided the chairs for the event faced uncertainty during the planning phase, due to scheduling, hierarchical, and practical issues. It was therefore crucial for the organisers to consider how to plan an event with minimum impact on the school's activities and schedule.

In retrospect, feedback after the event showed that some stakeholders did not feel sufficiently involved, even though the organisational team believed that they had actually reached them via the relevant networks and key stakeholders as multipliers. More direct contact and communication would therefore have been more effective in some cases. Finally, practical legal requirements were important points of attention in the overall organisation of the event, for example permission to have a drone flying on the day of the event, permissions to occupy the square, and data protection in the visual material.

Reflections on the transformative potential of the action

The event succeeded in raising awareness on multiple levels. The Dortmund City Council was made a little 'more' aware of the issue and was triggered to reflect upon its role in finding alternatives. The entire process, from designing a project description and flyer to shaping the event, prompted discussions about the scope of the school place shortages and possible solutions. Interestingly, in the political and scientific debate, the event also helped to revisit previous unfinished engagements with the topic, such as a discussion paper. Finally, the effective media coverage ensured that the public discussion continued even after the event on the square itself. Pictures from the event have been used as visual material in reports addressing the under-provision of school places.

TAKEAWAYS

Being aware of the different sensitivities of stakeholders helps keep everyone on board when planning and taking your action.

Gradually engaging local stakeholders optimises their contributions and respects mutual relationships.

Co-creation with partners should be balanced with the action's objectives to ensure coherence, as not all ideas can be realised.

Time and energy are limited resources for local stakeholders, and a lack of these often prevents their participation.

Effective media coverage can prolong the public discussion.

> For other stories from the Nordstadt site, see:

p. 61, Easing access to school in Nordstadt (Dortmund): identifying barriers and overcoming assumptions

p. 106, Mediating between Roma parents and teachers in Nordstadt (Dortmund): overcoming mistrust in public authorities through translation work

p. 153, Housing support for newcomers in Nordstadt: addressing housing exploitation, instability, and discrimination

> Further reading: In this story we refer to the 'Overall Newcomer Strategy' of the City of Dortmund. To explore this more, see: Stadt Dortmund. 2023. *Entwicklung Handlungsrahmen Neuzuwanderung 2021–2022*. Unpublished document.

> To view the video produced by our researchers documenting the event, use the following link: https://vimeo.com/838235191.

TOOL 14
DEVELOPING A ROADMAP FOR STAKEHOLDER INVOLVEMENT

MATERIALS: Paper, sticky notes, writing utensils.

TOOL SUMMARY: This tool guides you in strategizing your approach to involving stakeholders in an action plan. It involves identifying key people, organisations, and institutions, choosing essential allies, recognising multipliers, and pinpointing crucial organisations. This tool ensures a structured and inclusive approach to stakeholder engagement, enhancing the effectiveness of the action.

Taking action almost always implies 'seeking allies'. However, the diversity and number of stakeholders to be involved can vary a lot. No matter how 'allies' are selected, making a plan for approaching them is a key point. This tool presents a strategy for approaching and involving potential stakeholders.

STEP 1: Identify people to involve

Make a list of people and organisations you would like to involve. Write each name on a sticky notes. Include everyone that comes to mind, without thinking of the next steps. What you are now doing is in fact developing what is called a 'stakeholder mapping'.

In Dortmund, on the topic of the shortage of school places, the organising team wanted to involve (in no particular order): youth organisations, migrant families experiencing this issue, the mayor, the schools in the district, etc.

STEP 2: Chose key stakeholders: the ones that are essential to co-organising your action

Looking at your list, identify who you can involve from the beginning, before your idea is fully formed. It can be a good idea to invite these key stakeholders to co-construct the idea and the plan for the action. These key people can also refer you to other people who might want to be involved, for example organisations that are doing similar work that you did not know about.

In Dortmund, the team already had a network of civil society organisations who they knew would be interested. They invited them to present the idea and refine it collectively.

In your list of potential stakeholders, some people are particularly well positioned to spread the word to other organisations that might want to join. It is a great way to widen the base of organisers and supporters for your action.

> In Dortmund, one representative from one of the schools served as a 'multiplier', as she could reach and involve a broader network of people, who were therefore contacted through her.

STEP 4: Identify crucial organisations

Looking at your list again, identify organisations or people who are not yet a stakeholder, but are important for your action, either because they are essential for the event to happen or because you want to reach them with your action. What could be a strategy to involve them? How can you cater the message to them?

> In Dortmund, it was particularly important to make sure a local school would provide the chairs, and that the municipality would provide a permit for the action. As for policymakers, once the team had support from the ground and the event was going to be a success anyway, they were invited and were only faced with the choice of attending the event or not.

STEP 5: Decide on the order in which to involve stakeholders

Once you have a list of all the stakeholders you would like to involve and have identified the role(s) each of them can play, you can use sticky notes to discuss the order for involving them.

The sticky notes allow you to shift them around the work if needed, and identify new stakeholders to add through discussions with those you already contacted.

> In Dortmund, it was also crucial to follow institutional hierarchies to avoid tensions: contacting the school authority meant also contacting the mayor beforehand to reduce potential discord. At the same time, making sure to contact all the members of a group or network was also important.

REFLECTION

This tool shows how a structured approach to involving potential stakeholders is crucial for the success of any action plan. By systematically identifying and engaging key stakeholders, multipliers, and crucial organisations, the tool helps build a comprehensive and inclusive strategy. This method not only broadens the base of support but also enhances the effectiveness and sustainability of the action. The example from Dortmund highlights the importance of strategic and flexible planning and collaboration, to allow for meaningful engagements within the parameters stakeholders can practically operate.

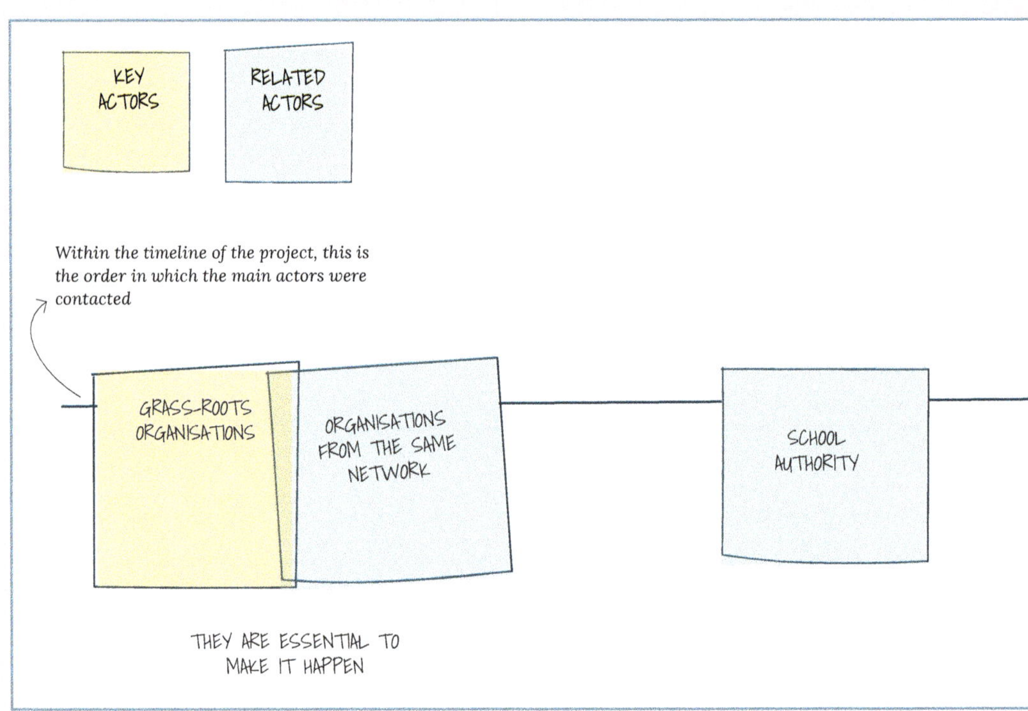

Figure 37. Diagram for developing a roadmap for stakeholder involvement.

CONTACT THE MAYOR BEFORE INVITING ANY POLICY MAKERS OUT OF RESPECT
FOR HIERARCHIES WITHIN THE MUNICIPALITY

PRIMARY
SCHOOLS

MAYOR

POLICY-MAKERS

TOOL 15
PREPARING YOURSELF FOR MEDIA COVERAGE

MATERIALS: Paper, writing utensils, computer for more in-depth engagement.

TOOL SUMMARY: This tool gives you practical tips for gaining accurate press coverage of awareness-raising events related to arrival, integration, and migration. It involves preparing a clear message, documenting the event through photos and videos, and strategically disseminating this information to the media and on social media platforms. This tool helps maintain control over the narrative and supports ongoing discussions and collaborations.

Working on arrival, integration, and migration carries the risk of being represented in unexpected, negative, or harmful ways in public discourse and in the media. To minimise these risks, it is essential to prepare your message in advance and have a strategy for the production and dissemination of the material documenting your event and its purpose.

Here are some steps you can follow:

STEP 1: Preparing your message

Before the event: Choose one key message you want to communicate, write a press release, gather images that are relevant.

> Choose your tone carefully: an objective tone or a more activist one will each achieve different results.

During the event: Make sure there is someone who is taking pictures, recording a video, and taking notes of impactful quotes. This material will be useful for later communication, beyond the specific instance of the action. This documentation can also serve as material for further discussion, and can be used to build new collaborations.

STEP 2: Disseminating your message

Contact journalists: Think strategically about which journalists you want to contact. You can contact journalists before or after the event, either to invite them or to let them know the event took place. When you contact them, you can also send the key points or press release to them.

Assign someone to be your media contact point who knows the key points to be communicated, and make sure all co-organisers know who they are.

Use social media: You can disseminate your message yourself through different social media channels, using meaningful keywords and hashtags to make your post findable. Make sure your post is catchy.

STEP 3: Keep an archive of your event (optional)

Save screenshots or download articles, news reports, and other media coverage of your event.

Gather all pictures, videos, and other documentation you made yourself and keep them together in a place you can find them when you need them in the future.

In Dortmund, great care was put into collecting images and producing videos of the chairs event. This allowed the discussion to continue after the one-day action. Not only was this documentation used to talk about the event itself, but it was also picked up by the media to report on the shortage of school places in general.

REFLECTION

Preparing for media coverage is essential for accurate representation of awareness-raising events related to arrival, integration, and migration. By crafting a clear message and strategically documenting and disseminating information, organisers have a better chance of maintaining control over the narrative. This tool not only helps in gaining media attention but also supports ongoing discussions and collaborations. The example from Dortmund illustrates how thorough documentation can extend the impact of an event beyond its immediate occurrence.

> SEE ALSO TOOL 21: 'Unsettle to attract media attention' (p. 238).

A website, seminar, and public discussion on social housing for migrant workers in Paris: different formats for exposing evictions and triggering public confrontation

This story is about the actions carried out by our researcher to address the struggle of residents in the Boulogne Foyer, a social housing project for migrant workers in Paris, who were facing eviction due to renovation plans. Together with *foyer* residents and local activists, our researcher initiated actions to raise awareness of the value and precarity of *foyers* in Paris. This story details our approach to reaching the broader community and policymakers through a website, seminars, and public debates. We reflect on best practices and significant challenges, including lack of support from neighbours and barriers to participation. Ultimately, the initiatives were able to shed light on the importance of *foyers* and advocate for the rights of their inhabitants.

The Boulogne Foyer's 'bad reputation' as a starting point for action

Foyers are a type of collective housing set up in the 1950s to host migrant workers arriving in France from its West African colonies. Today, *foyers* are an important part of the Parisian arrival infrastructure. They provide unique spaces for established and recently arrived newcomers to come together, to share resources and tips for navigating the French arrival situation, and to form essential relationships in a new place. Despite the value of the *foyers,* the French state is currently renovating them into more standardised social housing based on individual units in an attempt to open them up to a wider population, beyond newcomers and older arrivals from West Africa. In the face of a prevailing assimilation model of integration, *foyers* are often stigmatised as being 'closed communities' that host 'communal practices' such as Islamic prayer rooms or the transfer of residences between family members. This 'bad reputation' often isolates these facilities from the neighbourhoods where they are located. Consequently, many Parisians lack insight into the essential role these places are playing. This lack of knowledge also makes it difficult to build coalitions to mobilise against problems faced by inhabitants as a result of the renovations.

This is the case in the Boulogne Foyer, located in a suburb of Paris, where residents are facing mass eviction because of the renovation plans to transform the *foyer* with its collective facilities into standardised social housing. The renovation-related evictions triggered a conflict in 2016 with the building manager responsible for dismantling the collective kitchen. These collective kitchens are used by residents to cook when their rooms lack cooking equipment, which is common in the *foyers.* In addition, they are important social spaces where residents pass time, share meals, and build new relationships. To protest the removal of the collective kitchen, the residents started a rent strike, which led to the accumulation of a rent debt. In 2018, due to financial difficulties, the Foyer was sold and the residents continued their strike. The new management, looking to diversify its clientele, took legal action against the residents for not paying rent and won. As a result, 118 people received an eviction order. At the time, the only ones protesting against this situation were the residents themselves and some activists, whereas a larger mobilisation would have strengthened their position in the process. As for many *foyers*, residents of the Boulogne Foyer suffered from a lack of interest and encountered hostility from the surrounding neighbourhood. Neighbours' support would have been helpful for opening a dialogue with the municipality and securing access to the only form of housing *foyer* residents can afford.

To address this, we collaborated with *foyer* residents and a local activist group 'COllectif Pour l'Avenir des Foyers' (shortly COPAF, translated as 'collective for the future of the *foyers*') to devise an action to give visibility to the *foyers* and raise awareness of the precarious situation of many residents. Our strategy involved creating virtual and physical spaces to reach out and get in touch with a wider public about the *foyers*. We chose to highlight the Boulogne Foyer to illustrate broader issues because of our long-standing relationships with the residents, the management, and COPAF.

Multiple formats to reach different audiences: a website, a seminar, and a public debate

The planning phase

The main goal of our action was to highlight the issue and initiate a dialogue with a broader audience, laying the groundwork for future, larger-scale mobilisation. We aimed to tell the story of the *foyers*, contextualise the current controversy through a historical lens, and create spaces for constructive debate and reflection on similar housing issues. COPAF provided essential expertise and contacts, including those of residents, which were crucial for planning and smooth collaboration. Together with COPAF activists, we organised an initial event to invite inhabitants, scholars, and residents to discuss the history and future of the *foyer*. The biggest challenge we faced while planning our actions was involving new audiences and opening a dialogue with people unfamiliar with the topic. To address this challenge, we organised multiple types of actions to reach more diverse audiences and unpack the complexity of the issue in a format appropriate for the chosen audiences. Taking action ultimately involved creating a website, organising a seminar at the national parliament, and hosting a public discussion and book presentation near the *foyer*.

A website

The website is an online platform where the history of the Boulogne Foyer is presented, contextualising its tensions from the 1960s to today alongside the development of migration, integration, and housing policies in France. As we wanted to cater both to journalists and scholars and to local neighbours of the Boulogne Foyer, the design of the website is intentionally multi-layered while at the same time being user-friendly. The history is represented through a timeline show-ing material collected from archives and previous academic research. The user can choose to engage to the extent they are comfortable with or keep scrolling through the history. The most challenging component of putting together the website was presenting one coherent narrative that gathered together all the sub-narratives involved in the Boulogne Foyer's history.

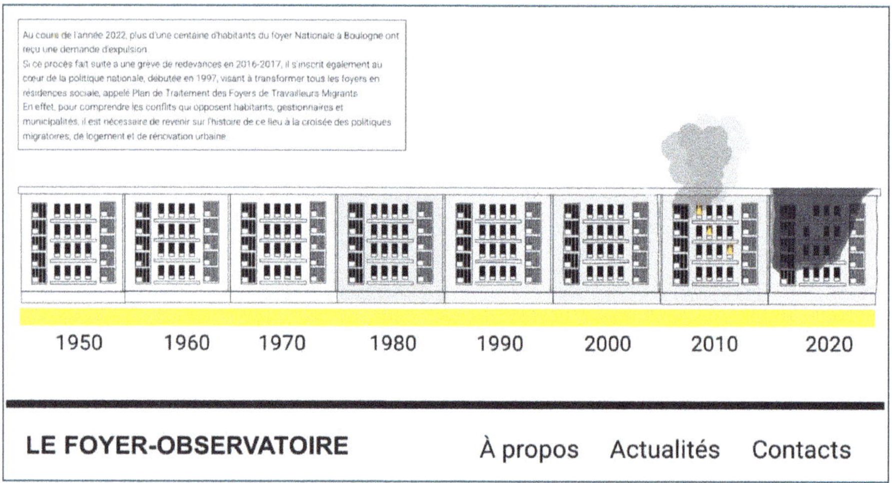

Figure 38. A website documenting the history and current events of the Boulogne Foyer

A seminar

To discuss the condition and struggles of the *foyers* in political circles, the second initiative involved the organisation of a seminar at the National Parliament, entitled 'Private life, collective life and representation: exploring the housing rights of *foyer* residents. In this case, the existing ties with civil society experts, *foyer* residents, and political stakeholders were key to a successful event. The seminar intended to address legal propositions on housing and living conditions for migrants. In this action, the event was not focused on the single case of the Boulogne Foyer, but rather on the general legal framework surrounding the *foyers*, with a specific emphasis on actions policymakers and elected officials can take going forward.

We organised the seminar around three roundtables following a short introduc-tion. Each roundtable included a representative of all the stakeholders involved: residents, activists, researchers, and a French elected representative. Interestingly, more than 150 *foyer* residents were present and contributed to the debate. Many of them took the opportunity of being able to express themselves in front of pol-icymakers to tell their stories of eviction, marginalisation, and injustice. The three roundtables concluded with a debate on a proposal to improve the everyday life in the *foyers*, according to residents and activists, and the role of social mobilisa-tion in the *foyers'* current transformations.

A public debate

The third action was a public discussion on institutional evictions in the neighbourhood of the Boulogne Foyer, framed around the launch of the book *Willingly and Not: How the State Evicts the Poor* (2023, in French) by scholar Camille François. The aim of this action was to highlight the similarities of the problems in the *foyers* with broader housing issues, within a less politicised – and hopefully more inclusive – setting. Organised jointly with the invited scholar François, local activists, and residents of the Boulogne Foyer, this debate was intended to open a common ground for a dialogue with neighbours and was therefore meant to be held near the Foyer in a 'neutral' place, around the book presentation. This event was more difficult to organise. The local bookshop where we initially intended to host the event did not agree to participate. In the end, it was held at a local café. More importantly, while there was an initial concern about the risk of attracting hostile audiences due to the sensitive nature of the topic, the real obstacle was that neighbours did not take part despite the many flyers that had been distributed. All three actions were followed by reflective moments shared by the core organising group to discuss success and failures.

Challenges and ethical concerns: representation

While working with diverse stakeholders to shed light on the *foyers* and their residents' struggles, our central concern was representation: all stakeholders were to have a voice in the discussions. To break this down, we have divided the challenges of representation into four sections: *foyer* residents, undocumented populations, language barriers, and the involvement and participation of neighbours.

Foyer residents

To ensure our actions were based on the needs of the *foyer* residents, it was essential they take part in every step of the process and that the diverse stakeholders had a place in the various events. The representation of residents was ensured through the involvement of some residents who were elected to represent the *foyers*. The election process itself took significant time during the collective discussions and organisation, in particular for the seminar. One retired *foyer* manager also took part in a roundtable.

Seeking a voice for undocumented *foyer* residents

Concerns about representation also included the question of how to represent those who cannot participate. Undocumented people are not allowed to access the National Parliament, as it is a requirement to show a valid ID and residence permit at the entrance. This prevented undocumented *foyer* residents from taking part in the seminar. To work around this issue, a migrant who had recently obtained a residence permit and was very active in the collective mobilisation of undocumented people was invited to speak. The question remained whether this effectively addressed the experiences of all those unable to attend.

Language as a barrier to representation

A third point on representation concerned the language barrier. In the public debate, many inhabitants – despite their participation in the preparation of the event – refused to speak in public. This episode triggered a reflection on inclusivity and on the need to consider all barriers to participation, both in the planning phase and in the implementation of the event.

Representation of neighbourhood residents

The main obstacle throughout the process was linked to the involvement and missed participation of some groups, especially neighbours of the Boulogne Foyer. Since the early phases, they were a main target group and had therefore been invited to take part in the events. Because of the potential of this topic to polarise audiences, we took specific steps to formulate the events in a non-polarising and non-political manner. This was especially the case for the invitation to the book launch in Boulogne. However, our efforts were not enough to bring them to the table. It was even difficult to secure a space to organise that launch, as the local bookstore's owner avoided the requests of the organising team without explanation. Interestingly, in other *foyer* contexts in Paris – often working-class neighbourhoods – neighbours proved to be much more supportive of the *foyers'* struggle. It was never made clear to us why the neighbours of the Boulogne Foyer did not attend or show more interest in events concerning the Foyer.

Figure 39. Flyer for the launch of Camille François' book *Willingly and Not: How the State Evicts the Poor* which addresses the eviction of the *foyers*, put on as part of the Paris site action

Reflections on the transformative potential of the action

The main aim of the action was to shed light on the condition of *foyers* in Paris. The creation of the website, the seminar at the National Parliament, and the public debate achieved this objective and in fact exposed the issue of the *foyers* by attracting the attention of policymakers and journalists. Indeed, several articles were published afterwards. Interestingly, this action had some further effects. On the one hand, it opened spaces where *foyer* inhabitants could have a voice, by participating in and co-creating the narrative on the *foyers*, as well as by co-organising and taking part in the seminar and public debate. On the other hand, it also tried to lay the groundwork for new coalitions for future strategic actions supporting the *foyer* cause. Likewise, reaching new audiences was a main aim, in order to both share insights with new audiences and get them involved in support of the *foyers*.

TAKEAWAYS

\# Local allies are invaluable when taking action. They bring first-hand knowledge, experience, and contacts, which can be crucial for understanding and addressing local struggles.

\# Direct representation of large groups is often not possible; working with smaller groups of delegates helps to remain inclusive.

\# Different audiences absorb information in various ways. Tailoring your approach and adapting communication formats to suit diverse groups can enhance engagement and impact.

> For other stories from the Paris site, see:

p. 92, Building managers in Parisian social housing: balancing hierarchical pressures and on-the-ground needs

p. 124, Sudanese restaurants in Paris: sharing knowledge among co-nationals and beyond

p. 159, Passing down one's room in Parisian social housing: claiming space in a rigid institutional housing system

> Further reading: The book that was launched as part of the awareness-raising action in Paris: François, Camille. 2023. *De gré et de force: Comment l'État expulse les pauvres* [Willingly and Not: How the State Evicts the Poor]. Paris: La Découverte.

> For a more in-depth reading on the role of *foyers* in Paris, see: Mbodj-Pouye, Aïssatou. 2023. *An Address in Paris*. New York: Columbia University Press.

TOOL 16
FINDING THE RIGHT ACTION FORMAT FOR EACH AUDIENCE

MATERIALS: Paper, writing utensils.

TOOL SUMMARY: This tool emphasises the importance of tailoring the format of activities to suit different audiences when addressing sensitive topics. It involves identifying the goal, listing potential activities, and determining the target audience for each activity, taking into consideration their interests and how best to engage them. Examples include creating an accessible website for journalists and scholars, organising policy meetings for lawmakers, and hosting a book launch to engage local residents and *foyer* residents.

Shedding light on a certain topic or situation may involve addressing issues that are uncomfortable for some stakeholders and, at the same time, may involve many different audiences. In this sense, the best way to involve each stakeholder may vary signficantly: in some cases, assuming a political or activist perspective could be productive, in others counter-productive. Some people may be interested in knowing more, others in giving their own opinion on the topic. When planning action in such cases, including multiple events in varied formats can be a great way to reach different types of audiences.

STEP 1: Identify your goal.

STEP 2: Make a list of activities you could organise to achieve that goal.

STEP 3: For each activity, identify the people who might be interested by that activity. To further your reflection, you can consider: What would it achieve for this audience to participate in this activity? Why would they be interested? How can I cater the activity to that specific audience?

In Paris for example:

Goal: to shed light on the situation in the *foyers* and ongoing evictions

Possible activities	People who might be interested	Reflections
Publish a website sharing the knowledge we have about *foyers*: it should be an easy-to-navigate website where people can access the archival history of one *foyer* as an example, with current news about the *foyers*.	Journalists Scholars Researchers University students Interested urban dwellers	The information on the website should be clear and accessible for those who have little time to go in depth. At the same time, we could add references and 'further reading' for students or scholars who have more time to go in depth.
A policy meeting with a number of experts. In addition, a partner organisation can prepare and print a law proposal ready to be picked up by any MP who would like to present it for adoption. We can also use this opportunity to bring in *foyer* residents as experts of their own lives and give them a tribune.	Policymakers Members of Parliament	Some policymakers expressed interest in the opinions of experts on the subject, so this can be an occasion to give multiple voices a tribune for expression. In addition, we can organise this policy meeting at the Parliament so that MPs can pass by whenever they have time. We can also contact their political team, who will have more time to sit through a whole day of discussions.
A sociology book launch at a local café followed by a public debate.	Local neighbours in Boulogne Scholars	Neighbours of the Boulogne Foyer have a strong bias against the Foyer, and do not want to engage much in a conversation about it. A book launch about evictions in general is a good attempt at engaging them from another point of view.

Figure 40. Diagram for identifying the right activities for the right audiences in the Paris research site.

REFLECTION

Tailoring activities to suit different audiences is useful for effectively addressing sensitive topics. By identifying the goal and customising the format of each activity, organisers can engage diverse groups in meaningful ways. This approach ensures that each audience's interests and perspectives are considered, enhancing the overall impact of the action. The examples from Paris demonstrate how varied formats can successfully reach and involve different stakeholders, fostering a more inclusive and productive dialogue.

TOOL 17
STORYTELLING AS A TOOL TO ILLUSTRATE BROADER ISSUES

MATERIALS: Paper, writing utensils.

TOOL SUMMARY: This tool allows you to experiment with using storytelling to address broad and structural issues by selecting a concrete example that illustrates a larger picture. This approach humanises the issue at hand, showing its impact on individuals, and helps identify and mobilise those involved in disseminating the story. The process involves identifying potential stories in your field, selecting the most relevant example, constructing a digestible narrative, and ensuring all necessary permissions and materials are in place to effectively tell the story.

Taking action often involves tackling wide and structural problems. Often it is difficult to paint a good picture of the impact of these structural problems in a concise way. However, a concrete example can be selected to sketch the broader picture. The example does not have to be representative of all situations, but it should have plenty of rich details that can be explored to understand different elements of the structural issue at stake. It allows organisers to humanise the subject by showing how it affects people concretely. Going into more depth on one story, rather than many superficial stories, also allows for the identification and mobilisation of those who should be involved in disseminating that story.

To identify the right example for broader illustration, follow the steps below.

STEP 1: Identify a few examples

For this, you can start by working intuitively: Which stories are the first ones that comes to mind? Which ones do you most often think of? Which stories represent the issue most convincingly?

STEP 2: Select your example

You can finalise your selection by asking a series of questions, such as:

- What are the main structural elements I want to talk about? Are they all present in the one example I am thinking of?
- Which elements are the most relevant for my audience's area of influence? Am I allowed to tell that story? Should I ask for the consent of anyone?
- Do I have enough material to talk about? Do I need to gather more information or pictures?

You can add more questions and criteria that are meaningful to your context.

> The case of the action in Paris is a clear example: the team meant to shed light on the conditions of *foyers* in general, but producing useful, cohesive information on all of them would have been very hard. Instead, focusing on the Boulogne Foyer allowed them to embed the action in existing networks of activists and residents and to produce detailed information on its story. Interestingly, a comparison with other *foyers* was also carried out and proved very helpful to contextualise it in the broader picture.

REFLECTION

Storytelling is a powerful method for addressing broad and structural issues. By selecting a concrete example, this tool humanises the issue, making it more relatable and impactful. It also facilitates the identification and mobilisation of key individuals who can help disseminate the story. The example from Paris underscores how focusing on a specific case can effectively illustrate larger systemic problems, fostering deeper understanding and engagement.

A participatory exhibition on agricultural labour in Westland and Haspengouw: facilitating conversations and changing narratives

> This story is about a collaboratively produced exhibition in the regions of Westland and Haspengouw, two areas highly reliant on agriculture and migrant labour. The exhibition was created by our researcher to change the narrative around migrant labour by showcasing migrants' contributions and fostering community dialogue. Despite challenges, this action highlighted the importance of migrant workers to local agricultural heritage and encouraged a shift in public perception.

Disconnectedness, invisibility, and unsustainability of migrant seasonal labourers: the entry points for action

The regions of Westland in the Netherlands and Haspengouw in Belgium rely heavily on agriculture and migrant labour for both their economy and cultural identity. Westland is known for its greenhouse farming of vegetables, plants, and flowers, while Haspengouw focuses on growing fruits like apples, pears, and strawberries. In these regions, the way migrant presence and labour are managed directly relates to worker isolation, invisibility, and exclusion from local resources. Temporary work and housing conditions, along with dominant ideas about how migrants should fit in and the placement of migrant workers in disparate locations, all contribute to making agricultural migrant work less visible. This also means there is a lack of proper support and access to essential services like healthcare, community support, and other resources beyond just providing jobs.

Policies and public opinions about migrant labour are divided: some believe no integration is needed as the workers are temporary, while others argue that migrants should be seen as well-integrated and long-term residents. When specific integration policies are implemented locally, they are conditional on the length of stay, intention to settle, official registration, and general 'deservingness'. Despite these challenges, migrant workers find innovative ways to stay or return for longer intervals, form social connections, and integrate in small ways within their work and living environments. This creates a local ecosystem where migrant workers are not fully accepted and sometimes face resistance, especially regarding how they arrive and their housing arrangements.

In the face of these conditions, we chose to focus our action on changing local labour migration narratives, to get residents and other stakeholders together without falling into the same polarising discussions. Our approach drew inspiration from sociologist Nirmal Puwar, who conducted a postcolonial intervention known as "Noise of the Past" in a church in Coventry. While Puwar used curation to interrupt narratives of war and death, our exhibition aimed to disrupt the commonly accepted and somewhat romanticised narrative of agriculture and agricultural heritage, in which migrant workers, despite their long-established presence and current contributions, often go unnoticed.

Co-creating and discussing new narratives: a multifaceted exhibition

The objective of our action was to encourage people to think differently about labour migration by discussing with key stakeholders the ways in which migrant workers are already integrated into both Haspengouw and Westland, without reverting to a reactionary debate about exploitation. This led to the concrete idea of co-creating an exhibition showcasing both new and traditional agricultural rituals and practices from farmers in Romania and Moldova, as well as from Central and Eastern European (CEE) migrant workers in the Netherlands and Belgium. We drew inspiration from agricultural rituals, particularly the annual blessing ritual in Haspengouw, where various religious and local dignitaries participate in a ceremony to bless the fruit trees' blossoms. This event serves as both a celebration of local agricultural heritage and a vital aspect of the regional fruit horticulture's tourist appeal. However, the other side of this story – the role of global export, industrialisation, and foreign workers in enabling local fruit farming success – is completely overlooked.

The idea of agricultural heritage in relation to the history and role of migration became a central topic for the exhibition, especially because heritage has the potential to be shared. What would happen if we contrasted this blessing with similar rituals from the countries migrant workers originate from? What if, by collaboratively creating an exhibition with migrant workers, we could introduce 'new rituals' from the fields into the existing important moments for agricultural heritage? What if we introduced stories, languages, and bodies into the small church where the blossom blessing occurs that are not typically present?

The planning phase

Taking action developed into a collaborative and co-creative process. It involved multiple events and actions of a rather performative nature. The co-creation of the exhibition was developed with local migrant workers; further setting up was done with farmers and farming organisations, who helped by providing materials (fruit-picking bags, timecards) and spreading the invitation. The organisation of the actual exhibition and dialogue was done in collaboration with other local organisations, such as the tourist office in Sint-Truiden (Haspengouw) and a welfare organisation in Westland.

A variety of stakeholders participated in the exhibition: organisations involved with agricultural heritage, retired farmers and farmers' organisations, local residents, and volunteers. In some cases, the collaboration with specific individuals proved crucial. In the context of Westland, this was an employee at the local welfare organisation, who shared the feeling of urgency to bring migrant workers and residents together. She had a wider network in the field of agricultural labour migration and other local support infrastructures. This helped in many ways: increasing the inclusivity of the platform, reaching a more diverse 'audience', and in mediating different positions of power.

After the co-creation process, the exhibition was physically set up in the two regions and it included an opening event and some dialogues; finally, an online version of the exhibition was made available. This action made was possible by collaborating with various stakeholders, who were involved at different levels.

About the exhibition: three contexts

The exhibition was entitled 'Picking Fruit, Sowing Stories', it was translated into English, Romanian, and Polish. It portrayed moments, objects, practices, and rituals of migrant agricultural workers, who were asked to provide photographs of a moment in their daily work that they felt was special. They could also write something in their own language about why they took this picture and what it meant to them. These photos were combined with an audioscape consisting of recordings from orchards in the Netherlands and Belgium and with interactive objects from modern-day horticulture. Visitors to the exhibition were also invited to share their memories, perspectives, experiences, and thoughts, thus 'harvesting' new stories for a more inclusive and participatory story of local (agricultural) heritage.

Figure 41. At the exhibition.

Figure 42. The exhibition flyer.

The exhibition took on a different life with each iteration. In spring 2023, the exhibition opened in Sint-Truiden, Haspengouw during the yearly harvest blessing ceremony. It was incorporated in the programme of activities and introduced during the ceremony in the church. People could interact with the exhibition by leaving behind messages in fruit-picking bags and registering their time on the timecards that are typical of agricultural labour sites. After the opening event, two dialogues were organised in the church, to which various stakeholders from the field were invited: farmers, tourist guides, NGOs, and agricultural heritage organisations.

In autumn 2023, the exhibition opened in a community centre in Westland. Unlike at the opening in Haspengouw, some of the migrant workers who contributed were present to talk about their photos and experiences in Westland. The exhibition then moved to a local church, where it became part of a local programme during which citizens of Westland are encouraged to meet each other through all kinds of activities. We were invited by the church to give a speech, or 'sermon', in our capacity as researchers to launch the exhibition in the church. There were informal dialogues, and the audience left behind messages about the questions raised in the exhibition and in the sermon. In both contexts, the exhibition attracted some media attention from various local and regional news outlets.

Challenges and ethical concerns

The main dilemma was how to deal with the in/visibility of migrant workers: while aiming at making them 'more visible' in the public narrative, it was not always possible to have them physically take part in the exhibition. Participants expressed a wish to be recognised for their hard work, their relationships with colleagues, and their presence in Westland and Haspengouw. Interestingly, even though they were asked to provide photographs of objects, places, or moments – rather than recognisable faces – because of privacy concerns, many pictures included people and relationships in the field that made the labour in the fields meaningful. On the other hand, despite this opportunity for visibility, those who were meant to be at the forefront of the intervention, especially in Haspengouw, were in the end still mostly represented through their photos, voices, and objects, and not by themselves. They were included in the creation of the exhibition but, due to the seasonal nature of the labour, were not physically present when the exhibition and the dialogues took place. Of course, the whole point of the exhibition and launching it during the blossom festival was to take this invisibility and temporality of seasonal labour as the focus point. All these difficulties raised the question of whether the action ended up reproducing the temporariness and invisibility it was trying to critique.

We faced a few challenges in creating the exhibition. First, it was tricky to get stakeholders involved and working together. Second, it was hard to decide who the exhibition was for and how to manage that audience. Lastly, it was difficult to handle and explain things clearly in a setting with many different power dynamics.

As regards the first issue, getting some people to visit the exhibition and actively participate in the dialogue was not always easy. This was particularly challenging with stakeholders from municipalities, policymakers, representative farming organisations, and the farmers. Sometimes the main obstacle was timing: in the case of farmers, the unpredictable nature of their work, which also includes evening work, often prohibits them from coming. In other cases, the parameters of participation had to be negotiated. An example is the exchange about communication choices with the welfare organisation and the church. In preparing promotional material about the exhibition, they expressed the wish (and official requirement) to disseminate information only in Dutch.

Even with regard to the content of the exhibition, the coordinator of a social welfare organisation was afraid it would not appeal to the 'average' Westlander audience, who would not be open to exhibitions that were too different from what they are familiar with. The second obstacle was the difficulty of identifying audiences: developing an open exhibition implied also being ready to welcome unexpected audiences and exchanges. On the occasion of the first dialogues, unexpected people came (e.g. mainly tourist guides) and there was an overrepresentation of members of the Royal Committee of Fruit, among whom were a couple of farmers. This made the dialogue difficult to mediate, as many farmers did revert to defensive language.

Reflections on the transformative potential of the action

The exhibition and the process of developing it triggered a shift in the narrative on migrant agricultural labour. In particular, its transformative effect had at least two dimensions. First, it ensured the recognition of migrant workers whose pictures and faces were showed in the exhibition. This recognition empowered both migrants and local communities: as mentioned, workers were willing to send photos that often visibly portrayed themselves. Beyond privacy concerns, this was a meaningful call for visual recognition of this hard, invisible work and the importance of the relationships between colleagues that form in the fields. Local communities benefited from another perspective on their own region, history, and agricultural heritage. For example, a visitor to the exhibition did not at first understand why there were so many pictures of Romanian farmers and Polish workers in a Belgian church, until he realised the exhibition was about those newcomers who work in the fields of Haspengouw and how agricultural regions in Belgium are therefore connected with other agricultural regions in Europe.

Secondly, the exhibition triggered an initial shift in the narrative of the two regions and their agricultural history. This was possible because of all the small actions that built the exhibition: the co-creation, the material that was shown, the collaboration and inclusion in local rituals, the dialogues. This shift can clearly be seen from the interest that a heritage organisation had in the exhibition and dialogues. Afterwards, an audience member working in the field of agricultural heritage said she would include more stories about migrant workers in a new heritage project on fruit horticulture from the 1960s. In fact, so far, she had only included stories from farmers, farming organisations, auction centres, and factories.

> Further reading: The online version of the exhibition is available for consultation at: https://rerootproject.eu/exhibition.

TAKEAWAYS

\# In polarised contexts, people may hold divergent views on certain issues. Utilising topics that are not contested as starting points for dialogue can help bring them together.

\# Identifying and collaborating with individuals who can navigate local contexts and power dynamics can facilitate the organisation of your action.

\# Lowering barriers to participation involves addressing various stakeholders simultaneously, as well as taking into consideration language, time, resources, and mobility.

WHAT ARE THESE PHOTOS OF ROMANIAN WORKERS IN THIS CHURCH?

IT MAKES ME REALIZE THAT THERE ARE PEOPLE AND SOCIAL WORLDS BEHIND THE APPLE I BUY IN THE SUPERMARKET

PERHAPS NOT A RITUAL, BUT AS A SON OF A FARMER I OFTEN THINK ABOUT THE HARD WORK IN COMBINATION WITH RAMADAN, BECAUSE MANY OF OUR EMPLOYEES (FROM TURKEY AND MOROCCO) WERE MUSLIM. THEY LEFT THEIR HOMES (IN THE HAGUE) VERY EARLY AND THEN THEY WORKED SO HARD WITHOUT DRINKING AND EATING. MUST HAVE BEEN SO DIFFICULT!

Figure 43. Lively encounters at the Haspengouw exhibition.

> For other stories from the Haspengouw/Westland site, see:

p. 99, Migrant hotel managers in Westland as key intermediaries: connecting seasonal labourers to vital services

p. 116, Mobile information points for EU migrant workers in and beyond Westland: broadening the reach of existing outreach services

p. 138, Fostering relationships through agricultural work in Belgium and the Netherlands: work as a vital place for socialising across languages and origins

p. 142, Community-building initiative for Polish women in The Hague: creating a safe space for encounter, exchange, and combatting loneliness and depression

TOOL 18
FIND A NON-CONTESTED STARTING POINT FOR DIALOGUE

MATERIALS: Paper, writing utensils.

TOOL SUMMARY: This tool helps you find a non-contested starting point in polarised contexts to facilitate dialogue among distant stakeholders. It involves identifying topics that lie at the intersection of all groups' interests, and therefore sometimes peripheral to their central concerns, and that are deemed non-threatening. This approach of focusing on shared, less contentious subjects helps trigger attention and initiate interaction and dialogue.

In certain polarised contexts, tense relationships between stakeholders can lead to a paralysis in action. Bringing together different stakeholders, especially those who are typically distant, presents the challenge of finding shared entry points for the conversation.

To define such entry points it is useful to think of topics that lie at the intersection of the interests of all groups of people and represent 'non-threatening' subjects for all. This means that this common ground should not be subjects that are vital or central for any stakeholder, but at the periphery of their interests. Such topics can have different meanings for each group but they should also be commonly recognised among groups. In this sense, they help trigger stakeholders' attention and become a starting point to interaction and dialogue.

STEP 1: To identify a non-contested common ground, make a list of the people who you would like to gather for dialogue.

STEP 2: Make a list of their subjects of interest according to how high the stakes are and how important the topic is for them. For each person, make a circle with the most central subjects for them in the middle, with less important subjects at the periphery of the drawing.

 Identify, in the peripheries, one or two subjects that these groups of people have in common in terms of interest.

For instance, in Haspengouw:

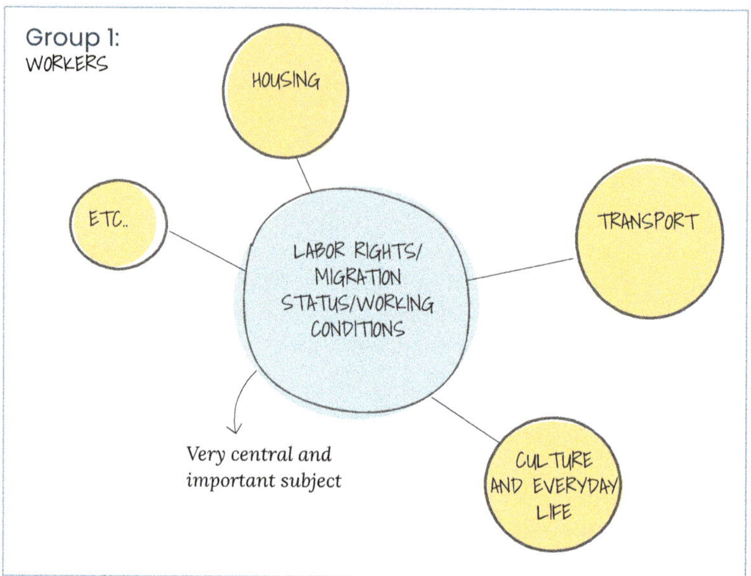

Figure 44. Diagram 1 for finding a non-contested starting point for dialogue.

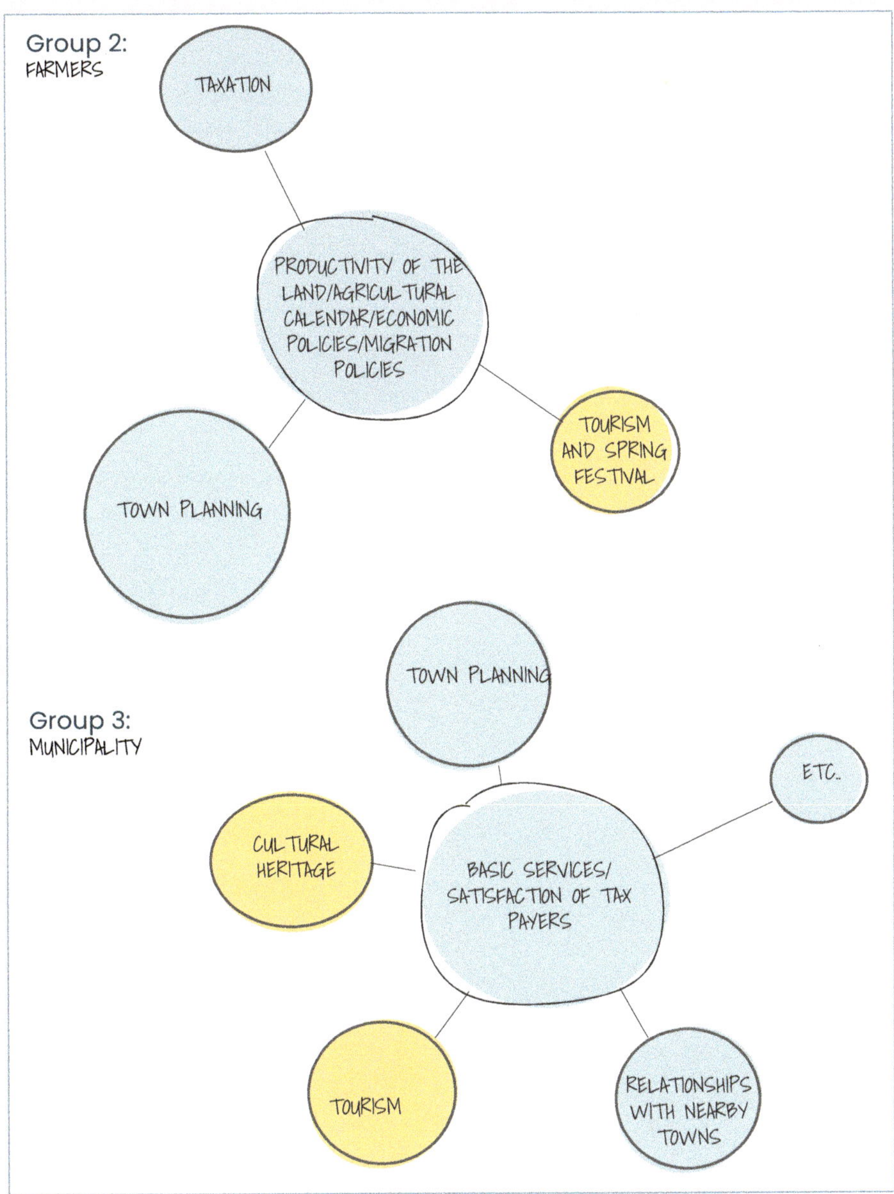

Figure 45. Diagram 2 for finding a non-contested starting point for dialogue.

In the exhibition we discussed in the story, cultural heritage, specifically rituals, represented a very effective topic, through which it was possible to involve different stakeholders, who usually are on opposite sides of a polarised discourse: farmers and workers. Since it was perceived as relatively non-threatening, the process of getting access, getting permission, and starting a dialogue with many different people was easy.

Finding a non-contested starting point is crucial in polarised contexts to facilitate dialogue among diverse stakeholders. By identifying topics that intersect with all groups' interests and are non-threatening, this tool helps initiate meaningful conversations. This approach not only has the ability to reduce tension but also fosters collaboration by focusing on shared subjects. The example from Haspengouw illustrates how cultural heritage can serve as an effective entry point, enabling dialogue and cooperation among historically opposing groups.

TOOL 19
PHOTOVOICE: A VISUAL TOOL TO LOWER THE THRESHOLD TO PARTICIPATION

*additional preparation time: 5 minutes for explanation and a week for collecting materials.

MATERIALS:
- Cameras or smartphones with camera functionality
- Notebooks and pens
- A space for group discussion (physical or virtual)
- A display area for the photographs (physical board or digital platform)

TOOL SUMMARY: Photovoice uses participant-taken photographs and narratives to showcase lived experiences, helping to overcome barriers to participation such as language, time, and distance. It emphasises identifying obstacles to participation and using creative, non-textual communication methods like drawing, mapping, and music to address them. Photovoice can be very accessible to different backgrounds and be effectively combined with digital tools to engage participants remotely.

Participatory actions bring with them the challenge of finding the right tools that allow people to fully participate in them. Indeed, people encounter multiple barriers to participation in activities, even when they are enthusiastic about their content or outcomes. Creative tools such as photovoice can be mobilised to address those barriers.

Photovoice is a method that gathers participant-taken photographs and narratives to showcase the lived experience of a certain subject. Like other visual tools, it is very useful in overcoming obstacles to participation, such as language barriers, lack of time, or distance from the activity's location.

It is important first to identify obstacles to people's participation, then mobilise creative tools to address those obstacles. In the case of photovoice, it mobilises non-textual communication to overcome language barriers, similarly to drawing, mapping, sculpting, dancing, and music. Taking a picture with one's phone is a very accessible activity that participants can decide to engage with. It can also be easily combined with digital communication tools to reduce the distance between interested participants.

Figure 46. A photovoice photo sent to our researcher by a migrant labourer.

Figure 47. A photo sent by Modeste with his caption "The Active Youth" using the photovoice method.

Figure 48. A photo sent by Wiktoria with her caption "The morning after a rainy night reveals nature's true beauty amidst the bustle of work".

STEP 1: Introduction to photovoice

Begin with a brief introduction to the photovoice method. Explain how it allows participants to capture and share their experiences through photographs, providing a visual and narrative representation of their daily work.

STEP 2: Setting the theme

Set a theme for the exercise, such as 'Documenting everyday rituals' or 'A day in our shoes', like our researcher did in Haspengouw. Encourage participants to capture moments that represent their daily experiences, challenges, and interactions.

STEP 3: Photo-taking phase

Give participants a week to take photographs that reflect their experiences. Encourage them to think about moments that are significant, challenging, or rewarding.

After the photo-taking phase, ask participants to select three to five photographs that they feel best represent their experiences. Have them write a brief description or story for each photo, explaining its significance.

STEP 5: Group discussion

Organise a group discussion where participants can share their photographs and stories. Encourage open dialogue, allowing participants to express their feelings and insights. Discuss common themes, challenges, and meaningful moments that emerge from the photos.

STEP 6: Creating a visual display

Compile the photographs and stories into a visual display. This could be a physical board (for example hanging the printed photographs on a wall) or a digital platform (for example sharing slides in an online meeting) that is accessible to participants and the broader community if desired.

STEP 7: Follow up

Conclude the exercise with a reflection session. Discuss what was learned from the exercise and how these insights might be useful for addressing the topic at hand. Consider developing further actions based on the themes and issues identified.

REFLECTION

Photovoice can be an effective method for lowering barriers to participation because of the accessibility of visual storytelling. This tool allows participants to share their lived experiences through photographs, making it accessible to people from different backgrounds. By considering obstacles such as language, time, and distance, photovoice fosters inclusive participation and deeper engagement. The combination of visual and narrative elements helps to create a rich, shared understanding of the issues at hand.

HOUSING
Protest actions in Brussels seeking media coverage: spotlighting the government's denial of asylum rights

This account recalls two examples of action work initiated by our researcher together with activists in Brussels, where many newcomers fight to survive on the streets because they are denied access to the reception centres for asylum-seekers. These actions built on and supported interventions already in play in long-standing activist mobilisations. The actions had two main goals and target groups. One goal was to improve the situation for people who are forced into homelessness due to the current Belgian and European migration politics. The other aim was to apply pressure on policymakers and raise awareness about the problem in broader society.

The context: solidarity initiatives fighting forced homelessness of newcomers

In Brussels, our actions were initiated at a time when more and more newcomers' asylum requests were being denied by the Federal Agency for the Reception of Asylum-seekers (Fedasil). Over the past decade, Belgium has undergone multiple periods where the government denied asylum because of a (self-created) lack of accommodation places for newcomers. Beginning in October 2021, Fedasil has regularly turned away in particular male asylum-seekers because a lack of beds in its asylum centres, leaving thousands to sleep on the streets for months. At the same time, the federal government refuses to offer alternatives like putting people in hotels, planning for local municipalities to take them in, making use of vacant buildings, or using emergency plans to set up temporary shelters.

Belgium's increasingly strict migration policies are supported by public opinion, which sees newcomers as a problem and a threat. This view suggests that strict migration policies are necessary because more welcoming asylum policies would attract even more newcomers to Belgium. Paradoxically, the perception of Belgium as being 'full' of newcomers is amplified by the federal government policy of not providing asylum accommodation as it leads to more newcomer homelessness visible on the streets, with many men sleeping in tents in central Brussels.

As migration policies get tougher and hostility towards non-European and non-Western migrants grows, support and protests for newcomers by civic groups, lawyers, and citizens have also increased. Activists and NGOs in Brussels challenge the government's stance and public opinion, highlighting the denial of asylum rights and seeking media attention. Less visibly, activists and those rendered illegal by the state – such as people on the move to England or newcomers required to request asylum in the first European country they enter, as stipulated by the Dublin Convention – collaborate to improve the living conditions of newcomers. Actions include providing food and social and medical support, organising protests, occupying buildings, and court cases.

Planning the action: being flexible, collaborative, and context-sensitive

Our active interventions in Brussels were approached as an opportunity to deepen previous research engagement with the everyday realities and needs of people excluded from state-provided services, by (co-)initiating actions. Central to these actions were two main goals and target groups: on the one hand, the aim was to improve the situation of those forced into homelessness; on the other hand, the actions intended to put pressure on policymakers and raise awareness about the problem among broader audiences.

We adopted a flexible approach that allowed us to account for the rapidly changing situation in the city, where spaces were continuously claimed and evicted, resulting in short-lived occupations that popped up across the city in rapid succession. Setting up sustainable initiatives in this situation was difficult. Therefore, we developed many spur-of-the-moment interventions with activists. They involved the improvement of basic and social infrastructure, education, social integration, and access to services, which required interaction with people from the neighbourhood, medical and other services, and local authorities.

Two examples of interventions that grew organically from the otherwise dispersed engagement with the situation were sleeping at the makeshift camp and a protest action involving a politically charged sofa. Both interventions sought to disrupt the anti-newcomer status quo, attract media attention to the failure of the federal reception process, and highlight the need for government accountability.

Sleeping at a makeshift camp

The idea for this action took root when homeless asylum-seekers set up a camp on a bridge opposite the Fedasil intake centre in Brussels. By pitching their tents at this specific location, they aimed to stay visible to Fedasil and keep informed about the latest developments and opportunities for shelter. As the makeshift camp grew, so did the concerns of neighbours and activists about the well-being of its residents.

Early on, a group of neighbours organised a solidarity sleepover event, or 'sleep-in', to support the asylum-seekers. Months later, with over 400 people living in the camp, together with activists, we revived this idea. By then, media coverage of Belgium's reception crisis had increased, prompting activists to begin organising widespread mobilisations. This old idea gained new momentum, culminating in a curated evening at the bridge with music, speeches, and a widely publicised sleepover.

The event led to an opinion piece that highlighted the warm, convivial evening spent with the camp's inhabitants, emphasising the hospitality and care they extended to their guests. The men living on the bridge offered their best tents, ensured the safety of female participants during the night, and provided breakfast in the morning. By reversing the guest—host relationship, both the sleepover event and the opinion piece reflected back to Belgian society, challenging negative perceptions of newcomers and demonstrating that there is much to learn from them about hospitality.

Living room of shame

Another protest action centred around using politically charged sofas as symbols and tools of protest. These sofas were confiscated from the Fedasil headquarters due to the federal government's unpaid fines exceeding 275 million euros. These fines stemmed from over 8,000 convictions by the Court of Brussels, holding the government accountable for failing to uphold its legal duty to respect asylum rights and maintain minimum standards for asylum accommodation. The sofas thus symbolise the government's self-created reception crisis and its failure to comply with its legal duties. When the sofas came up for auction, we and our activist colleagues got the idea to purchase them and bring these sofas to homeless asylum-seekers who had been denied access to the centres.

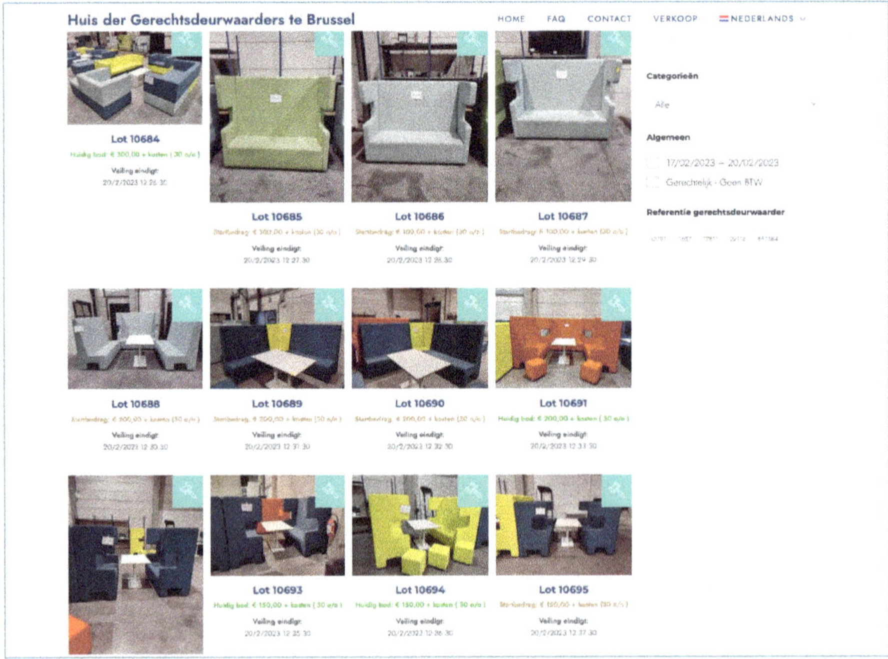

Figure 49. The online auction where the FEDASIL sofas were auctioned-off.

Propelled by the Stop the Reception Crisis movement, together with collaborating activists, we crowdfunded the purchase of the sofas and organised a protest action called 'Salon de la honte' ('Living Room of Shame'). For this action, the sofas were fitted with wheels, adorned with banners, and pushed across Brussels to a building occupied by homeless asylum-seekers who had been denied access to the centres, in order to bring them symbolically the asylum accommodation they were entitled to.

This action received significant media coverage, thanks in part to the contacts with journalists previously established by the movement. The action and the media coverage of it proved extremely effective and were later adopted by various stakeholders. The sofas remained in the city, moving with homeless asylum-seekers from one occupation and protest action to the next.

These sofas provided a provocative way to tell the story of the asylum reception failure. As items that moved from the Fedasil headquarters, through the auction house, and into pro-migrant protests and occupations, the sofas became tools to critique exclusionary policies and practices, serving as a symbol of and for the federal government of its unlawful actions.

In planning this intervention, the support of the inhabitants of the occupations, local stakeholders, and their previous investments proved crucial. Cooperation occurred with local organisations that provided space; inhabitants of occupations who shared in all the actions; experienced activists who professionally mobilised and organised numerous interventions and efforts; journalists who covered the protests; and civil society and individuals who invested their time and efforts in the cause.

Figure 50. Media coverage of the sofa action in the Brussels Times.

Reflections on the transformative potential of the action

Both actions discussed above had at least two effects: a short-term effect of empowering and supporting newcomers in their everyday lives and a long-term effect of producing counter-narratives about reception and the state's failure therein. A key lesson from these interventions is that it sometimes makes more sense to try and integrate actions into existing initiatives rather than creating new ones. This approach allowed for continuous learning and adaptation to the rapidly changing context in Brussels, where protest actions and solidarity initiatives emerged and disappeared quickly. This fluid situation made pre-planning ineffective, so an adaptive and inductive approach was necessary, though it was also demanding and resource-intensive. However, this fluctuating context and limited resources posed significant challenges, asking the organisers to evaluate whether it was possible to achieve the desired impact with the available resources.

One of the most widespread ethical challenges that arose concerned the potential exposure of participants. Actions were intentionally non-neutral and political, aiming to raise awareness and denounce issues. However, this exposure risked legal repercussions for some participants and could negatively impact their asylum procedures. It was crucial to ensure that everyone involved was fully informed and could choose their level of participation.

Finally, navigating power dynamics between researchers, activists, and newcomers was also important. Researchers and activists had to avoid being over-protective, while newcomers sometimes felt indebted. Additionally, exposing newcomers to difficult information, such as racism and discrimination, needed careful handling to avoid further demotivation.

"A series of slogans spread by the activists summarise well their shared values and public discourse. Some examples are: 'nobody is illegal', 'Belgium is breaking the law, respect refugees' rights now', 'Fedasil stop sleeping, it's time to take action', 'stop the reception crisis', 'this is not a crisis, it's a crime', 'no borders', 'police go home', 'everywhere police, nowhere justice', 'asylum-seekers on the streets, state guilty'"

—RESEARCHER FROM BRUSSELS SITE, BRUSSELS, NOVEMBER 2023.

TAKEAWAYS

\# Supporting existing actions begins with adapting to the (changing) context, which can be both an inspiring and energy-consuming process.

\# Setting reasonable objectives for your actions and continuously evaluating them is crucial when working in a rapidly changing context where many stakeholders are beyond your control.

\# Short-lived engagements and actions are not futile. They can provide opportunities to build connections for future projects.

In protest actions, there is a significant risk of becoming overexposed. It is essential for all participants, including yourself, to remain continually aware of this risk.

> Check **TOOL 11**: 'Mapping roles and relations in social activism' (p. 156) to identify different roles that can be taken in protest actions, and to position yourself within these different roles.

> For other stories from the Brussels site, see:

p. 82, Hosting newcomers in private homes in Brussels: remediating a politically constructed reception crisis

p. 114, Mobile medical services cruising from occupation to occupation (Brussels): Bridging healthcare gaps across the city

p. 148, Occupying a government building in Brussels: engaging in political mobilisation and creating community amid dire living conditions

p. 167, Reframing the 'refugee crisis' in Brussels as a 'reception crisis' in Belgium: holding the government accountable for violating the right to asylum

TOOL 20
FORECASTING FUTURES AND PLANNING YOUR ACTIONS

MATERIALS: Paper, writing utensils.

TOOL SUMMARY: Forecasting future scenarios can be a useful method for analysing the pressures and possibilities of the present. In this tool you will use your creativity to fabricate scenarios and identify potential avenues for transformative action in your arrival infrastructure.

STEP 1: Identify a topic for forecasting

Choose a topic central to the arrival infrastructure in which you are working.

For example, in the context of our research in Brussels we chose the failure of the asylum reception process.

STEP 2: Choose two factors that strongly influence your chosen topic.

For example, we chose (1) the degree of migration regulation and (2) the reception of newcomers.

These two factors become your horizontal axis and vertical axis in a diagram:

For the horizontal axis, we put 'less asylum accommodation available' on the left-hand side and 'more asylum accommodation available' on the right-hand side.

For the vertical axis, we put 'tighter asylum regulations' on the top and 'looser asylum regulations' on the bottom.

STEP 3: Forecast the future in newspaper headlines.

For each corner of diagram, write one or two fictional headlines (or scenarios) based on what the horizontal axis and vertical axis are forecasting.

For example, in one of the scenarios below, the regulations governing migrant arrival in Brussels are looser and there is less asylum accommodation available. We imagine that a headline in this scenario could read: 'Abandoned federal building converted into housing for asylum-seekers'.

STEP 4: Reflect on the possibilities and pressures that could be relevant for implementing transformative action.

Although the scenarios are fictional, the exercise allows us to identify potential problems and thus action areas. In this forecasting, possible action could involve protection of asylum-seekers from police violence and homelessness. It could also involve advocacy work for a better asylum reception system and more asylum accommodation.

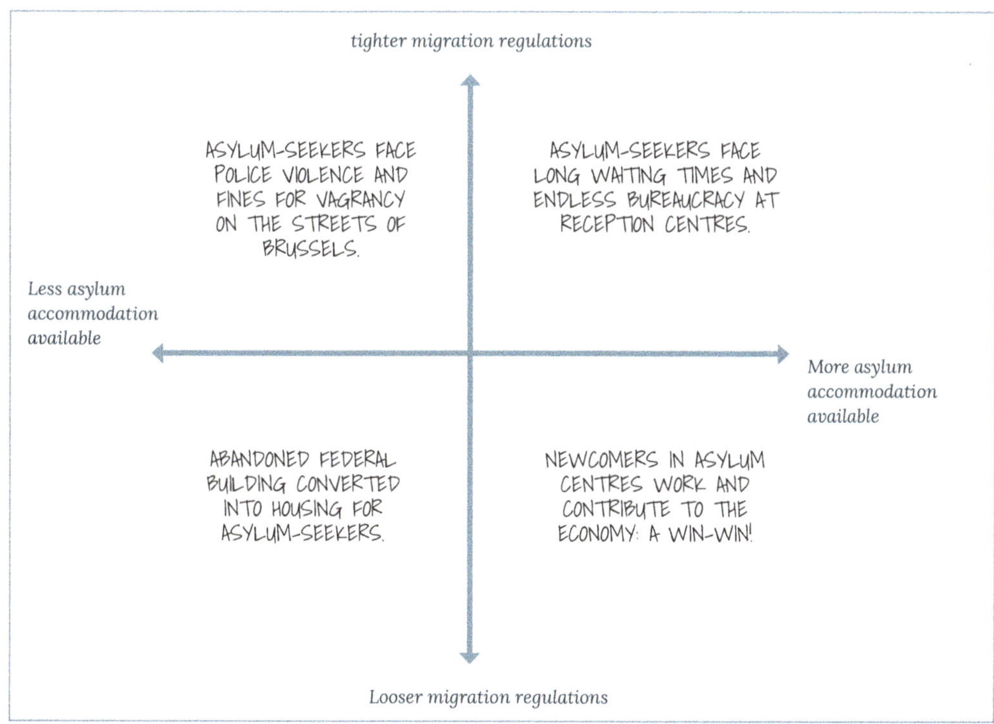

Figure 51. Diagram for forecasting futures and planning your actions.

REFLECTION

By creatively fabricating future scenarios based on 'real-life' conditions, we can identify potential challenges and opportunities within the arrival infrastructure that could inspire action. This method not only enhances our understanding of current pressures but can serve as a useful brainstorming tool for thinking, together with others, about current and future scenarios and assembling perspectives that may consider the future differently.

> FURTHER READING: For further reading on the strategic foresight possibilities used in this tool, see Ravetz, Joe and Ian Douglas Miles. 2016. 'Foresight in Cities: On the Possibility of a "Strategic Urban Intelligence"', *Foresight* 18(5): 469–90.

TOOL 21
UNSETTLE TO ATTRACT MEDIA ATTENTION

MATERIALS: Paper, writing utensils.

TOOL SUMMARY: This tool emphasises the importance of developing surprising and visually attractive public actions to expose topics and trigger discussions. By choosing symbolic objects, relevant spaces, and peak times, organisers can create memorable images that capture media and public attention. An example is moving politically charged sofas across Brussels to highlight the failure of the Belgian government to respect asylum-seekers' rights and provide them with shelter, which garnered significant media coverage.

Actions that follow the objective of 'exposing' certain topics and triggering discussion often also benefit from media exposure to attract the attention of broader audiences.

In addition to preparing media coverage by producing the relevant material, it is useful to remember that surprising sights can go a long way in making an impression on the memories of bystanders and journalists alike. To attract attention when organising an action or event, do not be afraid to think visually. The moment of the action is the moment when attention is at its peak, so you can use this key moment to produce impactful and impressive images.

Here are some questions to brainstorm about possible imagery for your action:

- Which objects are symbolic of the subject at stake?

  Don't be afraid of taking objects out of their context, it can make them shine.

- Which space would be relevant for my action?

  Don't be afraid to choose a symbolic space or one that has opportunities for striking photos.

- Which moment would provide the peak of attention I need?

  Don't be afraid to choose a time in the day when more people are about, like a public holiday.

  In Brussels, moving three sofas – confiscated from the agency for the reception of asylum-seekers – across the city, to an occupation housing homeless asylum-seekers, received significant media attention, as the image brought multiple ideas to the surface. First, it was a symbolic gesture of justice: if you do not fulfil your mission of accommodating asylum-seekers, we will bring the asylum centre to them. Second, the absurdity of rolling a sofa across the city provokes enough curiosity in the viewer to make them question the reasons for it and look for answers. As such, the image was reused many times by media platforms to illustrate the issue of the failure of the Belgian government to provide asylum-seekers with their legal right for shelter.

Using surprising and visually impactful actions can effectively attract media attention and trigger public discussions. By selecting symbolic objects, relevant spaces, and peak times, organisers can create memorable images that resonate with audiences. This approach not only gives you the opportunity to highlight relevant issues but also engages a broader audience, fostering awareness and dialogue. The example from Brussels demonstrates how a creative and symbolic action can powerfully illustrate systemic failures and provoke curiosity and reflection.

2. COALITION-BUILDING

Stakeholders involved in arrival infrastructuring work can vary widely. In some cases there are only a few, while in others they are numerous and diverse. The dynamics in long-established arrival neighbourhoods in large cities can differ significantly from those in smaller towns and rural areas. Some stakeholders are institutional, while others are not; some operate in alignment with prevailing policy frameworks, while others actively counteract them.

Often stakeholders working within the same area – such as municipalities, civil society organisations, and individuals – operate in a fragmented manner. For example, in our London story, limited opportunities for exchange and reflection hindered collaboration. Therefore, taking action may focus on building stronger networks among stakeholders around shared objectives, such as employment, as seen in Karditsa.

Building and facilitating networks often requires a gradual process of understanding the stakeholders, their interests, and their interrelationships. It is important to establish a network embedded in and adaptable to existing resources and to always negotiate objectives, approaches, and outcomes to ensure sustainability. While the goal may be to build networks, interactions with and among stakeholders can lead to a series of other, unexpected transformations, both in the short and long term.

ESSENTIAL SERVICES

A network of organisations in a London borough: counteracting fragmentation in newcomer support

The arrival situation at the London site was characterised by newcomers in diverse vulnerable positions, facing numerous and varying barriers. Opportunities for reflection and exchange were limited due to a fragmented, modestly resourced arrival infrastructure that was thinly spread across a wide range of social issues, often affecting both newcomer and established groups. For our researcher, the aim of the action was to help create and support a network of organisations providing assistance to newcomer residents, among other groups. This effort built on the foundations of an existing social initiative in the borough, which fostered the development of local networks and offered modest funding opportunities. Many services and organisations were not connected to or aware of the resources and opportunities provided by others, so the initiative helped to catalyse new conversations, mutual assistance, and collaborations between those supporting socially excluded newcomers in the area, improving coordination of support efforts.

Figure 52. An interactive booth for the coalition-building network at Refugee Week in the London borough

A network of organisations in a London borough: counteracting fragmentation in supporting newcomers and residents

Efforts to support migrants in diverse, vulnerable conditions in a London borough were hindered by a fragmented, modestly resourced support infrastructure. In response, we wanted to catalyse a network of organisations to better coordinate assistance for newcomer residents. This built on an existing social initiative to catalyse networks and help local organisations collaborate.

Building on existing foundations

Despite increasingly hostile national discourse on immigration in the early 2020s, the municipality in the borough remained committed to social inclusion through its policy 'No one left behind. We all belong'. This approach focused on supporting all residents, including those facing social exclusion due to migration or deprivation. The municipality's support for a free food distribution initiative and a research project commissioned to better understand the needs of residents with 'no recourse to public funds' (NRPF) exemplified this commitment.

The borough's landscape of organisations and services was diverse but fragmented, often addressing cross-cutting social issues with limited resources. A catalyst initiative supporting civil society networks in the local area offered us an opportunity to bring together disconnected services to create a more collaborative infrastructure. Together with these organisations, we initiated a network with the aim of improving support for newcomer residents by fostering stronger relationships between local organisations.

Developing the network

The decision to catalyse a network was made gradually and was shaped by practical needs, emerging through a process of trial and error. Despite our initial ideas, such as a project documenting the stories of homeless newcomers, we ultimately rejected these in favour of the coalition-building action. Rather than focusing on a single issue or group, we chose to support a more inclusive and flexible action—one that brings together diverse stakeholders and addresses the wide range of challenges faced by newcomers.

Our first step toward creating the network was convening local organisations who were interested in supporting newcomer residents. The starting point for the network was a meeting we organised to share key fieldwork findings. This meeting provided an opportunity for organisations, some of whom were unaware of each other's work, to come together and exchange information. In the meeting, we emphasised forging connections and fostering open dialogue among stakeholders that had previously worked in isolation.

Figure 53. A flipchart made in preparation for a stakeholder meeting to encourage communication and clear expectations.

To carry out the research, we took on roles as facilitators of the group. In this role, we were also crucial organisers in the network's early stages. Acting as the network's de facto 'secretary', we managed communication, coordinated meetings, and helped create opportunities for members to engage with one another. This role was vital, as many local organisations lacked the capacity to maintain a networking space, especially when the benefits of the network were not immediately apparent. Our proactive engagement as facilitators — through face-to-face communication, suggesting initiatives, and organising reflection opportunities — helped sustain the momentum of the group and guide its growth.

Over time, the network developed a diverse range of activities. Members held meetings, set up communication channels including a WhatsApp group, and offered each other help to solve problems or promote support activities that were shared in the group. The WhatsApp group in particular became a valuable tool for instant problem-solving and collaboration. For example, in one case, a network member was able to find emergency housing for an evicted asylum-seeker through quick coordination with another organisation, a solution that may not have occurred without the network. Other collaborative initiatives, such as the co-production of a welcome resource for asylum-seekers and a local policy review, highlighted the network's ability to address both immediate needs and longer-term systemic issues.

Challenges and ethical concerns

Despite the network's early successes, several challenges and ethical concerns emerged throughout the process. One key challenge was the lack of opportunities for reflection and evaluation. There was limited time for the network as a whole to step back, define its objectives, and assess its activities. This was partly due to the pressures of immediate service delivery and partly because the network was still in its formative stages, with evolving objectives. Time constraints and unpredictability meant that even though reflection was recognised as important, it was often abandoned due to lack of time.

Balancing our dual role as both facilitators and academic researchers added another layer of complexity. Our involvement in facilitating the network sometimes created tension between the goals of fostering a collaborative support structure and advancing research aims. Diversity within the network also required careful navigation. The participating organisations and individuals came from a wide range of backgrounds and areas of focus, including local government teams and civil society groups. While this broad representation enriched the network, it also required ongoing efforts to ensure that all members could engage meaningfully and have their voices heard equally. Some organisations were more experienced or better resourced, which could have created imbalances in participation.

Another obstacle was related to participation and representation. Limited availability of members often made organising meetings and collaborative efforts challenging. Some organisations lacked the capacity to attend regularly, which created barriers to consistent involvement. Additionally, while the network remained relatively conflict-free, it seemed possible that the time pressures faced by members might have led them to avoid conflict, which could have stifled constructive debate and prevented the network from addressing underlying issues that might hinder its long-term success.

Reflections on the transformative potential of the action

The network unexpectedly became a point of contact for larger organisations looking to engage with the borough. National and regional charity organisations and social movements sought the support of the network to connect with relevant local stakeholders. Additionally, the municipality was able to commission projects related to newcomer residents more inclusively, allowing network members to participate and receive compensation through a collective approach.

TAKEAWAYS

\# Taking action does not necessarily imply introducing a new project, but can involve supporting a new process of engagement to strength relationships and existing support efforts.

\# Supporting a network from within implies continuous adjustment and learning from the stakeholders involved. Remaining flexible and open is key.

\# Choosing to nurture engagement between a network of stakeholders in a given context requires the ability to set aside expectations and allow action to emerge organically through the network's interactions and timeline. It is important to be prepared to come to terms with 'network reality'.

> For other stories from the London site, see:

p. 58, Universal services in a London borough: challenging categorisation-based provision of material support

p. 97, Creative English classes in a London borough: promoting service access through language courses

p. 109, Practical support to see a doctor in London: the role of social contacts in overcoming language barriers to service access

p. 135, Volunteering at a community hub in London: building connections, skills, and confidence

p. 164, Repurposing abandoned buildings and public spaces for shelter in a London borough: claiming inhospitable spaces for making homes in displacement

TOOL 22
PREPARE FOR A COALITION MEETING USING THE ORGANISATIONAL TRIANGLE

MATERIALS: Paper, writing utensils.

TOOL SUMMARY: This tool is designed to help you build coalitions that prioritise transparency, inclusion, and alignment. It focuses on identifying the purpose, people, and processes to promote inclusivity, maintain transparent decision-making processes, and align members with the mission.

Collaborating with diverse stakeholders across organisational and disciplinary boundaries can be both generating positive results and challenging. With many perspectives, working styles, and experience levels around the table, it is essential to employ a transparent, inclusive, and sustainable governance strategy. This strategy should maintain the project mission, encourage active participation from all members, and consider general well-being and inclusion.

The organisational triangle is a useful tool for this. The organisation triangle has three points: purpose (your goal), process (how you achieve your goal), and people (with whom you collaborate to achieve your goal). It can be used in many scenarios: from strategic assessments of coalition health to simple tasks such as planning a meeting. In the following example, we will show how the organisational triangle was used to implement a coalition meeting.

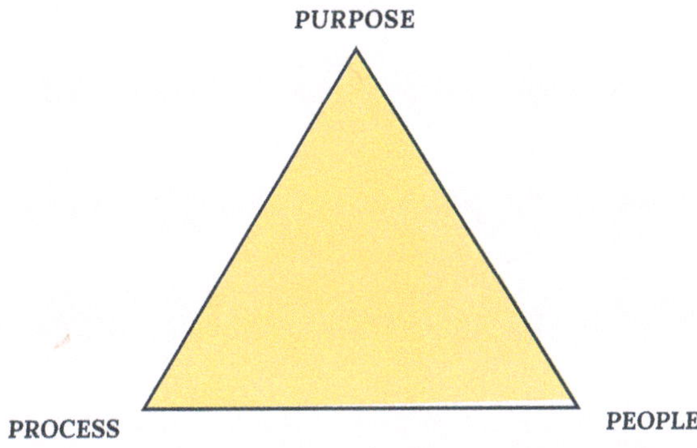

Figure 54. Diagram for preparing for a coalition meeting using the organisational triangle.

Purpose: For healthy collaboration, it is important that all members are on the same page as to its purpose. Furthermore, it is necessary to regularly come back to it to make sure everyone is still aligned on it, and that most of the activities fall within it.

Example purpose: Form a coalition of stakeholders working in the arrival infrastructure of a London borough to share resources and best practices and inspire change.

People: It is important that members of a coalition – people who are a part of it – feel safe and comfortable in its setting. Social activities in which members get to know each other allow for a stronger sense of cohesion and belonging. This is also where caring about inclusion becomes important, to make sure that no one is excluded for reasons outside their control.

In the London borough, the facilitator took special care to accommodate the diversity of members. For example, to account for mismatched work, religious, and life patterns among members, the facilitator was attentive to these differences and ensured for instance that not all meetings were called on a day or at a time that excludes a particular member.

Moreover, at the beginning of each meeting, an introduction round was organised, as the network was growing and not all members attended all meetings. Over time, it facilitated members' awareness of each other's roles, affiliations, and activities.

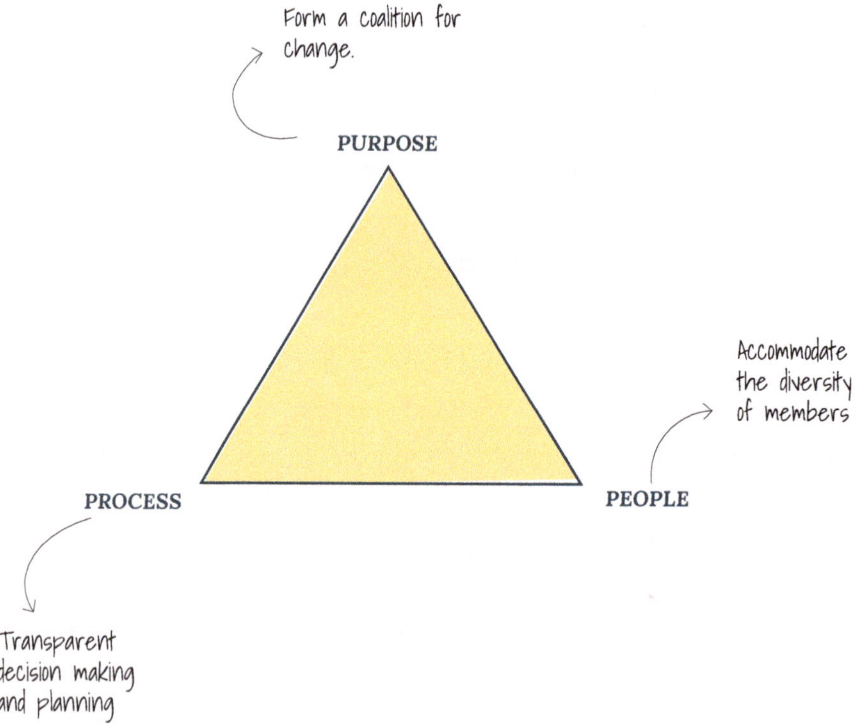

Figure 55. Diagram for preparing for a coalition meeting using the organisational triangle with examples.

Process: The structure of the network and decision-making processes should be clear and transparent to all. Ways of working and rules should be revised regularly to make sure they are respected or changed collectively if needed.

> In the London borough coalition, the facilitator would share the meeting agenda in advance, which enabled members to decide whether the content of the meeting warranted the investment of their time.
>
> Communication channels were diversified to ensure everyone could access internal communication. WhatsApp groups were useful to enable members to interact and solve problems in their day-to-day work. However, these benefit from having an agreed purpose and ground rules to ensure messages are relevant to group members.
>
> The meeting chairs were appointed in advance, and their role was to ensure that everyone had an opportunity to speak and that all, or at least the highest-priority, items were covered within the allocated timeframe. It is important both to have a meeting structure in mind, and to know in advance which parts of the agenda can be deprioritised and left out if necessary.

Can you think of examples of practices, within your organisation, for each of these three pillars? Is there any pillar that is less taken care of? Can you think of any activities or actions that could fill this gap?

REFLECTION

The organisational triangle is a useful compass to keep an eye on the overall health of a network, by making sure there is a balance in how energy and attention are distributed between its three pillars. It is common (and normal) for organisations to sometimes forget one of the pillars, and it is the role of the facilitator (and the collective) to remind the group to give it a bit more attention.

A job-matching platform in Karditsa: strengthening local collaborations and challenging dominant narratives

In Karditsa, as in other small- and medium-sized Greek towns, our researchers identified a paradox between the concentration of newcomers in prominent urban areas and labour demand in peripheral rural areas. Thus, the action described in this story aimed to empower newcomers by connecting them to employment and to address structural labour force shortages. In other words, action was taken to initiate a dialogue between different stakeholders, addressing employment as a common and pragmatic need of all parties, with the potential to create a 'win-win' situation. In Karditsa, our researchers collaborated with local stakeholders to create an online job-matching platform for newcomers and potential employers. The proposed intervention also drew attention to the diverse ways local municipalities implement national programmes.

Matching a structural labour demand and a potential labour force

This case study takes place in Greece, where national migration policies focus on migration control, management, and 'prevention' using a centralised system that largely overlooks and disempowers local municipalities. Such an approach results in diverse local responses and management of national aid programmes. In the case of Karditsa, a medium-sized town in central Greece, the local responses we studied did not align with the dominant view of migration as a temporary situation. Rather, confronted with the long-term migratory dynamics in the area, both the municipality and local stakeholders implementing national policy and aid programmes addressed the arrival and presence of migrant newcomers as an opportunity and tried to maximise existing resources, even beyond their designed aims.

Like many other small- and medium-sized Greek towns, Karditsa simultaneously faces structural labour force shortages and the presence of under- or unemployed newcomers who often lack permission to work. Therefore, Karditsa is defined as a 'disempowered city': a city with a low population, inadequate labour force, poor tax revenue, and little economic, political, or cultural power. The lack of labour force is concentrated in specific sectors of the economy – agriculture, construction, and hospitality. At the same time, following the significant arrival of refugees and asylum-seekers in 2015, newcomers in Karditsa experience a state of limbo produced by legal frameworks and policies that directly limit their mobility and agency.

Within the limiting national context and specific socio-economic challenges facing Karditsa, we proposed to plan an action to address the relationship between the lack of labour force and the disempowerment of newcomers to see what could be learned, shared, and innovated at the local level.

Building spaces for dialogue: a job-matching platform and communication hub

The overarching objective of the action undertaken in Karditsa was to build or strengthen connections and networks among local stakeholders to tackle newcomer empowerment and labourer shortages. This objective was defined with two main rationales: identifying a reasonable field of action and working around a topic of interest for both locals and newcomers. Avoiding issues under national jurisdiction, such as the length of asylum procedures, and focusing on local implementation was crucial in order to foresee transformative effects. Addressing the labour market shortages allowed for a 'win-win' initiative, motivating all parties to participate.

The action involved engaging with local stakeholders from the beginning and co-producing insights, best practices, and outcomes. This included many planning meetings and brainstorming sessions with local stakeholders, as well as individual interviews and informal discussions with other stakeholders (newcomers, participating municipal and NGO personnel) to gather feedback and share views. In Karditsa, the collaboration between the municipality and local stakeholders was already well established. Together with these collaborators, we decided that the most fruitful way forward would be to establish a platform to match newcomer job-seekers with potential employers.

In addition to planning interventions, these exchanges also helped establish a common vocabulary and understanding around the term 'newcomer', countering dominant stereotypes and emphasising the importance of viewing migration as an ongoing process rather than a temporary phenomenon. All of the meetings were also an opportunity to understand how stakeholders perceived the broader framework of migration and integration and the interplay with the micro-politics of their region. Sharing standpoints and awareness of the local micro-politics, alliances, rivalries, controversies, social networks, and personal relationships proved to be a useful element in the pursuit of successful actions.

In Karditsa, the aim was strengthening an existing organisation that carried out important arrival infrastructuring work in the area, namely Stavrodromi (meaning 'Crossroads' in English). Stavrodromi functioned as an intercultural centre in Karditsa from 2019 to 2022, providing support to refugees and immigrants with their settlement and integration needs, and connecting them with Greek society. Funded by the ESTIA programme of the European Union (providing urban accommodation and cash assistance to refugees and asylum-seekers in Greece) and supported by UNHCR, it operated until the funding ended, forcing the centre to close. During its four years of operation, the centre provided educational, cultural, and recreational activities, significantly aiding newcomers' social inclusion through cooperation with local organisations.

Figure 56. The "Crossroads" or Stravrodromi community centrewhere newcomers and local stakeholders come together in Karditsa.

WE WORKED TOGETHER WITH STAVRODROMI
STAKEHOLDERS AND THE DEVELOPMENT AGENCY
OF KARDITSA (ANKA) AND CAME TO THE
CONCLUSION THAT THE EXPERIENCES AND
INFORMATION FROM STAVRODROMI SHOULD BE
TRANSFERRED TO AN ONLINE ENVIRONMENT.

We worked together with Stavrodromi's stakeholders and the municipal development agency of Karditsa (ANKA) and came to the conclusion that the experiences and information from Stavrodromi should be transferred to an online environment. Through the co-production process, we mapped out what the website functions should be based on Stavrodromi's previous service offerings, added the specific feature of job listings, and handed the plans over to ANKA for development and operation. Eventually, e-Stavrodromi was launched, continuing to support newcomers with critical information about the region. Now newcomers can find information online regarding employment opportunities, living conditions, and facilities offered for temporary and/or permanent settlement in the area. Following the development of the website, ANKA helped us present it at a public event, attended by representatives of key organisations such as UNHCR, IOM, and the Cities Network for Integration, Region of Thessaly, where the initiative was well received, inspiring ANKA to seek official funding to further develop it.

Figure 57. The website for e-Stavrodromi compiling resources and particularly employment and accommodation information for newcomers and local stakeholders.

Limitations and challenges

The main challenges for our actions were time limitations and unforeseen circumstances. The proposed actions sought to address the mismatch between the demand for labour and newcomer empowerment, but they required significant time and commitment from the partners, many of whom, such as grassroots and voluntary organisations, worked on a voluntary basis. It quickly became evident that the initiative's timeframe and its impact would extend well beyond the research period. Building the website and networks was time-intensive, and local partners agreed that the initiative should be seen as a starting point rather than a final outcome, with long-term benefits in mind. To ensure success, it was essential to actively involve local partners from the outset and co-design the process collaboratively.

By the end of 2022, most newcomers benefiting from the ESTIA programme were relocated to camps as the funding programme ended, prompting many to leave Karditsa. To address this challenge, we organised workshops with local residents and planned broader discussions for later stages. Yet several unforeseen events posed additional challenges, including regional and municipal elections in October 2023, which delayed activities to avoid political tensions, and severe storms in Thessaly in September 2023, which diverted attention to managing the natural disaster. These events underscored the politically sensitive nature of migration and integration, requiring careful timing and consideration of stakeholders' varying positions.

Reflections on the transformative potential of the action

Looking back at the initiative in Karditsa, it was clear that although there were limitations of time and resources, all partners embraced the opportunity to work together, paving the way for transformation. This transformation can be seen in three long-term dimensions. Firstly, beyond the website's role, the initiative fostered connections among local stakeholders. Secondly, the actions in Karditsa, especially the public event attended by international stakeholders, inspired other cities to consider similar engagements. Lastly, the process involved a shift in the narrative on migrant integration. This included introducing a more neutral vocabulary, such as 'newcomer', 'minor integrations', and 'arrival infrastructure', and launching the e-Stavrodromi platform. This platform has the potential to transform how migrants are treated, recognising them as vital contributors to society.

TAKEAWAYS

\# Coalition-building efforts often serve as starting points rather than final solutions, acting as catalysts for medium- and long-term transformations by fostering sustained collaboration and innovation.

\# Effective coalition-building requires engaging diverse stakeholders with a context-specific approach. Even with shared goals, tailored strategies are essential to navigate local dynamics and unique challenges.

\# Coalition-building has the potential to challenge dominant narratives and foster alternative perspectives, even in contexts resistant to change, by highlighting the value of inclusivity and collaboration.

> For other stories from the Karditsa/Katerini site, see:

p. 54, Volunteering in exchange for material support in Katerini: from charity to dignity and autonomy

p. 71, Mother-tongue language courses by asylum-seekers in Karditsa: nurturing transnational communities and cultivating trust in institutions

p. 145, Informal council of asylum-seekers in Karditsa: strengthening community ties and joining forces in advocacy for shared needs

p. 162, Friday meetings of newcomer women in public parks in Katerini: everyday convivial claiming of public space in the city

TOOL 23
DRAGON DREAMING FOR TRANSFORMATIVE ACTION PLANNING

MATERIALS: Paper, sticky notes, writing utensils.

TOOL SUMMARY: This tool is useful for brainstorming concrete ideas for transformative action. The exercise helps create an environment for ideation based on four principles of project implementation: dreaming, planning, doing, and celebrating. In four steps, participants take turns dreaming up solutions to a common problem or question, defining commonalities and key terms, turning dreams into objectives, and engaging in collaborative processes.

Dragon Dreaming is a method for project development that emphasises belonging, participation, and the sustainability of life as a whole. It is founded on three key principles: personal growth for all participants, community building, and environmental stewardship. Participants are encouraged to consider whether their actions benefit themselves, the community, and the environment. This method, created by John Croft and Vivienne Elanta, draws inspiration from their work with indigenous communities worldwide, particularly the Noongar people, nomadic indigenous inhabitants of southwestern Australia.

This method is particularly useful for thinking together with a group of people with diverse backgrounds, with the aim of creating a shared goal that is representative of the values and desires of the different participants.

What we present below, is inspired by the Dragon Dreaming method. We urge you to follow the link to the fully explained version if it triggers your attention. It is important to realise that Dragon Dreaming demands a lot of brain work and can not be speeded it up much, because then it loses its transformative potential. You have to count at least 2 hours for each step mentioned below and ideally, these parts are spread over multiple days and at the end of each step a celebratory moment can take place.

STEP 1: Initiate the dreaming circle

Prepare a question or prompt that is relevant to the arrival situation and the people gathered to participate, and share it with participants.

> For example (for the above story): 'Describe the asylum reception process in Karditsa 20 years from now, so you can say: Yes! It has improved significantly'. Or as another example from a workshop we organised together with the ATLAS-project at the Brussels site: 'How would people be housed in Brussels in 20 years from now, so that you can say: Yes! It could not be better'.

Sitting in a circle, take turns sharing responses to the prompt. Ask the participant to the right of the speaker to take notes while their neighbour shares. This way the role of note-taker is shared, active listening is practised, and you will have a collection of themes when the sharing period comes to an end.

 Identify shared themes

Once you have finished with the dreaming circle, work together to arrange the responses into groups. You can do this by gathering the sticky notes on a surface and arranging them by shared topics.

 Define key themes and objectives

For each group of responses, identify the key themes. Based on the key themes, define an objective.

> For example, say within one column you have the following responses grouped:
> - Multilingual service provision
> - Tailored support for newcomers designed by people with lived experience of seeking asylum
> - Childcare and child-friendly accommodation
> - Geographically accessible facilities
>
> Key themes could be multilingualism, tailored support, childcare, and accessibility. Based on these themes, the objectives could be: the creation of a multilingual arrival info-point, and provision of childcare facilities within one kilometre of each residence.

 Celebrate

Celebrating is an important part of the Dragon Dreaming process and involves acknowledging the value of collaboration and collective achievements, reflecting on the collaborative journey, sharing successes, deepening connections, and developing rituals and traditions.

Ask all participants to reflect on and share observations about the dreaming process. Acknowledge the collective work and shared experience. Consider a closing activity: sharing a meal together, taking a group photo, or starting a group chat where participants can continue connecting if desired.

> FURTHER READING: This tool is based on the Dragon Dreaming method and can include more steps for project ideation and implementation. For more information see: https://dragondreaming.org/. For more on the ATLAS-project, see: https://atlas-bxl.eu/.

3. EMPOWERING

Arrival often encompasses a condition of high vulnerability linked to intersecting mechanisms like gender inequality, legal statuses, temporariness, and discrimination. This chapter collects stories where the vulnerable condition of newcomers navigating the arrival context were key triggers for taking action and building coalitions. A case in point is the story about the recently arrived women in the Fatih district in Istanbul experiencing intersectional discrimination, hence discrimination that is not solely based on one characteristic, such as gender, race, ethnicity, religion, or class, but rather as a combination of these and other factors that interact in complex ways. Other stories concern undocumented people on the move in Thessaloniki and Stipendium Hungaricum (international scholarship) students in Budapest.

Coalitions can be activated to empower newcomers in vulnerable situations in their everyday lives and empowering can happen through transferring specific skills and competences or by sharing experiences. In the three accounts below, this objective took different formats. In Istanbul, our researcher organised a self-defence training that provided practical empowering tools and a safe space for sharing traumatic experiences. In Thessaloniki, the main action consisted of a participatory mapping project. In Budapest, our researchers carried out a community-building course with international students. Our researchers found that empowering initiatives require open safe spaces for exchange and mutual support. Starting from there, participants are able to share everyday experiences and build their power collectively.

A self-defence training in Istanbul: empowering participants and opening spaces of shared reflection

Gender-based and intersectional discrimination and violence have played a prominent role in the arrival processes of newcomers in the Fatih district in Istanbul. Our researcher organised self-defence trainings where participants acquire practical tools to empower themselves against different types of violence. Further aims of the training were creating a safe space to discuss taboo and sensitive topics as well as establishing community bonds based on a shared experience of violence.

Gender-based and intersectional discrimination

In the last decade in Turkey, anti-immigrant sentiments have been on the rise, with migrants and refugees getting the blame for the declining economy. Simultaneously, this public discussion intertwines with a rising anti-feminist narrative, strengthened by the public promotion of the 'Turkish familial unity' ideal, consisting of heterosexual Turkic Sunni Muslim individuals. In such a national context, where anti-immigrant and gender-normative sentiments intersect, the issue of violence against migrant women has become pressing.

Gender-based and intersectional discrimination has played a prominent role in the arrival processes of newcomers in the Fatih district in Istanbul. Over recent decades, some parts of the district (such as Aksaray and Laleli, see map in introduction p. 34) have emerged as places where young and middle-aged women from post-socialist countries have been arriving as shuttle traders. A shuttle trader is an individual or small business that travels across borders to buy goods in one country and then sells them in another, often taking advantage of price differences between regions. This type of trade is usually informal and can involve a wide range of products, from consumer goods to electronics. Other women have found work in low-paid jobs in the service and textile sectors, as well as the entertainment/sex work industry.

Many migrant women engage in complicated relationships with (local) shopkeepers, real estate brokers, and café managers that lie on the continuum of business and love, sex and friendship, or mutually benefiting partnerships. These relationships and the simultaneous development of migrant sex work in these localities have reinforced the public notoriety of the area as a place of prostitution. Such notoriety makes movement through public space and finding employment and housing particularly difficult and sensitive for (young) women newcomers. As a 'foreigner' in the space, it is not uncommon to be exposed to verbal and/or physical sexual harassment. In these neighbourhoods, there is limited presence of non-governmental and civil society organisations working with migrant populations.

Figure 58. Women in Istanbul attending a self-defence workshop in a safe space for newcomers.

The prominent role of discrimination and violence in the neighbourhoods and the limited presence of support services inspired us to organise self-defence trainings where participants acquire practical tools to empower themselves against different types of violence.

Identifying allies, spaces, and participants: the complex process of organising self-defence workshops

Organising self-defence workshops had the explicit objective of empowering women to defend themselves against different types of violence. However, the trainings also aimed at creating a safe space to discuss taboo topics relating to sexual violence and create a community bond based on the shared experience of violence among people with diverse backgrounds and roles. Many women in the area have very different national and ethnic backgrounds and often compete over the same jobs and have conflicting and hierarchic relationships with each other. To pursue these workshop objectives, collaboration with local stakeholders was crucial.

Developing defence training tailored to women in the arrival situation

To improve the relevance and reach of this action, we assembled a network of local experts. The first key stakeholder was the association Body Movement Vulnerability (BoMoVu), which provided the technical training. BoMoVu develops programmes and projects that use sports and body movement to help fight discrimination. They offer a specific type of self-defence called WenDo. WenDo is a participatory self-defence technique designed and taught by women. The technique aims to provide participants with the knowledge and skills to safeguard themselves against gender and sex-based violence and to empower women through building a connection with each other over the shared experience of violence.

Other 'allies' played crucial roles in refining the trainings, reaching potential participants, and in some cases also providing spaces for the trainings. A private health clinic that treats migrants in the Fatih district was essential in spreading the word and improving our offering. We held a first self-defence session with female employees of the clinic who are in contact with victims of sex and gender-based violence. They gave feedback on the session and advised on our training development based on their knowledge of the specific needs of the target group. Another training was held at the YOLO Art Centre, which owned by a Syrian woman who worked on gender-based violence issues as a social worker. This link had a double benefit. First, we were able to rent her space in the centre, thus contributing to her business, and second, her established contacts and reputation helped us spread the word about the trainings to the wider (young) Arabic-speaking population attending the centre's events.

Based on the success of these first trainings, we then offered further sessions at similar local associations with Arabic-speaking migrant women and association volunteers. In these workshops, the trainer explained about the different types of violence against women and young girls. She provided various tips on self-protection to keep in mind in different situations and gave demonstrations of self-defence techniques. In addition to word of mouth and the allies already described, we also launched an open call for women employers from various civil society initiatives, NGOs, and institutions.

Figure 59. The flyer for the self-defence Istanbul action.

Challenges and ethical dilemmas

In organising the training sessions we faced several challenges, particularly with stakeholder involvement, logistics, timing, participation, and sustainability. Engaging stakeholders meant dealing with diverse interests and availability, which sometimes varied even within the same organisation. In some instances, the extensive involvement of employees in the workshops conflicted with their organisations' commercial and administrative priorities, hindering the action's longevity and participation willingness. For example, one migrant organisation could not participate due to funding restrictions, as they needed to justify the involvement of migrant women in another project to their funders.

The training schedule was affected by significant events like the February 2023 earthquake and the May 2023 presidential elections, which pushed the sessions to summer. This period was not ideal due to holiday schedules and childcare needs. Additionally, the five-hour session length was difficult for many working women. This raised an ethical question about compensating participants for their time. Instead of monetary reimbursement, which seemed ethically questionable, participants received small gifts from the NGO Migrant Women Enterprise, and their transportation was covered.

Visibility also posed an ethical dilemma. With rising anti-immigrant sentiments, many support organisations had to operate discreetly. Migrants, especially undocumented ones, often avoid public spaces and events in this political climate. Addressing gender-based violence, a sensitive issue, required creating a safe space by ensuring the anonymity and security of the location and participants, and avoiding openly targeting migrant women. These factors should be seen as a catalyst for forming coalitions and should be integrated into existing initiatives of permanent organisations.

Reflections on the transformative potential of the action

Our action was guided by the umbrella objective of empowering women in the Fatih district, in the face of widespread gender-based violence and discrimination. Interestingly, the trainings produced further effects: participants were provided with knowledge and tips on violence and self-defence. They also found the trainings to be a space in which they could share individual experiences and create bonds. The solidarity that emerged between the local stakeholders, BoMoVu, the private clinic, other support associations for migrant women, and the individual women who took part in the workshops triggered and established new connections and coalitions that may be of further use in the future.

TAKEAWAYS

\# Newcomers often experience vulnerable conditions and can therefore be hard to reach. Seeking allies should be one of the first steps when taking action.

\# When planning a co-organised action with stakeholders who are not familiar with each other, it is important to determine roles and define responsibilities for each stakeholder.

\# Arrival contexts are highly dynamic, making it often impossible to ensure the continuity of activities. Relying on existing local organisations provides a way to navigate this challenge and achieve a longer-lasting impact.

> For other stories from the Istanbul site, see:

p. 65, Paperwork facilitation for residence permits in Istanbul: profiting from people's needs or enabling access to rights?

p. 78, Affordable childcare in Istanbul: mutual support facilitating access to work for migrant women

p. 103, Referring newcomers to other migrant organisations in a private clinic in Istanbul: access to services beyond healthcare

p. 129, A day off for Central Asian domestic workers in Istanbul: sharing knowledge on how to navigate challenging working conditions

TOOL 24
CHOOSING AN OUTREACH STRATEGY: OPEN CALL OR WORD OF MOUTH?

MATERIALS: Decision tree worksheet.

TOOL SUMMARY: This tool helps you decide between using an open call or word-of-mouth strategy for outreach in contexts where people face pressures like overstretched work schedules and restrictive migration laws. Open calls can reach a broad audience but may make the event too widely publicised, while word of mouth is more personal but limited to existing networks. The tool includes a decision tree and examples, such as in the case of Istanbul where a combination of targeted flyers and personal referrals effectively engaged the desired audience.

When working in an arrival context, taking action might involve reaching out to people who live under pressure, because of overstretched work schedules, the accumulation of multiple factors of vulnerability, or even tightening civic freedoms and restrictive migration laws. In light of this, tools to communicate a certain event have to be carefully chosen depending on the nature of the event and its target.

To reach the audience you are looking for, it is important to balance the pros and cons of different outreach methods. Open calls – though posters or other forms of invitations, through online of offline communication – can reach a wide audience. However, they can also exclude those who do not already have access to the chosen channels. On the other, the direct referral method allows for information to be shared personally by word of mouth, but will only reach people who are already part of a network.

Here is a decision tree to guide your outreach strategy:

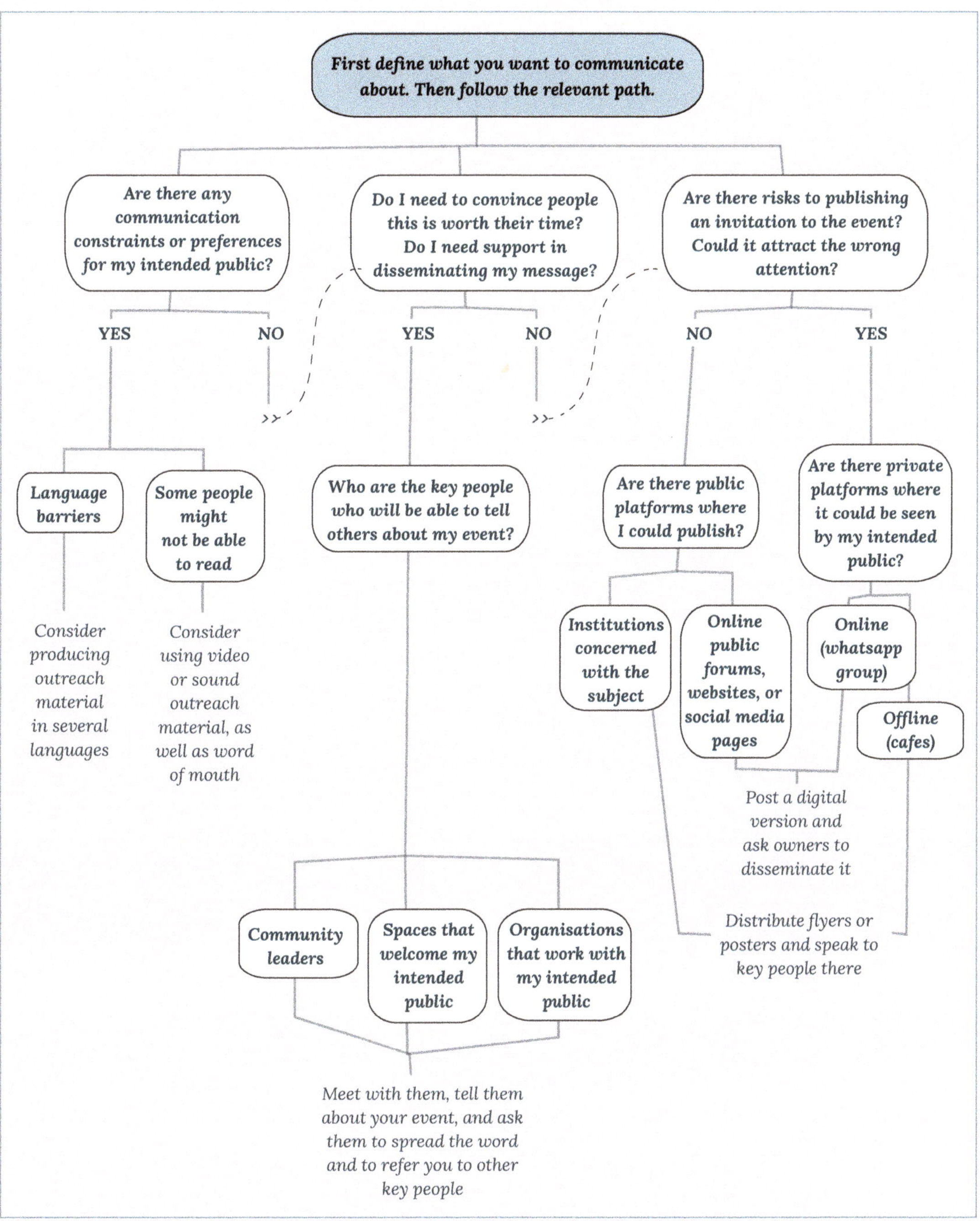

Figure 60. Diagram for choosing an outreach strategy.

In Istanbul, publicly inviting migrant women to a self-defence workshop was risky due to the xenophobic and sexist environment at the time of organising it. A more 'private' open call consisted in sending flyers to relevant organisations and community leaders, as well as posting the flyer on social media groups for migrants. This was successful in bringing together women who were employees at different migrant organisations, but not migrant women themselves. A creative solution was therefore adopted: key women who worked in key organisations were invited to a first self-defence training session, which allowed them to experience the workshop first-hand and see its benefits. They were then asked to spread the word among the beneficiaries of their organisations, which succeeded in bringing migrant women to the subsequent trainings.

REFLECTION

Choosing the right outreach strategy is crucial in contexts where people face significant pressures. Balancing the broad reach of open calls with the personal touch of word of mouth can effectively engage the desired audience. The decision tree provided helps you navigate these options, ensuring a tailored approach. The example from Istanbul demonstrates how combining targeted flyers with personal referrals can successfully connect with and involve the intended participants.

TOOL 25
SHARING CIRCLES: INTRODUCING A HORIZONTAL APPROACH TO GROUP SETTINGS

MATERIALS: Physical space to gather and form a circle with participants, writing utensils, notebook for note-taking (optional).

TOOL SUMMARY: This tool promotes a horizontal approach in group settings through 'sharing circles' to create safe, non-hierarchical spaces for exchange and trust-building. Facilitators participate equally with participants, breaking the pattern of unidirectional discussions. The tool includes steps for 'check-in' and 'check-out' moments to identify expectations, share feedback, and ensure a participatory and voluntary environment, as demonstrated in a successful training in Istanbul.

To create safe spaces of exchange and sharing, the format and approach of the action matter a lot. Horizontal approaches help participants to build connections and trust, especially in arrival contexts where there are a lot of unequal power relations. In group contexts, having the facilitator or trainer participate equally with the other participants makes it possible to achieve a less hierarchical environment by breaking the pattern of unidirectional discussion in which asylum-seekers and other migrants are asked to share about themselves without any reciprocity.

For an example of a 'check-in', try asking all participants to share when the last time they laughed or cried was.

An example of such an approach is to integrate 'sharing circles' into different steps of the process, especially to 'check in' and 'check out'.

STEP 1: Make a circle with everyone.

STEP 2: Ask each person to share a few words about the subject of your choice.

STEP 3: Recap. Address some questions that arise in the circle, share the plan for the action, make necessary changes according to the needs of the participants, and remind them that the action is participatory, voluntary, and non-hierarchical.

To foster a non-hierarchical environment:

For an example of a 'check-out', ask all participants to reflect on one thing they will take away from the exercise.

- Use a 'check-in' moment at the beginning of an activity to identify expectations and goals of participants.
- Use a 'check-out' moment to allow participants to share a final word, as well as their evaluation of the activity.

- Avoid a classic teacher–student relationship by sharing your own expectations and feelings, and more generally by participating in being vulnerable at the same level as the rest of the participants.

In Istanbul, the proposed training was not a 'classic' training format with a trainer at the front deciding on all the aspects of the training session. Instead of a top-down approach, the trainer ensured the non-hierarchical involvement of the participants by reminding them of principles such as voluntariness of participation, safe space, and anonymity. This openness and non-vertical approach helped participants to connect to each other and build trust. Once the participants realised that it was not a straight-forward knowledge/skill-sharing workshop but rather an open, reflexive space, they felt more relaxed and confident.

REFLECTION

Adopting a horizontal approach through sharing circles fosters a safe and non-hierarchical environment. This method encourages open dialogue and trust-building by allowing facilitators to participate equally with participants. The use of 'check-in' and 'check-out' moments helps to align expectations and gather feedback, ensuring a participatory atmosphere. The successful implementation in Istanbul highlights how such an approach can make participants feel more relaxed and confident, enhancing the overall effectiveness of the training.

A mapping project in Thessaloniki: co-producing and sharing knowledge to navigate the city

Many people on the move seek to cross northern Greece and the city of Thessaloniki without being registered and documented by the country's authorities. They attempt to cross the Balkans and apply for asylum in a central or northern European country. Due to a fear of detection by the authorities, their contact with the city and especially with the city centre is limited. Without this contact, people on the move miss out on crucial information about available services and support infrastructures. Therefore, the following action developed by our researcher revolved around mapping available and accessible arrival infrastructures. This included cataloguing locations of organisations and solidarity groups. Through workshops, information about safe and dangerous areas in Thessaloniki was collected. The handout paper map that was the outcome of this initiative was later distributed to people on the move temporarily living in the city.

Invisibility as a condition for people on the move to inhabit the city in northern Greece

People on the move often cross northern Greece and the city of Thessaloniki to reach the Balkans and later central or northern Europe. The European Dublin Convention requires new arrivals to Europe to seek asylum in the first country of arrival. Once registered there, they cannot move on further without permission. Given this restriction, it is a common practice to try to pass 'unnoticed' in first arrival European countries – such as Greece – and only formalise the asylum request upon arrival in the desired country.

Thus, journeys are planned in such a way as to avoid formalised encounters with local police authorities. Furthermore, people on the move often face the risk of deliberate pushbacks or attacks from local far-right groups and deportation. Remaining invisible is therefore a key priority of people on the move in northern Greece, who prefer isolated and 'less visible' places to live and therefore intentionally reduce their contacts with the city and the quite touristic city centre in particular. In Thessaloniki, an area with abandoned train wagons in the west of the city represents a stop-over for many people on the move. Here, they find shelter and a 'safe' space to temporarily pause on their journey.

Remaining invisible often also implies disconnectedness from local resources, and hence missing out on information about the services and support infrastructures that are available. To address this issue, we organised an action to empower people on the move that simultaneously respects their need for remaining invisible while strengthening their connection to available resources.

Building trust and 'safe spaces' for engagement: co-producing a map

Building a coalition and improving outreach

With the overarching aim of empowering people, taking action involved the production of a map with two objectives. The first was to create and share information about dangerous and safe urban spaces and available arrival infrastructures that might be unknown to newcomers. A second objective was to 'co-produce' this information. We did this by forming a coalition with like-minded local stakeholders, people on the move, and old and newcomers and involving them in the mapping process.

To begin the mapping process, it was essential that we could rely on existing relationships and trust built during previous fieldwork, given the specific circumstances of the people involved. Personal contacts were crucial entry points for taking action. Connections with grassroots humanitarian organisations enabled their inclusion on the map and facilitated contact with the people they assist. Established relationships with newcomers and long-term residents of Thessaloniki were also vital, as trust had already been established.

The action

The main focus of our co-production took place around co-creating a map. The plan was to make a map based on desk and field research and the views, perceptions, and experiences of newcomers. We broke the development and sharing of the map into three main components: desk research, workshops, and getting the word out.

First, we did desk research to make a comprehensive list of the locations of applicable organisations and solidarity groups active in Thessaloniki. Then we began the participatory interactive workshops with newcomers. At the beginning of each workshop, we informed participants about the mapping activity's objective and asked them to draw their own perception of Thessaloniki on A3 paper using markers. They highlighted important areas, streets, points of interest, and meeting places, as well as unfriendly parts of the city. In the second part of the workshop, we used a printed map of the city centre, only showing the urban layout, onto which participants pinned relevant infrastructures such as NGOs, cafés, restaurants, barbershops, mini markets, and places frequented by people on the move. They also marked their favourite spots where they had had pleasant experiences.

On the same map, using a different colour, we asked them to indicate areas where they felt uncomfortable, such as police checkpoints or places where they had experienced racism. In the final stage of the workshop, participants drew their typical daily routes through the city. Interestingly, some areas visible on all tourist maps were invisible on our participants' maps. Conversely, areas with a high concentration of arrival infrastructures in the city centre were overrepresented, and certain spots were clearly avoided in their daily routes. After the workshops, we used the results to make a distributable map combining the findings. We then shared and discussed the resulting maps (in which several types of mappings were overlapped) with newly arrived people on the move.

Who was involved?

Co-production and sharing of the map were the core of the initiative: in the first place it was very important to create a 'safe space for engagement', a friendly atmosphere where the workshop could take place and where new relationships were often formed. Participants included migrants living in Thessaloniki, aged between 18 and 32 and mainly coming from Afghanistan, Algeria, Iran, Iraq, Morocco, Palestine, and Syria. Importantly, it became clear that each participant produced a unique map and collectively a plural geography of the city emerged, where each group – longer-established immigrants, newcomers living outside the city, and people on the move – emphasised a different urban area.

Figure 61. Participatory map-making in Thessaloniki with people on the move.

Challenges and ethical considerations

The main obstacle we encountered was directly related to the issue the action aimed to address: improving the temporary stay in Thessaloniki for people on the move. Their short stays often meant they lacked a comprehensive under-standing of the urban environment, making the mapping process challenging. More importantly, their brief time in Thessaloniki often did not allow enough time to build new relationships of trust. In this context, the support of local residents became crucial. These individuals acted as intermediaries between the organisers and the people on the move who were invited to participate.

An ethical dilemma also arose: how to discuss and share the routes of people on the move without making them too visible? There was a balance to be struck between the usefulness of sharing navigation information and the need to protect the privacy of these individuals, whose invisibility is often vital for their safety. To address this, we adopted different strategies. The map clearly showed only the locations of solidarity groups, NGOs with public profiles, and other public arrival infrastructures. Other layers, such as safe and dangerous areas and everyday routes, were sketched and discussed with newcomers only when the map was distributed. This approach not only protected the participants but also added a reflective element to the process, where further knowledge was both shared and co-produced.

Reflections on the transformative potential of the action

The co-creation of a map became a valuable tool for newcomers in their daily lives and navigation of the city. Beyond empowering people on the move, our collaborative mapping also illuminated the spatial experiences of undocumented migrants, who often face exclusion and insecurity. The insights gained through participatory mapping can therefore inform civil society organisations and enabled them to better address the needs of undocumented migrants.

Moreover, our mapping project also showed that conventional navigation systems like Google Maps fail to capture newcomers' complex spatial realities and strategies for survival because places that are important for their survival are not depicted. Through the workshops, undocumented people on the move also redefined their relationship with urban space, challenging dominant narratives and reconfiguring notions of belonging and safety. Their reflexive gaze challenges the city and raises the question: which parts of the urban fabric, and the arrival infrastructure of the city, are experienced by people in vulnerable positions as more welcoming and which as more inhospitable?

TAKEAWAYS

\# Invisibility is both a survival strategy and a barrier. The need to remain unnoticed underscores the precariousness of newcomers' journeys, but it also limits access to vital resources. Balancing these competing priorities is a recurring challenge for actions engaging with newcomers.

\# In contexts of vulnerability and temporariness, building trust as a foundation for action is essential. Leveraging pre-existing relationships with individuals or organisations that act as intermediaries can provide a strong starting point for fostering engagement and collaboration.

Empowering individuals to share their experiences and knowledge can reshape perceptions and highlight diverse ways of navigating challenges. As such, it offers an opportunity to counteract dominant narratives on migration and integration and co-create alternative perspectives and urban imaginaries. Yet collaborations must be aware of the potential for power imbalances, ensuring that the voices of people on the move are not overshadowed by those of other stakeholders.

While sharing information is vital, making certain knowledge public risks compromising safety. The selective inclusion of data, such as publicly known infrastructures over sensitive routes, demonstrates a thoughtful approach to mitigating risks.

> See also **TOOL 12**: 'Analysing discourses and their impacts'. p. 170

> For other stories from the Thessaloniki site, see:

p. 52, Self-organised community centre next to the abandoned train wagons in Thessaloniki: solidarity beyond borders

p. 80, Occupying abandoned buildings as temporary shelter in Thessaloniki: vacancy as resourcefulness in the city

p. 127, Coming together in abandoned train wagons in Thessaloniki: transforming desolate spaces into hubs of solidarity for people on the move

p. 172, From 'migrants', 'asylum-seekers', and 'refugees' to 'people on the move' in Thessaloniki: resisting government labelling of people

TOOL 26
COLLABORATIVE MAPPING TO MAKE VISIBLE MARGINALISED SPATIAL EXPERIENCES

MATERIALS: Paper, writing utensils, coloured markers, stickers, map printouts.

TOOL SUMMARY: This tool promotes collaborative mapping as a way to foster communication and share knowledge. Participants co-create maps, drawing on blank paper or printed base maps, either collectively or individually, and represent important waypoints, landmarks, and feelings. The process emphasises the conversation and activity over the final product, making it an excellent tool for collective dialogue that is able to overcome language barriers and make visible marginalised spatial experiences.

Collaborative mapping is a method that aims to foster a space for communication through the co-creation of maps. Collaborative mapping workshops can be lead in different ways, for example:

- participants are invited to draw on a blank piece of paper, or on a printed base map showing the geography of an area, with pens, paint, or other materials;
- they are invited to draw collectively or each on their own paper;
- they are asked to draw landmarks or to represent feelings;
- the workshop can be two hours long or span over several weeks.

In short, the formats of the collaborative mapping processes are varied. It is important to reflect on the best approach, which will depend on the context of the workshop you are organising, the time you have, and the trust of participants. However, all formats have a few important things in common:

- they take, as a starting point, a space or geography to be drawn and commented on;
- the conversation around the activity and the process of producing a map is more important than the final product.

Collaborative mapping, then, is an excellent tool for opening up a collective dialogue.

In the following we provide a step-by-step plan to launch your own collaborative mapping workshop (based on the story above).

STEP 1: Pre-workshop preparation:

- Desk research
  Identify and document the locations and addresses of organisations and solidarity groups that provide support to people on the move.
- Building trust
  Leverage existing relationships with local stakeholders, grassroots humanitarian organisations, and local residents to establish trust with newcomers.

STEP 2: Participatory workshops:

- Creating a safe space
  Ensure a friendly and welcoming atmosphere for the workshops.
- Informing participants
  Explain the objective of the mapping activity to the participants.
- Mental mapping
  Provide A3 papers and markers. Ask participants to draw their perception of the arrival context (the example was Thessaloniki), including important streets, points of interest, meeting places, and unfriendly areas. Do not worry about accuracy.
- Collaborative mapping
  Use a printed a blank map of the city centre. Ask participants to:
  Pin relevant infrastructures (NGOs, cafés, restaurants, barbershops, mini markets, etc.).
  Mark spots where they feel uncomfortable (e.g. police checkpoints, areas with incidents of violence or discrimination).
  Draw typical routes they follow daily.

STEP 3: Reflection and analysis:

- Combining maps
  Overlay the mental maps with the printed maps to identify patterns and areas of concern.
- Identifying key areas
  Note areas that are overrepresented or avoided and understand the reasons behind these patterns.

STEP 4: Sharing the map (optional)

- Distributing the map
  Share the final map with people on the move and/or temporarily living in the arrival context.
- Discussing findings
  Engage with new participants to discuss the map and gather additional insights.

Tips for success:

- Engage local stakeholders. Collaborate with local organisations and individuals who have established trust with the target group.

- Create a welcoming environment. Ensure that the workshop setting is comfortable and conducive to open discussion.

- Be flexible. Adapt the process based on the participants' feedback and needs.

- Respect privacy. Ensure that the information shared does not compromise the safety or anonymity of the participants.

Collaborative mapping is a powerful method for fostering communication and sharing knowledge. By co-creating maps, participants engage in meaningful dialogue, emphasising the process over the final product. In the context of migration, some ethical aspects of collaborative mapping are particularly salient, one of them being the risk, when producing a map, of exposing certain information that should remain invisible. In Thessaloniki, the mapping process tackled this issue by only sharing information that would not harm people on the move if revealed to the public, and keeping some sensitive information private or only verbally shared.

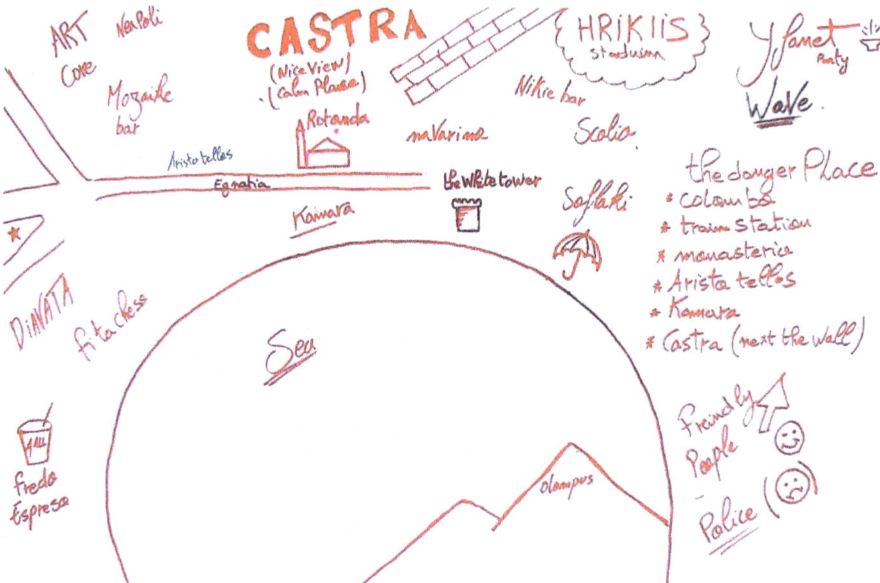

Figure 62. Mental mapping with people on the move in Thessaloniki.

> FURTHER READING:

This tool and the mapping project in Thessaloniki were inspired by other collaborative mapping projects in contexts of migration. To see what they were able to achieve, check out the following projects: Crossing Maps (Fabien Fischer, Lauriane Houbey, Marie Moreau, Sarah Mekdjian, Anne-Laure Amilhat-Szary) and Mapping Journey Project by Bouchra Khalili.

Crossing Maps
For several months, twice a week, Sarah Mekdjian and Marie Moreau hosted a space where asylum-seekers mapped their migration trajectory in non-conventional ways, breaking with the tradition of representing migration through a single unobstructed arrow. Some migrants made their maps out of clay or embroidery. Slowly, the group converged towards the creation of a common legend for their maps (with red representing danger, for example), thus allowing them to have a 'universal' common language across language barriers. These maps were then used in geography classes and exhibited in museums to tell a different story of crossing borders. The mappers were given authorship and therefore receive credit every time their maps are published. You can learn more about the project here: https://www.antiatlas.net/fischer-houbey-moreau-mekdjian-amilhat-szary-crossing-maps-cartographies-traverses/.

Mapping Journey Project
The Mapping Journey Project is a series of videos produced by Bouchra Khalili with migrants who had crossed the Mediterranean. While they narrate their journey, their hand, visible on camera, traces their journey with a permanent marker on a printed colour map. The maps are the product of the dialogue between the artist and the person in front of her. With these, Khalili aims to bring to the fore practices of resistance to the borders of nation-states. These maps succeed in producing stories about migration. The video format makes it possible to bring the voice of the migrant to life. You can learn more at her website: https://www.bouchrakhalili.com/the-mapping-journey-project/.

A community-building course in Budapest: supporting students in connecting and addressing shared challenges of repression

> Stipendium Hungaricum (international scholarship) students in Budapest encounter common problems when trying to integrate, such as language barriers, discrimination on the housing market, unemployment, lack of information, loneliness, exclusionary bureaucratic practices, and culture shock. These individual elements appear as part of a broader framework of weak and limited social connections between the students, especially between Hungarians and internationals. This limiting context prevents students from developing collective initiatives to influence their environment and cope with the problems at a community level. The main goal of the initiative taken by our researchers was to help students connect and enable them to articulate their challenges, find solutions, and actively generate changes. Thus, a project-based community-building course was designed where students learn how to implement collective activities within the arrival environment of the university.

Universities as arrival infrastructures in a hostile political framework: strengthening social bonds between students

Hungary is seeing an increasing number of third-country nationals, in particular people who are not citizens of an EU member state. However, the national political debate promotes a hostile, ideologically driven stance on immigration, and the country lacks a comprehensive integration strategy at the state policy level. Instead, the state has adopted an ideology that deliberately sidesteps issues related to integration and citizenship. In this challenging political climate, local contexts and institutions take on a vital role. Universities, in particular, serve as key arrival spaces.

The case of the Stipendium Hungaricum scholarship is an example of controlled migration without support for integration. Stipendium Hungaricum is a governmental programme that invites international students to study in Hungarian universities, through controlled entry and access to services. The formal aim is the internationalisation of higher education. Locally, at the university level, this also implies the university becoming part of the arrival infrastructure. This requires a new set of competences and generates challenges that often extend beyond what is expected of the university. Despite universities expressing interest and developing internationalisation strategies, the lack of arrival infrastructuring competences can lead to beneficiary international students missing out on the support they need to settle in Hungary.

In the face of a national anti-migration discourse and despite the efforts of some local organisations to counter this, the everyday life of international students is

Figure 63. Taking action in the university classroom to build community and belonging among international students in Hungary.

still largely affected by exclusionary, power-driven political speech. Students told us that they face language barriers, discrimination on the housing market, unemployment, lack of information, loneliness, exclusionary bureaucratic practices, and culture shock. These individual elements appear as part of a broader framework of weak and limited social connections between the local and international students.

Based on this limiting context, we proposed an action to support students in connecting and enabling them to articulate their challenges, find solutions, and actively generate changes. This took the shape of a project-based community-building course where students learn how to implement collective activities in order to strengthen arrival infrastructuring work, grassroots, bottom-up governance, and democratic functioning.

Strengthening the arrival infrastructure 'from the inside': organising a project-based community-building course

Given the hostile context, we decided to act within the university institutional framework to empower international and Hungarian students by proposing to add a community-building course to the curriculum. By having it formally included in the university, we were able to overcome a key question: how can we reach students effectively? As opposed to an extra-curricular event or external workshop, students could easily access the seminar. It fit into their schedules and took a familiar format without requiring new roles or identities, and a common language and set of behaviours was already in place.

Building on previous positive interactions established during our fieldwork, we decided to collaborate with the Social Science Faculty at Eötvös Loránd University (ELTE). The choice of this stakeholder was twofold. First, it was important to work with a stakeholder willing to be included in our effort to build coalitions around our common goal. This meant they had to be willing to be an active part of the initiative and to take an active role in decision-making. Second, it was crucial to be able to align the action proposal with the criteria and conditions of the university course, which in the case of ELTE turned out to be possible. The process was further followed by a group of stakeholders that we identified and engaged with ad hoc: the Student Council, the Vice Deans, the International Office of the Faculty, and the Heads of Departments.

The university course, entitled 'From Strangers to Members – Community-Building in Practice', targeted international and Hungarian students of the Social Science Faculty of ELTE in Spring 2023. It was made accessible to bachelor's and master's students. The course was organised so that we, the researchers, acted as mediators. We adopted a critical pedagogy methodology that involved open reflection on how an education system can counter institutionalised repression and inequality. Adopting egalitarian positions and roles instead of a classic teacher–student relationship was essential, as was creating a common space that also represents equality in its layout and arrangement. In addition, this pedagogical model required the joint establishment of rules within the seminar community, giving students as much autonomy as possible. At this stage, sharing the analytical approach of our research proved useful to support and trigger a reflection on these issues.

The activities of the course included four consecutive modules:

(a) Community building, focusing on the individual's place in an intercultural setting. Students experienced 'community in action' by playing a cooperative problem-solving game.

(b) Identification of problems, obstacles, and challenges in integration. By sharing their stories individually and in groups, students made obstacles more visible and developed reciprocal solidarity.

(c) Forming project teams around potential interventions. Students learned how to plan an intervention and how to take action themselves by listening to the experience of us as researchers and by reflecting upon it through a self-reflection exercise.

d) Intervention, planning, needs assessment, stakeholder meetings, and actions. The participants formed two teams, one engaging in an awareness poster campaign and the other in active intervention. They also held a meeting with the Vice Dean and student coordinators to plan and discuss their proposals.

Finally, together we organised an extra event outside the university to reflect upon the course experience and share evaluation criteria with the students and the faculty leadership.

Obstacles and ethical concerns

The seminar was carefully prepared thanks to the extensive experience of our researchers in training and working with newcomer youth. In this sense, the main obstacle consisted in balancing the conditions and obligations set by the institutional framework and individual needs of the students. These challenges were often hard to plan for. On the one hand, academic obligations and workloads during certain periods hindered the full and continuous participation of all students in the course. Similarly, the assigned time slot of 90 minutes proved a challenging format for conducting in-depth community building. On the other hand, students also presented individual and specific needs depending on their situations, for instance the need to match the university commitment to employment. In this sense, the preparation work done for the seminar was crucial. Continuous attention to collective and individual needs and an effort to make communication as effective as possible was also important. This involved complementing the seminar with ad hoc exchanges, and sometimes covering one-to-one communication with students who, for instance, missed some classes. In this regard, an interesting topic of discussion was finding a common understanding of 'success'. This was useful when student ambitions did not match the given timeframe and became an important part of the development process.

The major ethical dilemma concerned our position as researchers within the university framework. To retain the trust of our collaborating stakeholders, we worked to maintain an 'outside-inside position'. We saw ourselves as working from within the arrival infrastructure to strengthen it, while still ensuring a certain degree of independence from it. This meant finding a balance between highlighting shortcomings and exclusionary mechanisms of institutional functioning and developing trust based on cooperation. A balance also had to be struck found in student–teacher relationships, where a strong emphasis was put on our role as facilitators so as to leave the stage as much as possible to students.

Reflections on the transformative potential of the action

Our action aimed to empower students and the arrival infrastructure in general by working on community building. Interestingly, this experience resulted in an opportunity to achieve at least three goals: create a common space to share knowledge and reflect upon common interests, provide students with tools to generate transformative actions in their communities, and build a replicable experience within the university.

The grassroots community-building process was intended to reflect upon the systemic exclusion that dominates Hungarian public debate, with its anti-immigrant rhetoric. This kind of attention to the micro-level needs of small communities and the mapping of where processes of inclusion break down, made it possible to create a community that, by taking the steps of agency, inclusiveness, social intervention, and activism, could generate a sense of belonging and empower community members to act against exclusion. Finally, it was also very productive to propose an initiative that had the potential to be continued within the arrival infrastructure, and indeed the Faculty's leadership invited us to replicate the course in the next academic year.

TAKEAWAYS

Local institutions, such as universities, often have an important role in the arrival infrastructure. Taking action within these institutions can aim at strengthening the arrival infrastructure 'from the inside'.

Building coalitions within an existing setting involves negotiating reciprocal positioning and goals and can be a nice opportunity for replicability.

Community building can empower people in diverse ways: creating bonds, making them more aware of existing exclusionary frameworks and dynamics, and developing skills to strengthen inclusion.

> For other stories from the Budapest site, see:

p. 89, Student dormitories in Hungary: spaces of integration or segregation?

p. 174, Rejecting the word 'migrant' in a shrinking civic space: the balancing act of civil society organisations in Hungary.

TOOL 27
BARNGA: A COMMUNITY-BUILDING EXERCISE WITH A TWIST

MATERIALS:
- Several decks of cards (only cards A to 7).
- Printed copies of the set of Barnga rules for each group (available for download).
- Blank paper and pens for silent communication (writing is not allowed).
- A timer.

TOOL SUMMARY: Barnga is a community-building card game that simulates intercultural communication by having participants play with different sets of rules without knowing it. This exercise helps players experience and reflect on the dynamics of intercultural interactions, such as assumptions and biases stemming from cultural differences. A debrief session follows the game, allowing participants to discuss their experiences and relate them to real-life intercultural communication challenges.

Community-building exercises are tools aimed at helping participants to get to know each other and create bonds. They are essential when starting to build coalitions, especially with a group of people who do not know each other yet. They reinforce group cohesion and communication, they create trust among its individuals, and they allow participants to get to know each other beyond the surface level. They include games, field visits, cooperative problem solving exercises, ice-breaking exercises, and more.

As a community-building game, Barnga has the added value, in arrival contexts, of imitating intercultural communication. In this card game, participants play a card game silently without knowing that they are each operating with a different set of rules. Through the game, players experience first-hand (with frustration and a certain amount of tension) some of the dynamics of intercultural communication, such as:

- What happens when people assume that others are working with the same 'rules' they apply to themselves?
- Who is adapting to the rules of whom? Who integrates or assimilates, and who dominates culturally? Whose social rules are considered the 'right' ones?
- How do we develop unconventional means of communication to overcome differences in perspective?
- An essential debrief moment at the end of the game allows players to vent about their experiences and relate this moment of simulated intercultural communication to real-life instances where they experienced similar social dynamics.

In the following, we explain step by step how to play Barnga.

Preparation (10 minutes)

Set-up:

- Download and print the rules of Barnga: https://sites.lsa.umich.edu/equi-table-teaching/barnga/. There are separate rules for each group, with the option to form up to eight groups.
- Divide the participants into groups of 3–4 players.
- Each group should have a deck of cards and a set of rules.
- Ensure that each group receives a different set of rules without knowing that other groups have different rules.

Introduction (15 minutes)

Explain the game:

- Briefly explain that they will be playing a card game in silence.
- Emphasise that communication should only occur through gestures and non-verbal cues.
- Distribute the rules to each group and give them 5 minutes to read and understand their rules.

Start the game:

- After the rules are understood, collect the rule sheets.
- Inform the participants that they will rotate tables after each round.

Game play (15 minutes)

Rounds:

- Each round lasts 5 minutes.
- After each round, participants rotate to a new table with a new group.
- Ensure that participants do not take their rule sheets with them.

Observations:

- The facilitator should observe the interactions and note any confusion, frustration, or adaptation strategies.

Debrief (20 minutes)

Discussion:

- Gather all participants and start a discussion about their experiences.
- Ask questions such as:
  - How did you feel when you realised others were playing by different rules?
  - What strategies did you use to communicate and adapt?
  - How does this experience relate to real-life intercultural communication?
- Encourage participants to share their thoughts on assumptions, and cultural dominance.
- Discuss how these dynamics play out in their personal and professional lives.

Conclusion

- Summarise the key learnings from the exercise.
- Highlight the importance of understanding and adapting to different cultural norms and communication styles.

In Budapest, international students face barriers to inclusion with regard to language, employment status, lack of information, loneliness, exclusionary bureaucratic practices, and culture shock. Community-building exercises helped students build relationships and find allies across geographical and cultural differences.

REFLECTION

Barnga is a community-building exercise that simulates the complexities of intercultural communication. By having participants play a card game with different sets of rules, it brings to the fore the challenges posed by assumptions and biases stemming from cultural differences. The debrief session is crucial, allowing participants to discuss their experiences and draw parallels to real-life intercultural interactions. This exercise not only fosters group cohesion but also deepens understanding of diverse communication styles and cultural norms.

> FURTHER READING: Full rules for the game of Barnga can be found at: https://sites.lsa.umich.edu/equitable-teaching/barnga/. Thiagarajan, Sivasailam, and Raja Thiagarajan. 2006. *Barnga*. Boston & London: Nicholas Brealey.

REFLECTION AND ADVICE

This chapter gathers advice and reflections on taking actions in arrival infrastructure contexts. It is directly based on the experiences of our researchers. In several meetings, we discussed their actions and reflected back on the process of action-taking, as there is much to learn from both their successes and failures. Out of these discussions, cross-cutting issues emerged that proved critical and useful when taking action in arrival infrastructure contexts, which we are glad to share here.

A. BALANCING VISIBILITY: TAKING CARE NOT TO OVEREXPOSE YOURSELF OR OTHERS

When taking action involves organising public events or seeking media coverage, as in some of the cases described above, you as well as the people with whom you collaborate will be exposed in one way or another. This process of becoming visible cannot be fully controlled, and as an organiser you can encounter unexpected situations, as our researcher describes below:

> "Some of the people that came, I didn't expect and some of the people
> I wanted to come, didn't show up. Other people that I had never met
> before, also showed up and were offensive. That was not the intention.
> I wasn't capable of managing that"
>
> —RESEARCHER FROM THE HASPENGOUW/WESTLAND SITE, OCTOBER 2023.

More generally, taking action and engaging yourself in arrival infrastructuring almost always involves unexpected encounters and publicity that can be challenging for you and your co-organisers. It is important to be aware of this unpredictability before you start your action and take mitigation measures beforehand.

Even more important is to acknowledge that taking action in the context of arrival infrastructuring often involves working with newcomers in very precarious and vulnerable situations. For them, there is a significant risk of overexposure, for instance when privacy details about people without papers are released. In the Brussels action, activists, researchers, citizens, and newcomers got involved in activities that were widely covered by the media. As described by our researcher, this raised concerns about the extent to which exposure of newcomers in vulnerable positions should and could be controlled:

> "It went so fast and it was hard to foresee that there would be so many cameras. I brought someone to a talk about the housing precarity they experience. I then realised that you can put a lot of work into creating safe spaces, but the danger [of overexposure] remains, even when you have a rather planned event. We have to keep talking, discussing, learning from it"
>
> —RESEARCHER FROM THE BRUSSELS SITE, OCTOBER 2023.

The unexpected media attention put the safe space created among the collaborators at risk, as newcomers were exposed to a hateful or inflammatory public debate that they might not have been ready to hear, for instance anti-migration speech of politicians or discussions about housing precarity when they had only recently arrived.

The question of exposure of the people with whom and for whom you take action is a core issue whenever you intervene in the arrival infrastructure. Being aware of the differing levels of risks that exposure entails and the varying degrees of vulnerability is key. It is therefore always important to reflect on your own position in relation to others when taking an action and to try to acknowledge how other people are situated differently from you and that the action might put them in even more vulnerable positions.

> "Be mindful of the situations you expose your collaborators to, such as interactions with media outlets or sensitive information they might prefer to avoid"
>
> —RESEARCHER FROM THE BRUSSELS SITE AND RESEARCHER FROM THE ISTANBUL SITE, SEPTEMBER 2023.

B. FLEXIBLE PLANNING FOR AN OPEN-ENDED PROCESS

Taking action within the complex social, political, and economic realities of arrival infrastructure contexts often requires walking a fine line between ambition and flexibility. External factors such as polarising political debates, elections, natural disasters, etc. can impose significant constraints on your action and change stakeholder availability considerably. One of our researchers highlighted this reality:

> "There were unforeseen elections, we had heavy rainfall. We were set back two months and it took a long time before the stakeholders could meet us. Patience is important. In September, we re-elected a right-wing government [that promoted strict border policies]. Yet, two months after the elections, a politician said that we should regularise many undocumented migrants in Greece, because they are actually needed for labour. This provided the perfect momentum to get all the stakeholders back together"
>
> —RESEARCHER FROM THE KARDITSA/KATERINI SITE, OCTOBER 2023.

The dynamic and volatile nature of arrival infrastructure contexts means that a patient, adaptable, and not overly goal-oriented attitude is essential. While it is important to plan ambitiously, flexibility and not overprioritizing end results can help you view your action from a longer-term perspective, as explained by our researcher: "We really learned that plans should be ambitious, but we needed patience for those findings and ambitious plans to work out" (Researcher from the Karditsa/Katerini site, October 2023).

Thus, while ambition is critical for driving meaningful action, it must be tempered with an openness to adapt to changing conditions – both within the arrival infrastructure and more broadly.

Moreover, keeping in mind that the process of action-taking is as important as the outcome will help you not only enjoy it more, but also value even its unpredictable parts. Acknowledging that the final event or occurrence of an action is only one of the many important phases of it is also an invitation to stretch what it means to work towards transformation and change. Indeed, you can also be transformative by doing things otherwise and by introducing a mindful, fair, and inclusive approach to action-taking. In fact, this may even increase the transformative potential of your action.

> "Accept that it's not going to be perfect, it has a life of its own, and you don't have control over everything"
>
> —RESEARCHER FROM THE LONDON SITE AND RESEARCHER FROM THE DORTMUND SITE, SEPTEMBER 2023).

This perspective not only helps manage the unpredictable but also encourages embracing trial and error with a good dose of realism: "Accept that it's not going to be perfect, it has a life of its own, and you don't have control over everything" (Researcher from the London site and Researcher from the Dortmund site, September 2023).

There is also a lot of wisdom in viewing your action as an open and unfinished process. Organisational tools and schemes should not only plan for outcomes but also include mechanisms to accommodate redefinitions of interventions, timing adjustments, and shifts in stakeholder involvement. The flexibility to adapt to unforeseen circumstances can transform small and scattered interactions into meaningful contributions.

> "When I prepared for taking action, I picked a location for the first event:
> a park. I had a lot of plans, building, mapping, walking, podcasting. Even
> though I wanted to start in a park, another place emerged: a building, which
> became a hotspot. I dropped all the plans I had. I still like them, but it did
> not feel right. I started volunteering, seeing where I can help. From there on
> I started to do very small actions, asking for left-over bread, I helped with
> a tour and translation, I started to talk to neighbours, to create contacts in
> the neighbourhood. This became my action; from there on, bigger and
> mediatized actions emerged"
>
> —RESEARCHER FROM THE BRUSSELS SITE, OCTOBER 2023.

Moreover, understanding the value of smaller, everyday exchanges and collaborations crucial. These interactions build the foundation for larger, more structured actions, even if they do not immediately appear transformative. By recognising the intrinsic value of the process itself, you can reframe success to include the transformative potential of incremental, situated actions that include multiple iterations of action and reflection. In navigating the challenges of arrival infrastructure contexts, a mindset of experimentation and adaptation is thus essential. Trial and error become tools for learning, and the process – with all its unpredictability – offers its own lessons and findings.

C. NAVIGATING POWER RELATIONS AND CREATING SAFE SPACES FOR ENGAGEMENT

A critical step when taking action is to seek 'allies' from the earliest stages of planning. These are often local stakeholders and often bring essential context-specific knowledge and valuable networks that can support you in tackling the relevant issues and navigating power relations when implementing your action.

Moreover, within arrival infrastructure contexts, it is of vital importance to address unequal power dynamics when taking action. At the same time, it is important to also be attentive to the new power dynamics that emerge during the process of taking action. Power is often unevenly distributed among stakeholders, influenced by factors such as language skills, employment status, migration status, cultural backgrounds, etc. and people experiencing intersectional discrimination based on a combination of their race, gender, class, etc. are often in the most precarious power positions. To ensure that your actions remain equitable and inclusive, it is important to continuously recognise and respond to these dynamics.

"As a facilitator of the action: lower the barriers to engagement, keep it easy and understandable"

—RESEARCHER FROM THE LONDON SITE AND RESEARCHER FROM THE DORTMUND SITE, SEPTEMBER 2023.

As such, taking action in arrival infrastructure contexts inevitably involves creating safe spaces for engagement with local stakeholders, particularly newcomers. A key focus in this regard is the creation of safe spaces where people feel empowered to contribute. The nature of these spaces depends on the objectives, the format of the action, and the intended audience. Safe spaces should enable participation while striving for 'horizontal' or equal relationships among all involved. In Thessaloniki, for instance, cooking sessions inspired active participation, allowing individuals to take on meaningful roles rather than being passive observers. A researcher from Thessaloniki noted how the act of cooking transformed roles:

"The guest becomes the host in the cooking process. Through this, participants gain confidence and feel more comfortable expressing themselves. Unexpected similarities often emerge, sometimes challenging deeply ingrained views"

—RESEARCHER FROM THESSALONIKI SITE, OCTOBER 2023.

Taking action also requires a reflexive approach, where you remain aware and critical of your own methods. This reflexivity must be accompanied by a willingness to continually redefine methods and question who is involved and who is not (yet) involved. Building a safe space thus requires careful consideration of who it is for and who will participate in its construction.

However, defining these groups is not always straightforward, especially when working with people on the move or within actions that are inherently open-ended. In the case of the participatory exhibitions in Westland and Haspengouw, the need for a continuous redefinition of the participants and of the ways of involving them was crucial, as our researcher discusses:

"As the literature and experiences with Participatory Action Research show, using co-creative, artistic, audio-visual, and collaborative methods – all of which have been part of the process of creating the exhibition – are a great stepping stone to make this type of action inclusive. However, I keep wondering if I should have thought out better who exactly the exhibition had to 'include' in which part of the process: the creation of it, the visitors, the dialogues, the action/transformation that I hope it inspires"

Ultimately, the dynamic and evolving nature of stakeholder involvement under-scores the importance of flexibility and continuous reflection in creating truly inclusive and safe spaces for impactful actions. Building safe spaces thus requires carefully chosen methodologies through which an environment can be co-created in which everyone can engage meaningfully.

"We needed to find a methodology to create a safe environment, for instance thinking about how to change or circulate roles"

ILLUSTRATION CREDITS

All drawings based on field researchers' notes and photos © Martina Bovo;
The maps that introduce the fieldwork sites © Aamina Shahid and Aliki Tzouvara;
The diagrams are co-authored by the four first authors;

Copyright photos:

Fig. 11. Money transfer store © Maps Data: Google, 2024; Church © Maps Data: Google, 2024; Stored belongings © Shila Anaraki, 2021; Multi-lingual libraries © Tortoise Path, 2021; Targeted newcomer services © Swetha Mathan, 2023; Repurposed infrastructure © Shila Anaraki, 2022; Free food provision © Tamlyn Monson, 2022; International student services © Márton Bisztrai, 2021; Information points © Carolien Lubberhuizen, 2022; Multi-lingual offerings © Carolien Lubberhuizen, 2022; Shipping services © Marhabo Saparova, 2021; Multi-lingual menu © Márton Bisztrai, 2023; Satellite dishes © Tina De Gendt, 2024; Cell shops © Marhabo Saparova, 2021; Political graffiti © Charalampos Tsavdaroglou, 2022; Laundromat © Maps Data: Google, 2024.

Fig. 12. © Charalampos Tsavdaroglou, 2022.

Fig. 14. © Marhabo Saparova, 2022.

Fig. 17. © Charalampos Tsavdaroglou, 2022.

Fig. 18. © Shila Anaraki, 2023.

Fig. 20. © Carolien Lubberhuizen, 2022.

Fig. 22. © Luce Beeckmans, 2022.

Fig. 25. © Tamlyn Monson, 2022.

Fig. 26. © Carolien Lubberhuizen, 2023.

Fig. 27. © Shila Anaraki, 2023.

Fig. 28. © Shila Anaraki. 2023.

Fig. 30. © Esmée Maluta.

Fig. 31. © Athina Desli, 2023.

Fig. 35. © Dounia Salamé, 2023.

Fig. 36. © Ruhr Nachrichten, 2023.

Fig. 38. © Laura Guérin, 2023.

Fig. 39. © Laura Guérin, 2023.

Fig. 41. © Luce Beeckmans, 2023.

Fig. 42. © Carolien Lubberhuizen, 2023.

Fig. 46. © Luce Beeckmans, 2023.

Fig. 47. © Modeste, 2023.

Fig. 48. © Wiktoria, 2023.

Fig. 49. Screencapture by Shila Anaraki © 2025.

Fig. 50. Screencapture by Mary Hogan January 20, 2025. © The Brussels Time, 2025.

Fig. 52. © Martina Bovo, 2025.

Fig. 53. © Tamlyn Monson, 2023.

Fig. 57. © e-Stravrodromi, 2025.

Fig. 59. © Marhabo Saparova, 2024.

Fig. 61. © Charalampos Tsavdaroglou, 2023.

Fig. 62. © Charalampos Tsavdaroglou, 2023.